TURKISH DEMOCRACY TODAY

TURKISH DEMOCRACY TODAY

Elections, Protest and Stability in an Islamic Society

ALİ ÇARKOĞLU
ERSİN KALAYCIOĞLU

I.B. TAURIS
LONDON · NEW YORK

For Gül and Sema

Published in 2007 by I.B.Tauris & Co Ltd
6 Salem Road, London W2 4BU
175 Fifth Avenue, New York NY 10010
www.ibtauris.com

In the United States of America and Canada distributed by Palgrave Macmillan
a division of St. Martin's Press, 175 Fifth Avenue, New York NY 10010

International Library of Political Studies 15

ISBN: 978 1 84511 185 4

A full CIP record for this book is available from the British Library
A full CIP record is available from the Library of Congress

Library of Congress Catalog Card Number: available

Printed and bound in Great Britain by TJ International Ltd, Padstow, Cornwall
From camera-ready copy edited and supplied by the authors

CONTENTS

ACKNOWLEGEMENTS

Our initial enthusiasm for a study of political participation and national elections in Turkey were met with similar interest of Hakan Altınay of the *Open Society Institute* (OSI) – İstanbul. Ali Çarkoğlu was at the time in charge of developing the research agenda of the then newly expanding *Turkish Economic and Social Studies Foundation* (Türkiye Sosyal ve Ekonomik Etüdler Vakfı – TESEV). Turkey was approaching a new general election within relatively denser uncertainties not only concerning the winners and losers, but also as to the extent to which the new National Assembly to be formed in its aftermath would be able to meet the challenges awaiting the country. TESEV adopted the idea of providing a reference information baseline for the years to come concerning the electoral character of the November 2002 election and the issues that shaped these dynamics. Besides the two authors of this volume Üstün Ergüder of Sabanci University participated in the design and analysis of our study.

Following these initial stages of research design, the fieldwork and analysis of the study survived many challenges and rapidly changing environment. On and off we have been working on this project for nearly four years now. When the study was being designed, both authors had just newly moved to Sabancı University, which had ever since provided a calm and supportive environment for this project. Our original financial plans for the funding of the project had to be modified many times along the way. At the very end, the Sabancı University Research Fund and the Swedish Consulate General of Istanbul funded the study generously. Çağlayan Işık of Frekans Fieldwork Company was from the beginning not only a considerate and reliable research aid but also a generous and understanding supporter of the project. At the end, Frekans *de facto* became our third major funder for the project. We are grateful to all our sponsors for their generous support for this project.

We not only intensely enjoyed working with Üstün Ergüder on this project but also are greatly indebted to him for insights and reliable guidance during the design and early analyses of our data. Unfortunately, he could not participate in writing up the findings of our study as presented in this book.

We presented our results at Sabancı University, St. Anthony's College – University of Oxford, Tel Aviv University, and Bar-Ilan University, where many valuable insights and feedback into our interpretations and analyses were provided. We are thankful to these institutions and the participants in our lectures and presentations who made valuable criticisms.

Melvin Hinich of the University of Texas-Austin and Eric Uslaner of the University of Maryland-College Park provided much needed insights and inspiration along the way for finalizing the study and this manuscript.

Sinan Ciddi read and edited the manuscript at different stages providing valuable comments as well. Abigail Fielding-Smith and Carolann Martin of I.B.Tauris were both not only very helpful but also accommodating and understanding for our difficulties in finalizing the project. We would like to thank İpek Dübüş of Işık University for her secretarial assistance in both the preparation of the manuscript and facilitating communication between the authors of this book.

Finally, as it is common in all long running projects, we are indebted to our families. Unlike many occupations, there simply is no vacation or off hours in academia. For three consecutive summers, our wives, Sema Kalaycıoğlu and Gülgün Çarkoğlu had to listen in our never ending conversations on our project. Ayşe Çarkoğlu was not even born when we collected the pre-election data. For at least one of us, there simply was no more important "intervening variable" than her birth in between the pre and post election fieldworks. Can Çarkoğlu seemed to have grown up from childhood to adolescence while listening to the diatribes of his father and Ersin Kalaycıoğlu over the political behavior of Turkish voters.

1

INTRODUCTION: TAKING PART IN POLITICS, A HISTORICAL OVERVIEW

Turkey's November 3, 2002, general elections ended with a predicted but still impressive victory for the Justice and Development Party (*Adalet ve Kalkınma Partisi*-AKP), the first party since 1987 to secure a clear majority in the Turkish Grand National Assembly (Türkiye Büyük Millet Meclisi-TBMM).[1] Although the AKP gained about a third of the valid votes, it nevertheless controlled a two-thirds majority of the seats in the TBMM.[2] The results reflect several important trends taking shape in this country of popular enthusiasts of the European Union (EU) membership where despite deep economic crises and political tensions, fourteen national legislative elections have been held since May 1950, following a questionable first experience in 1946.

First, the elections brought a landslide victory for yet another pro-Islamist party to power following the Welfare Party's (*Refah Partisi*-RP) experience as the senior coalition partner in the aftermath of 1995 general election. However, this time the AKP controlled an overwhelming majority in the TBMM. The nature of AKP's electoral victory, its leadership and ideological rhetoric and policy commitments at the start of its tenure, started a vibrant debate as to the extent of its similarity with its precedents within the pro-Islamist tradition in the country. The increase of support for the AKP marks the progression of electoral collapse of centrist politics in the country. From an optimistic perspective, one could claim that centrist politics was simply transformed during the course of the November 2002 election where some centrist parties have been pushed into the sidelines while others, namely the AKP, has replaced them. From a more somber perspective however, one could point to marginal right-of-center origins of the AKP as a potential threat to long-standing centrist orientations in the Turkish party system. The AKP has its roots in the pro-Islamist electoral tradition of the early 1970s, which until mid-1990s had stayed in the margins of Turkish electoral spectrum. With the rise of RP to the electoral forefront in the municipal elections of 1994 and then in 1995 general election, the pro-Islamists became a major electoral force in Turkish politics. With rising electoral power came not only reactions of the secularists, spearheaded by the influential military, but also divisions within the ranks of the party which eventually led to a split between Necmettin Erbakan's old-guards who controlled the pro-Islamist parties ever since the days of the National Order Party (*Milli Nizam Partisi*-MNP) and the younger generation led by the ex-Istanbul mayor Tayyip Erdoğan.[3] Erdoğan managed to free the AKP from the stubborn challenges of the old guards for the secularist establishment. He adopted a softer tone in portraying the AKP's conservative political outlook, which rendered the party more palatable for a larger and centrist electoral constituency. A key question in this context concerns the nature of AKP constituency: to what extent are they a continuation of the pro-Islamists of the 1970s, 1980s and 1990s and to what degree do they include a more centrist group of voters who had voted for other traditionally more centrist parties in earlier elections?

Second, the election saw the continued volatility in electoral preferences with a somewhat more concentrated support behind two parties in the system. The left-leaning Republican People's Party (*Cumhuriyet Halk Partisi*-CHP) is the only other party, which was able to pass the 10 percent nationwide electoral support threshold to gain seats in the Parliament. However, the CHP remained about 14 percentage points below the AKP, at around 20 percent (See Table 1.1 below). The nature of the constituencies, which were effectively denied representation in the TBMM, is going to define the character of the opposition to the AKP government. Moreover, it is clear that those constituencies, which make up nearly 45 percent of the electorate, will define the direction of party competition in the country for the next elections. Do these constituencies have a tendency to gather behind a certain ideological orientation, or a party, or do they tend to remain dispersed and unorganized and moving from one party to another without much of a momentum? Answers to these questions obviously have implications for the way Turkish party system's fragmentation and volatility indices will move in the future and thus have implications for the way the whole party system functions.

Third, the fact that none of the former coalition partners were able to pass the 10 percent electoral barrier suggests the great importance attached by the voters to the devastating impact of the recent economic crisis on their personal lives. Compared to the 1999 election, the coalition partners together lost about 39 percentage points of electoral support. The two major opposition parties, the other pro-Islamist Felicity Party (*Saadet Partisi*-SP) and the True Path Party (*Doğru Yol Partisi*-DYP) both incurred significant losses. The SP was closely associated with the old guards of the pro-Islamist movement, and thus the Virtue Party (*Fazilet Partisi*-FP), in consequence suffered a loss of 12.9 percentage points compared to 1999. The DYP on the other hand, did not perform any better and lost 2.5 percentage points. Why was it the case that none of these parties were able to reap the expected benefits of being out of power during a serious economic crisis? To what extent has the economic crisis been responsible for the rise of the AKP and for differentiating party constituencies in November 2002?

Fourth, the collapse of the centrist parties brought a populist newcomer to the Turkish electoral scene: the Young Party (*Genç Parti*-GP). With the help of financial backing from its leader Cem Uzan, the business tycoon of perplexing success, the GP was able to attract about 7 percent support away from the centrist hopefuls. The GP experience remains unique in Turkish electoral history and is full of tenets that may cause a loss of appetite for the followers of Turkish politics. The GP was a typical one-man show. It is hard to remember anyone other than its leader from the party. The campaign was a slick commercial show using Uzan's TV and radio stations, as well as his cellular phone network. Uzan's speeches were also full of populist promises, which were blended with anti-establishment rhetoric similar to those of Ross Perot in the USA and Sylvio Berlusconi of Italy. Especially Uzan, and to some degree Erdoğan, turned their campaign speeches into a ceremony of hatred expression against the establishment and the government where masses were asked to repeat certain slogans and make populist pledges out loud. The masses seemed to have been gathered first by free meals or distributions of other gimmicks financed through a non-transparent campaign mechanism by the Uzans. Such questionable campaign financing is nothing new in Turkey. However, Uzan's show exemplified that Turkish politics is vulnerable to a well-financed concerted attack. With the existing informal underground economy and loopholes in party campaign financing laws the whole party system is vulnerable to abuse by businessmen turned politicians, with cash to spend. Besides the institutional character of Uzan's campaign what is more interesting for our purposes concerns the demographic and ideological character of the constituencies it was able to attract through such a campaign. Who were the GP voters? What were the main reasons they voted for GP? From which party do they seem to have been diverted?

Fifth, besides the CHP and AKP the only other opposition party to gain votes over their 1999 levels of support was the ethnic Kurdish Democratic People's Party (*Demokratik Halk Partisi*-DEHAP). Ever since the pre-election coalition of the social democrats in 1991 general election with the Kurdish elements in the southeastern Anatolian provinces, there remains a distinct Kurdish electoral constituency in the country. This constituency is concentrated in less than a dozen provinces of the Eastern and Southeastern Anatolia where vote shares in excess of 35 percent is not uncommon for parties like the People's Democracy Party (*Halkın Demokrasi Partisi*-HADEP) or DEHAP. However, what the micro-individual characteristics of these voters are, is of yet unclear. Solid empirical observations concerning the Kurdish constituency are not readily available and thus the issue and attitudinal bases of ethnic Kurdish vote is at best blurred.

The electoral success of the AKP was also helped significantly by a number of other factors. First among these is the long-run inability of the center-right and left parties to follow a responsive uncorrupt policy agenda to attract mass support and thus the erosion of leadership credibility in the centrist parties of ANAP and DYP. Another is the almost continual economic crisis environment primarily due to irresponsible populist policies of the center party coalitions. Equally important is the inability of the then incumbent government and state establishment to come to the rescue of the victims in the 1999 earthquakes. Lastly, the historical impact of the rising salience of the EU membership bid for Turkey helped create an election context with large masses of the electorate that was alienated from the political establishment and ready for change. All of these factors considered together, along with the long-term rise of right-wing ideological predispositions of the electorate, created a historical window of opportunity for the AKP leadership to capture executive office, which they eventually seized and capitalized upon.

Before we highlight all of these points at some length and thus contextualize the November 2002 election we first provide a historical overview of patterns of political participation and the temporal peculiarities in which it developed.

Politics of Influence in Turkey

Making an impact on the substance of political decisions so that they turn out to be favorable to one's interests, though comes as so natural and legitimate in this day and age, have only recently come to play in the life of men and women in the streets. For an extensively long period of time, politics was the game that a select few dared to play with extremely high stakes. Turkish political past is no different in this regard. Historians tend to draw up a picture of the Ottoman Empire, from the ruins of which emerged the modern day Turkish Republic, as a medieval sultanate with patrimonial traditional

Table 1.1 Election results 1999–2002

	Vote Share (%) 1999	2002	% points wins and losses	Seats in the Parliament 1999	2002
DSP	22,19	1,22	-20,97	136	0
MHP	17,98	8,34	-9,64	129	0
*FP**	15,41	2,48	-12,93	111	0
ANAP	13,22	5,13	-8,09	86	0
DYP	12,01	9,55	-2,46	85	0
CHP	8,71	19,40	10,69	0	178
*HADEP***	4,75	6,23	1,48	0	0
BBP	1,46	1,02	-0,44	0	0
AKP	-	34,28	34,28	0	363
GP	-	7,25	7,25	0	0
Independents	0,87	0,99	0,12	3	9
Total	96,60	95,89		550	550
Other	3,40	4,11	0,71		

*In 2002 DEHAP, **In 2002 SP.

authority structure (Mardin, 1973, 169–174).[4] Political rule was defined as the prerogative of a dynasty, the legitimate right of its credentials to govern rested fully on a tradition, the roots of which were presumed to extend back to pre-medieval Central Asian tribal mores, customs and rites. The Ottoman Sultans seemed to base the legitimacy of their right to govern on the Turkic customary law (*törü* or *töre*), which dated back to an immemorial past (Inalcik, 2000, 44). Such roots tended to stress the pre-Islamic roots of style and substance of government in the Ottoman Empire. However, this is not quite far enough to argue that they had a secular style of government, fully autonomous from religious influence and control. Indeed such customary styles may be no less related to shamanism, which in essence is also religious, as much as it rested on expediency of the tribal politics of an earlier era.

The population over which the Ottoman Sultans ruled was mostly Muslim, though in such Ottoman territories as the Balkans, local majorities tended to be Orthodox Christians. Various Christian and Jewish communities lived under the Ottoman rule for more than four centuries without any major stirrings until nationalism began to make inroads into the Empires of Europe in the late eighteenth and early nineteenth centuries. Therefore, it seems as if it is quite certain that the Ottoman rule extended over large swathes of religious and even pious communities of all the monotheistic religions. Historians also concur on the fact that the Ottoman political system had considered the religious communities of Christians, Jews and Muslims as legitimate social entities deserving of respect and status (Lewis, 1995, 321–322). They called such communities as "*millet*" and respected and treated them as legal and social entities. Each religious community (*millet*) had been permitted to preserve its own peculiar institutions, continue practicing their own style of religious and social rites, preserve their educational and vocational practices, and practice their own standards of conflict resolution through their own legal systems. Under the circumstances it is unavoidable to reach the conclusion that whether the traditions they had rested upon to rule such religious communities had been secular or not, the Ottoman Sultans and their governments had to possess immaculate credentials in the eyes of their pious religious subjects. The calm and docile communities of subjects, who accepted the legitimate right of the Ottoman Sultans to rule, had done so on traditional grounds, which are not secular at all. The Ottoman Sultans and their governments were considered "just" or acted with "justice" as the understanding of fairness and justice of the rulers went in the eyes of the pious subjects. Ottoman subjects lived in communities immersed in religious practices, and as individuals had a traditional understanding of justice and fairness closely intertwined with their religious teachings. The Muslim subjects of the Sultan heeded the political guidance of the Holy Koran, which stressed that the "rule with justice" is a must.

The Ottoman patrimonial traditions of political rule enabled the Sultans to rule according to traditions, which were a mixture of Turkish customary law (*törü*) and obedience of traditionally minded subjects, who were ready to accept any form of rule so long as their understanding of religiously defined justice is preserved (Inalcık, 2000, 106). A heavily decentralized "*millet* system" enabled the Sultans to give just that impression as they prodded on with whatever suited them as tradition. In practice, tradition is a hazy concept, quite hard to define. It seemed as if the rebellion of his traditional minded subjects was the only real danger to the rule of a Sultan who seemed to veer away from tradition as the subjects believed in it. Such rebellions did occur. However, they were far apart, sporadic, and never provided an effective restraint on the arbitrariness and excesses of use of force and power by the Sultan and his government.

One ostensible outcome of such a style of political rule had been the remoteness of government to the people. The subjects considered the government as a mechanism of a traditional or even sacred order, in which they had no partnership at stake. Government was a mechanism to defend the state against foreign invasion, provide security and order, and collect taxes and conscript soldiers. The Ottoman practices also widely differed in these regards. Muslim men served in the military for indefinite periods of time to fight wars and conquer territory, which provided larger budgets thanks to agricultural production and taxation, which in turn helped to fund bigger armies and navies. This in turn helped conquer more lands and increased agricultural production of the Empire. The Christians and Jews did not serve in the military; they paid taxes instead, until the modernizing reforms of the nineteenth century. A minimally capable state existed with a pretense for full monopoly of power, and loaded rhetoric on central control and tutelage over the local institutions. Education, healthcare, welfare had all been provided by the "*millet* associations" and so was conflict resolution through the communal and religious court system and judges.

When the Ottoman Empire extended its power and control over large swathes of territory in Eastern and Central Europe, Russia, the Caucasus, Middle East and North Africa, their traditional system created few problems. However, they eventually met stronger rivals and resistance, and eventually began to lose ground. The government looked and functioned as a corrupt mechanism of mobilization of societal resources. The subjects of the Sultan tried to invent ways of avoiding and evading its officials, who turned into the plunderers of their own societies. The relations between the subjects and the officials of the Sultan further deteriorated when the modernizing reforms began to take off. The traditions that had instilled a sense of subservience in the subjects of the Sultan, the privileges of the previous order, and the decentralized millet system began to lose ground to genuine attempts at centralization. The non-Muslim subjects of the Sultan began to vent their frustrations with the decaying system through developing their own brands of Eastern European nationalism. Muslim subjects felt increasingly squeezed between the modernizing Ottoman center, which began to change the rules of the social order as the religious school system, health care and welfare institutions began to be taken over by secular and state run institutions, and the nationalist demands and attacks of their non-Muslim neighbors.

The Turks of the Ottoman society, who constituted one of the main Sunni Muslim communities of the Ottoman Empire, were forcibly evicted from the Balkans as old Christian communities started to gain their independence and establish their "nation-states". The ethnic nationalist Christian Orthodox elements who ascended to power in the Balkans turned against their Turkish populations, for they saw the Turkish communities as the vestiges of the

Ottoman power and future tool of Ottoman irredentism. The dislocation of the Turkish populations from the Balkans reached staggering numbers in the latter half of the nineteenth century and reached its climax in the Balkan Wars of 1912. Turkish speaking Muslims, who were mostly of Slav and other local origins, were forcibly evicted from the new Balkan states as the Ottoman Empire contracted between 1821 and 1922. They began to migrate to the seat of the Empire in Istanbul, and Anatolia, where larger communities of Turkish speaking Muslims lived. They were no longer wanted in the Balkans. However, they had learned a hard lesson in nationalism in the Balkans through the mass exodus, massacres, and various atrocities they suffered in the Balkans. By the early twentieth century, Turkish nationalism was converted from an intellectual vocation to a mass movement.[5]

In the early years of the twentieth century the Ottomans encountered a new nationalist awakening, this time to their south, among their Arab subjects. World War I further ignited Arab nationalism and turned it into a mass movement against the Ottoman armies. Large groups of Arabs, who were also mostly Sunni Muslims, turned against the Ottoman Sultan, who they had earlier recognized as the Caliph of Islam, their religious and spiritual leader. The Arab subjects of the Sultan had also recognized that the old traditional order was no longer sustainable, and the Turks had also been developing their nationalism. It was their perception of Turkish nationalism that they reacted to, through developing their own brand of nationalism, and in the process helping the British and French imperial aspirations over the Ottoman lands, to gain their independence from the Ottoman state.[6]

Thrown out of the Balkans and driven out of the Middle East into Anatolia and Eastern Thrace, the Turkish nationalists found themselves facing a new geopolitical reality in 1918. It was the occupation and further dismemberment of Ottoman Anatolia, which made them feel as if they had their backs to the wall. They now had nowhere else to go, but stand their ground, declare the last bit of mostly Muslim and Turkish Anatolia and Eastern Thrace as their national homeland and fight for it. It was the tormenting birth of nationalism and the Turkish nation–state, which occurred through the process of the War of Liberation between 1919 and 1922.

If nationalism constitutes one factor that characterizes the Turkish political system, the simultaneous drives of secularism and modernization were the other two main factors. Secularism began to make inroads into the Ottoman culture in the eighteenth century. However, it gained momentum after the modernizing *Tanzimat* (Beneficient) Reforms, which began to unfold in 1839 and lasted until 1876. The overall impact of the *Tanzimat* reforms was the creation of a new socio-political reality in the Ottoman Empire. The influence of religious institutions in social and legal systems of the Ottoman Empire eroded rapidly. Religious education which had attracted some of the best and the brightest sons of the Ottoman Empire to the ranks of the clergy, and functioned as the only social ladder for upward mobility in society began to lose ground to medicine, engineering and science education in general. The court system came under the influence of the *Tanzimat* reforms and began to lose its special contact with religious instruction and religious law, except in the special realms of marriage, divorce, inheritance and other issues closely related to the family in Ottoman society. Such developments drove a rift in society between those who stuck to the "image of good society" built around tradition/religion and those who promoted an alternative "image of good society" built around progress/science.[7]

The modernizing reforms of the nineteenth century also transformed the Ottoman society, on the one hand, and the relationships between the government and the Ottoman subjects, on the other. The most remarkable consequence of the reforms was the ground swelling transformation of the role of the individual in the Ottoman society. The *gemeinschaftlich* structure of the religious communities of the Ottoman Empire began to give way in the first half of the nineteenth century. The submerged role of the individual in the religious community began to erode, and the individual members of different *millet*s began to interact with each other with greater frequency. There is evidence pointing to the increasing interaction between Muslims and non-Muslims, including foreigners, in many substantial ways, which went beyond polite greetings (Hamlin cf. Inalcik, 1964: 619). Analyses of the literary traditions and the changes that occurred in them of the same era indicate the development of the "individual" as a valuable entity per se (Tanpınar, 1982, 78–79). The autonomy of the individual from the religious community in which he was born into and raised in was reflected in the value of the individual member of the Ottoman community as a human being, separate from one's identity as member of a *millet*. One major political consequence of such a major transformation of the social role and significance of the individual subject of the Ottoman Sultan was the transformation of the political transaction between the government and the subjects of the Sultan. This transformation became most ostentatious in the realm of contacts through appeals to the government in the form of petitions.

The Ottoman palace had always received petitions from its subjects. The subjects of the Sultan could always write a letter of appeal to the Sultan pleading for help. Indeed, they had been officially called "*imdatname*" (pleas for help), which were somewhat like S.O.S. calls to the Ottoman center. They were overwhelmingly written by communities of people who were requesting the Palace to intervene in some form of intractable conflict between two settlements or communities. Some were no more than reports of observations or gossips about the intent of the enemies of the Ottoman realm, such as the re-deployment of Russian or Austrian armies. Those pleas had overwhelmingly been communal petitions for help or conflict resolution until 1820s. However, a few years after the declaration of the *Tanzimat* reforms of 1839 the very substance of the appeals from the Ottoman periphery started to change. They became overwhelmingly personal pleas to request help with the objective of improving the welfare of single individual subjects of the Sultan. As of 1847 the Ottoman state began to refer to the pleas as "*Arz-ı Hal*" (presentation of one's state of affairs), with no obvious connotation of pleas of help. Indeed, the nature of the political contacts between the Ottoman subjects and their government had become so radically different by the mid nineteenth century that even the official terminology defining written contacts were amended to fit the new reality. Consequently, the start of mass political participation of the modern era in Turkey may be dated back to the 1840s.[8]

It is also a well-recorded fact that associational life of the Ottoman Empire started in the 1850s (Tunaya, 1952, 12–14). Indeed, Ottoman politics came under the influence of several political associations in the last decades of the nineteenth century. Among them the most famous turned out to be the Committee of Union and Progress (*Ittihat ve Terakki Cemiyeti*-ITC), which became increasingly influential in the early twentieth century. However, several ethnic and religious political organizations were established and rapidly grew in the same era. The Balkan territories of the Ottoman Empire especially served as a cauldron or incubator of protest movements and clandestine nationalist organizations. The anti-regime political organizations, which opposed the rule of the sultan (Abdülhamid II), and anti-system associations, which launched secessionist movements, emerged to change the Ottoman political landscape once and for all. The same era also experienced the development of representative organizations such as the provincial and city councils, and the Imperial Assembly (*Meclis*) in Istanbul.

The foundations of the representative institutions of the Ottoman and later Turkish were laid in the nineteenth century. Concomitantly, the Ottoman and later Turkish politics began to host local and national elections for public office. In the nineteenth century most elections were two-tier events, whereby only male and relatively distinguished members of the Ottoman millets participated as the voters. However, the practice of organizing and running elections and institutions of popular representation began to be established. The practices of *conventional* and *unconventional* political participation emerged and developed in tandem.[9]

It seemed as if it was the unconventional participation that impressed the Ottoman political authorities, and they were least reluctant to devolve power to the elected assemblies. The challenge of the elected assemblies and unconventional political participation rose to new heights during the Russo-Ottoman war of 1877, which leveled new existential challenges to the Ottoman government, and the load of political participation rose too high for the sultan's government to tolerate. Sultan Abdülhamid II used the prerogatives of the newly established written constitution of 1876 and suspended the activities of the Imperial Assembly for thirty years and outlawed all forms of associations in political life. However, although conventional political participation took a downturn in the years between 1878 and 1908, the structures of unconventional political participation went underground and moved outside of the Ottoman realm and into Europe. There emerged the famous phrase of "Young Turks", who became increasingly active in the relatively hospitable political environments of Western Europe. The Young Turks began to engage in peaceful associational life in Europe and increasingly anti-regime activities in the Ottoman Empire. Almost all acts of political participation became unconventional political participation by the early 1900s in the Ottoman Empire. Such anti-regime activities reached a climax in 1908, when an outright rebellion against the Sultan became very successful and resulted in the re-institution of the activities of the Royal Assembly. However, unconventional political participation continued to make its impact on the Ottoman politics. Ethnic nationalist violence and religious uprising of "March 31st, 1909" presented new challenges for the ITC, the leading organization of the 1908 freedom movement. The reactionary religious uprisings, which some believed were instigated by the Sultan and others argued that they were the accomplishments of some splinter groups of the Young Turks, could only be put down by force, after they wreaked havoc in the city of Istanbul for a few days in early April 1909.

The calm that was restored in the aftermath of "the March 31st incident" did not last long. Popular elections with representation limited to the relatively more distinguished male members of the Ottoman society were successful in changing the composition of the new Imperial Assembly, amending the constitution of 1876 in 1909, limiting the powers of the sultan and extending further guarantees for a constitutional monarchy. However, they could not prevent the ITC to come to power by force, through a military coup in the Balkan Wars of 1912–13 and terminate the budding multiparty system of the Ottoman Empire. World War I and the War of Liberation that followed it, also provided little fertile ground for conventional participation to mushroom. A large spectrum of ethnic, religious, nationalist, and even socialist organizations went underground and engaged in internecine conflict from 1913 through 1922, when the Ottoman Empire collapsed. Again, all political participation became unconventional participation.

The end of the First World War resulted in both a military defeat for the Ottoman Empire, as well as the occupation of its territories in the Middle East and Anatolia. This not only triggered the start of the War of Liberation, but also confirmed that a monumental change had taken place in the mindset of the Ottoman intelligentsia and perhaps to a lesser extent, those of the masses. That mind shift concerns the sources of political legitimacy. Starting with the *Tanzimat* movement, elites and to a lesser extent the less informed Ottoman masses no longer searched divine roots but only worldly sources of legitimacy and found those in the people. The idea of a representative assembly was only natural for the leaders of the War of Liberation in search of political legitimacy. In a sense, the biggest hurdle in front of a modern democracy was already passed by leaving the divine patriarchal family roots behind and by seeing the ordinary people as a legitimizing source of political authority. The leadership of the liberation movement used this opportunity and built its legitimacy by effectively using representative provincial assemblies and later by instituting the TBMM to even guide and govern the War of Liberation.

The War of Liberation also provided fertile ground for all forms of unconventional political participation to mushroom. Ethnic and religious nationalists, resistance organizations, myriad forms of clandestine societies, etc. emerged to battle each other and the Armenian, British, Greek, French, and Italian occupation forces during the War of Liberation (1919–1922). The successful end of the war for the Turkish nationalist forces consolidated the role of national representation and representative organizations, and a nebular two party system seemed to have struggled to emerge between 1923 and 1925.[10] From 1925 until 1945, the single party government of the CHP rendered unconventional participation too costly. Nevertheless, some government sponsored repressive participation seemed to have taken place in the 1930s and the 1940s. Various trials and police action taken against the clandestine and Muscovite Turkish Communist Party (*Türkiye Komünist Partisi*-TKP) also indicates that some protest activity went on, in spite of the stiff cost to be paid by the perpetrators. What blurs the picture of the 1920s and the 1930s were the events of a cultural revolution, which secularized the polity and society and extended political rights representation of women. The Civil Code of 1926 also extended many rights to women, which were considered revolutionary at the time, though they seem like humble accomplishments now. The single party governments held regular national elections, though they were mere plebiscites. However, building upon the

Tanzimat legacy, the act of taking part in national and local elections began to develop into a stable behavioral pattern by 1945. One clear difference in terms of classifying participation in pre and post Republican times was the fact that under the republican regime, at least in rhetoric, public participation was deemed legitimate and served as the basis of the republican authority.[11]

The Republican transformation into a modern nation however has from the very beginning taken a strictly secular path that was in stark contradiction with the very foundations of shari'a (or şeriat in Turkish) and has confronted a deep and continual resistance by Sunni religious circles which on occasions has exploded into bloody conflicts. These circles continued to oppose the regime, and persisted in pressuring other minority sectarian communities, especially the Alevis. The early Republican era was witness to a number of unpleasant incidents where reactionary forces gathered around a loud reactionary demand for *şeriat* and the protection of the Sultanate and Caliphate. The anti-nationalist peasant movement of the so-called Green Army instigated a number of uprisings in Anatolia during the Kemalist struggle for national liberation. These uprisings seriously threatened the nationalist army forces under the direction of Mustafa Kemal during the early phases of the liberation struggle. The Şeyh Said rebellion in the Kurdish dominated provinces of Anatolia that broke out in February 1925 had a strong Kurdish nationalist element in it. However, 'the terms in which it was launched and sustained was entirely religious' (Ahmad, 1993, 58). Conservative religious groups that backed both the Progressive Republican Party (*Terakkiperver Cumhuriyet Fırkası*-TCP) as well as the Free Republican Party (*Serbest Cumhuriyet Fırkası*-SCF) also seem to have absorbed or have been absorbed by all reactionary movements during the early years of the Republic. In the early years of the Republic when public opinion polls were not available to the leadership of the young regime, these short-lived parties and the kind of enthusiastic support they seem to have carried with them in Anatolian provinces proved to the Republican reformers how deep rooted were the religious loyalties and networks in the country.[12]

The bases of a secular regime were laid down with the adoption of the 1921 Constitution, which established the basis of sovereignty in the nation and people's preferences (Article 1). Dismantlement of the Ottoman *şeriat* rules continued with the abolition of the Sultanate in 1922 followed by the abolition of the Caliphate in 1924. *Şeriat* courts, the medreses (or religious education institutions), tombs and shrines of saints were closed. Grass root organisations of the religious orders, that is, all Islamic brotherhoods, their meeting places and coisters, titles and offices were abolished. The continuing symbolic authority of these brotherhoods in the use of terms such as *hacı, hafız*, and *mollas* as religious titles in official life were banned together with their use of distinctive attire (Berkes, 1964; Ahmad, 1993; Parla and Davison, 2004).

At the end of World War II and the beginning of the Cold War, Turkey began to approach the club of democracies in the world and a transition to multi-party politics and competitive elections began. The introduction of multi-party elections in 1946 was brought by a combination of both domestic and foreign policy related considerations. Domestically, the Republic managed to keep out of World War II and thus saved a generation of young Turkish citizens from perishing in its fire. However, as part of cautionary measures, men had to be kept under arms for years and the overwhelmingly agricultural Turkish economy suffered a number of consequences. The economy suffered seriously because of restricted production and imports. Many war riches were created in an era when shortages were rampant. As a consequence, there occurred a rising uneasiness on the domestic scene which found a sizeable group of opposition within the ruling RPP. On the foreign policy front the young Republic was relieved to have been able to avoid the horrors of fighting in WWII, only joining the allied coalition at the very end. However, now Turkey faced a new threat on its eastern front. The Soviets encouraged by their success against Germany, made territorial demands on the Turkish provinces of Kars and Ardahan. Turkey managed to counter both the domestic discontent and the Soviet threat by reverting to a functioning multiparty democracy. Allowing free elections to take place gave the electorate a real and free choice, whilst the adoption of democratic standards allowed Turkey to forge a new alliance with the West in general and the United States in particular.

The 1946 national elections were a transition election with the impressions of the immediate past haunting the electoral process. Many irregularities and deficient voting procedures rendered the 1946 elections unfair (Eroğlu, 1971). Nevertheless, the TBMM began to host two major political parties from 1946 until 1960. The 1950, 1954, and 1957 elections further contributed to the institutionalization of the multi-party elections in Turkey. Although the multi-party era of Turkey experienced three democratic breakdowns and military coups in 1960, 1971, and 1980, popular elections for national and local public offices have become institutionalized in Turkey. Elections, campaigns, political demonstrations and meetings by political parties, political party membership and work have become institutionalized practices in Turkey. A recent study of the Turkish civil society has unearthed that among all voluntary associations political party membership attracts the highest number and percentage of participants in Turkey, and in that category Turkey outperforms the rest of the countries included in the World Values Survey of the early 1990s

(Kalaycıoğlu, 2002, 63). Conventional political participation has become organized and institutionalized around the practices of local and national elections.

As noted earlier, an important dimension of political development during the republican era was shaped by a continuing struggle between secularist as opposed to pro-Islamist groups in the country. As soon as the multi-party elections were held in the country (1946), the original fears of the Republican regime of an Islamic reactionary opposition became one of the corner stones of the tension between the centrist CHP and the parties of the rising periphery. Following the 1960 coup, the centrist umbrella of the Democrat Party (*Demokrat Parti*-DP) collapsed into separate branches. These newly founded parties appealed to the ultra-nationalist and pro-Islamist electoral forces that significantly added not only to electoral fragmentation, but also to ideological polarisation in the system, which was also reflected in street clashes between opposing groups that have their separate ties to the political parties. The anarchic days preceding the September 1980 coup witnessed a new peak of rising pro-Islamism in the country which formed the basis of the tension between the secularists and the pro-Islamists. The National Salvation Party (*Milli Selamet Partisi*-MSP) organised the 'Save Jerusalem' demonstration in Konya which is a well-known religious centre in central Anatolia. In this demonstration open calls for the establishment of an Islamic state were made (Hale, 1994 237–238).[13] The military cadres which were at the time preparing the September 1980 coup had taken this new resurgence of Islamic fundamentalism apparently very seriously and became more convinced of the necessity of their actions in order to save the state from total collapse.

Re-emergence of the secularist versus pro-Islamist conflict did not wait for long after the normalisation of Turkish politics, with the lifting of the ban from politics of the pre-1980 period leaders to dominate the agenda. As outlined above, the new peak of the tension came with the success of the pro-Islamist RP, first in the local elections of 1994 and then in the general election of 1995, which eventually culminated in the so-called 28th of February Process in the aftermath of the infamous National Security Council (*Milli Güvenlik Kurulu*-MGK) meeting on February 28, 1997.

The continuing political struggle around the issue secularism should not cloud what perhaps is the boldest characteristic of Turkish political participation pattern, that is, the high rates of participation in elections. Taking part in the national and local elections has always attracted a lot of popular support, and the Turkish voting participation rates have been relatively high (see Figure 1.1). However, we should caution our readers to the fact that although it is certain that some of those who participate in the act of voting in the national and local elections lack any political motivation to do so. The landless peasants, uneducated women, and generally the have-nots have been subject to the manipulations of well-oiled patronage mechanisms at all times. Village elders, landlords, male chiefs of extended families, and in the eastern parts of the country the tribal heads, religious sheiks, labor union bosses have been notorious for their patronage records (Kutad, 1975, 66–70). Some studies have cast doubt on the fact that women with post-elementary education (middle school or high school education) possess the capacity to develop their self-image of politics, government, and the party system, and develop attitudes toward political objects, which in turn may be used to make their autonomous choices at the polls (Özbudun, 1976, and Kalaycıoğlu, 1986). In consequence, it is difficult to know what percentage of the vote is "mobilized" and what percentage is "political action". However, since the percentage of women without any post-elementary school education has been dropping, and more women move to the urban centers of the country with their parents and husbands, we can speculate that in the recent decades the "mobilized vote" has tended to drop in size. Nevertheless, participation rates in the national and local elections stayed high for another reason as well.

In 1982 Turkey adopted a new constitution and a new election law, which defined the act of voting as "mandatory". Those who failed to take part in the act of voting can be subject to punishment, if the eligible voter in question fails to declare a credible excuse, such as serving in the army, for soldiers have been exempt from voting since 1983. There were a few such people who were legally prosecuted and punished with a fine in the 1980s. However, recently, the political authorities tended to be more lax about non-participation in the elections. The media also seems to have lost any interest in such acts of prosecution as well. Consequently, the voters increasingly felt less intimidated from non-participation in the elections, and the rates of participation in the national and local elections started to decrease recently (see Figure 1.1)

In the meantime, through university student activism, and eventually labor union, and other interest group activities, protest movements emerged in the early 1960s and grew rapidly throughout the 1960s and beyond. Protest behavior and political influence through protestation have consisted of the acts of the less powerful groups and interests in Turkey. They often tended to take a violent nature and often attracted police reaction, which further increased the chance of bloodshed. However, although their frequencies showed some volatility over time, a stable pattern of protest behavior took hold by the early 1970s. Ever since the 1970s Turkey has witnessed widespread use of protest tactics, such as traffic blockages, boycotts, building occupations, demonstrations and rallies which disrupted public order, often on anniversaries of past protest events where bizarre incidents took place. For

Figure 1.1 Participation in the National and Local Elections in Turkey (1950–2004)

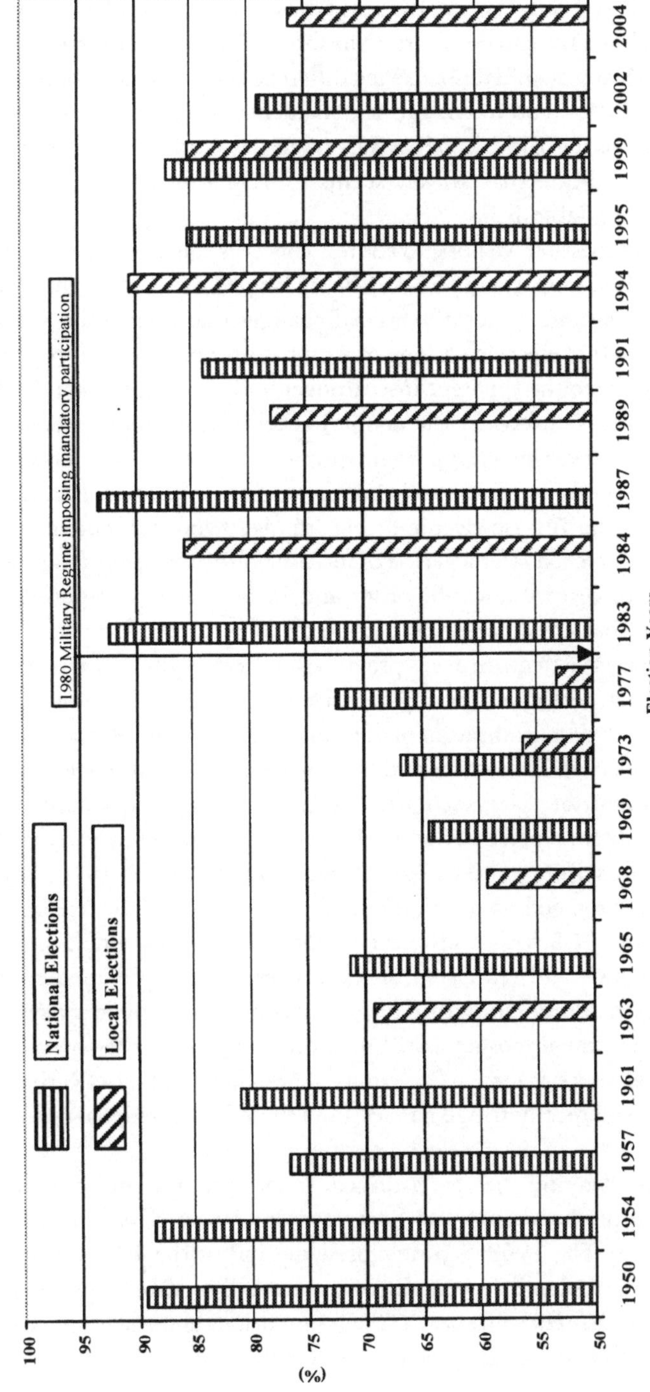

Source: Tuncer, (2003, 363–379) for national elections and İncioğlu, (2002, 77) and *Official Gazette*, no. 25460, (May 12, 2004, 55) for local elections.

example, May 1 of every year constitutes such a date since 1977 when, during May 1 Labor Day parade, more than forty people were killed in downtown Istanbul. Many such dates exist for different associations, groups and movements, and they tend to trigger new incidents of protest behavior every year. The results of the Turkish Values Surveys of the World Values Surveys of 1990 and 1997 indicate that Turkey seems to have a relatively rigorous protest potential (see Table 1.2).

A major question we hope to address concerns the degree to which patterns of political participation in Turkey have changed over years. This becomes an important question given the crucial changes that took place following the November 2002 election. A longer-term basis for our focus on continuity and change is due to the apparent institutional breaks brought about by recurrent military interventions in the country. Lack of continuity, persistent high volatility and ever increasing fragmentation of electoral preferences can all be linked to recurrent military regimes and their impact on the institutional structure of the Turkish electoral scene. In May 1960 and September 1980 the military intervened after a period of intense political tension and social unrest, arguably to restore law and order and in both times imposed new constitutions that are diametrically opposed to each other in their basic principles.[14] The 1961 constitution provided a relatively liberal framework within a bicameral parliamentary system that allowed a considerable role for judiciary and decentralisation of administrative powers. Gross representation biases of the plurality system with multi-member constituencies was replaced with a proportional representation system leading a large number of small parties to obtain representation in the Parliament that eventually undermined government stability and cohesion, especially during the 1970s.[15] The 1982 regime, being chiefly a reaction to the chaotic late-1970s, replaced the constitution of 1961 with a prohibitive constitution that emphasised centralisation of state and reduction of judicial powers. It provided considerable powers to the President within a single chamber parliamentary system while at the same time imposing a still in effect, ten percent nationwide threshold of electoral support for Parliamentary representation that effectively pushed smaller, ideologically fringe parties and ethnic based regional ones out of the Parliament.[16]

Besides changing the constitutional framework, the military regimes also directly intervened into the party system by chiefly eliminating some competitors. The 1960 regime closed the DP of the 1950s, the leaders of which were tried and sentenced to various terms, while three of its leading figures were sentenced to death. Their executions and the ensuing ban of the DP from political activity precipitated a still continuing contest for its legacy among a series of newly founded political parties in the 1960s. The electoral umbrella of DP that once included the reactionary forces to the centrist CHP with a pro-Islamist and ultra-nationalist character was broken. One by one, these groups formed their own parties within the liberal framework of the new constitution and the new proportional representation system, to challenge the two-party system of the previous decade.

Table 1.2 Comparative Protest Potential in Consolidated Democracies and Turkey*

(Percentage of those who recall participation in the corresponding acts)
Unconventional Acts of Political Participation

Countries	Petitioning (%)	Boycotts (%)	Legal Demonstrations (%)	Wildcat Strikes (%)	Occupation of Buildings (%)
Austria	45,5	4,8	9,8	1	0,7
Belgium	44,5	8,3	21,2	5,7	3,6
Britain	74,5	13,2	13,6	9,6	2,4
Denmark	50,3	10,2	27	**16,7**	2
France	51,4	11,3	31,2	9,4	**7,2**
Germany-West	55,1	9,2	19,5	2,1	1
Iceland	46,6	21,1	23,4	*0,1*	1,3
India	22,4	15,2	15,3	5,4	0,7
Italy	44,2	10	**34,1**	5,6	7
Netherlands	50,1	8,4	25	2,5	3,1
Portugal	24,8	*3,5*	19,2	3,1	1,4
Spain	17,5	4,7	21,2	5,7	2,4
Sweden	69,9	15,8	21,8	2,9	*0,2*
USA	**70,1**	**17,4**	15,1	4,4	1,8
Turkey-1990	*12,8*	5,2	*5,3*	1,4	1,2
Turkey-1997	13,5	6,3	6,1	2	0,5

Sources: World Values Survey (1989–91), Turkish Values Surveys (1990, and 1996).
*The figures in bold are the highest percentages per column and the figures in italics are the lowest.

The 1982 regime imposed a ban on all of the then existing political parties. Once again continuity in ideological rhetoric and its consequent electoral patterns were blurred. This time the ban was much more comprehensive and effectively lasted until 1987 when it was lifted after a referendum. In the meantime, brand new parties emerged to fill the vacuum. Indeed, the Motherland Party (*Anavatan Partisi*-ANAP) which came to rule the country in the 1980s, emerged as a novel party disowning any heritage of the previous parties. Eventually however, all of the former parties of the pre-1980 period re-emerged. Some of these new parties adopted their pre-coup names, some others drew up new names and symbols under their pre-1980 leadership. Completely new left and right wing parties have also been established. Consequently, the moderate left and right-of-centre voter alliances got split into two or three parties, while new varieties also emerged on both sides of the left and right extremes.

Simple observation of constancy in elite leadership cadres in many of these parties is enough to question continuity in mass electoral patterns as a reflection of a broadly defined ideological perpetuation. However, the macro indicators of the party system defy any sense of stability. Compared to the pre-1980 period where an average value of 2.95 is observed for the effective number of parties index, four elections in the aftermath of 1983, have an average value of 5.85.[17] Volatility of Turkish electoral support also remained remarkably high throughout the last five decades.[18] What is most striking is that, this near doubling of the effective number of parties and persistent high volatility of electoral support in the system came about despite new electoral laws that made it quite difficult to gain representation in the National Assembly for smaller parties.

Conclusion

The history of political participation in modern Turkey can be traced back to its origins in 19th century Ottoman Empire. The critical mind shift in the aftermath of the French Revolution that started to take shape in the Ottoman lands with the Tanzimat movement brought the worldly sources of legitimacy to the forefront of political agenda and thus prepared the ground for participatory institutions in the 19th century. Most of the Ottoman period was spent with little if any effective political participation. However, towards the end of the 19th century unconventional participation slowly turned conventional and by the time of the War of Liberation, the elites and to a limited degree the masses started to see the ultimate source of legitimacy in the hands of the masses. The War of Liberation was fought with an effective and active elected Assembly and the ensuing Republican era witnessed many legal and institutional changes to enhance participation in the country. Nevertheless, until the end of World War II the Republican Turkish polity remained a single party system with only acclamatory elections.

Starting with 1946 however, mass mobilization in competitive multi-party elections gradually became the sole source of legitimate government in the country. In this process, recurring interruptions due to military interventions took place and they all had enduring impacts on the functioning and behavioral patterns of all parties that exist in the party system. The spheres and zones of political participation expanded due primarily to institutional changes but also due to rapid socio-economic change. A recurrent theme in the ensuing chapters will thus be to underline patterns of continuity and change in recent Turkish political history. More specifically, we will aim at depicting the *sui generis* character of the November 2002 election and underline in what specific ways it marks a turning point in electoral patterns and in what specific ways it also carries signs of continuity in the system

We have so far covered nearly two centuries of developments in the acts of political participation. The modes of participation are outlined in a historical fashion underlining the end of the Ottoman Empire and the switch to a nation-state in the 20th century. However, we have not outlined most of the Republican developments in great detail. Besides the very basic comparative participation, either conventional or unconventional, we did not delve into the factors that contributed to the shaping of political participation, which we will return to in later chapters. In the following chapter we first present a short description of the parties and the nature of the Turkish party system and then present a more detailed account of the contextual characteristics that brought the AKP to victory in the November 2002 general elections.

2

POLITICAL PARTIES IN 2002 ELECTION

A number of overlapping ideological cleavages coexist in Turkish politics. These are shaped around discussions of left versus right, Islamism versus secularism, and ethnic Turkish nationalism versus the "Kurdish identity". Accordingly, fitting all the political parties into a multi-dimensional ideological space is more appropriate.[1] However, a longitudinal analysis of ideological cleavages and the shifting electoral support behind them is only available for the conventional left-right scale within which we will continue the following discussion. Table 2.1 attempts to provide a shorthand reference point for the parties' ideological and programmatic orientations. As expected from such an undertaking, the table leaves many of the subtleties concerning Turkish parties, their ideology and constituencies out of the picture. There is also a great deal of variation within each category of parties as well. Perhaps more importantly, this table only reflects the pre-conceived notions about the parties before our in-depth analyses that follow. Clearly, some have already claimed that the AKP is rather a centre-right party and that the GP should actually be placed on the extreme-right. As will be shown below, our analyses support the particular classification in Table 2.1 rather than others. However, our analyses are on the basis of the data collected at the very beginning of the AKP's term in the executive branch and subsequent analyses during the tenure of the AKP could reveal a somewhat different picture. Obviously, parties and their constituencies are never fully anchored into unchanging commitments and are rather dynamic in their ideological orientations.

The Party System in November 2002

Extreme left: For lack of a better category along the conventional left-right spectrum, the HADEP, and the DEHAP, have been placed in the extreme-left category. Although DEHAP/HADEP's rhetoric clearly has Marxist roots, its distinguishing trait is its emphasis on ethnic Kurdish identity and related

Table 2.1 Ideological Groups in the Turkish Party System

Extreme-Left (EL)	Centre-Left (CL)	Centre-Right (CR)	Extreme-Right (ER)
HADEP/DEHAP	CHP, DSP, YTP	ANAP, DYP, GP	Pro-Islamist SP, AKP Nationalist MHP, BBP
	Programmatic/Policy Platforms		
			Pro-Islamist
Ethnic Kurdish nationalist	Strictly secularist (CHP), some sympathy toward Fethullah Gülen's network (DSP)	Secularist on policy matters but courting the Sufi brotherhoods	Islamic revivalist, close relations with Islamic radical organizations
Pro-EU	Pro-EU Relatively more étatist (state interventionist)	Pro-EU Market oriented	Relatively more Euro sceptic State interventionist, populist in economic policy
Relatively more rural	Relatively more urban	Support from relatively more developed farming and other rural voters	Increasingly more popular in urban shanty towns
	Alevi support (CHP) Charismatic leader (DSP)		Sunni supporters Charismatic leader (AKP)
Support base is east and south-eastern Anatolia	Support base is western and coastal provinces	Support base is western and coastal provinces	Support base is central Anatolia
			Nationalist Ethnic Turkish nationalist Anti-European Sunni supporters Populist in economic policy Relatively more state interventionist Support base is central Anatolia

Source: Çarkoğlu (2003a).

issues. From the perspective of mass politics it is hard to find a policy area other than those concerning Kurdish identity politics and topics related to the EU on which these parties have distinguishing positions from the rest of the party system. There are a number of Marxist – Leninist and anarchist political movements and parties in Turkey, however few take part in elections and none receive more than a few thousands of votes from 42 million voters. Therefore, none of those political parties show any capability to influence the outcome of the national elections, or demonstrate any blackmail or government potential.

Centre-left parties: The two dominant social-democrat parties, that is, Deniz Baykal's CHP and Bülent Ecevit's DSP share a common historical root. DSP leader Bülent Ecevit led the CHP for a long period prior to 1980, effectively shaping its turn toward a modern left-wing policy stand in the late 1960's. However in the aftermath of the 1980 coup, Ecevit broke his ties with the CHP. He founded a separate party of his own under DSP and dominated its organisation together with his wife Rahşan Ecevit, effectively keeping the social-democratic elites away from his party. His charismatic leadership distinguishes the DSP from the rest of the parties and was responsible for the party's steady rise to dominance in the 1999 elections.[2]

Policy wise, the most striking difference is DSP's clear nationalist and Turkish ethnic tone compared to the CHP. While both parties were for a long time sceptical of market-oriented economic policies, both have adopted a more liberal economic policy stand over the last decade. Nevertheless, compared to the centre-right, their economic policies have always been more nationalist (anti-privatisation) and state interventionist. Facing the rising pro-Islamist agenda, the CHP especially, has consistently depended on a sizeable Alevi support.[3] Both the CHP and DSP have been pro-EU in their foreign policy preferences. However, at times, especially concerning domestic policy, their nationalist left policy stance formed a serious obstacle in front of their ability to support policy adjustments in line with the Copenhagen political and economic criteria. Both parties have been reluctant in changing their positions concerning the Kurdish issue and privatisation of state owned enterprises. Sharing a common root in the CHP, whose leadership cadres were the leading figures in Turkish modernization of the early Republican era, both parties have remained firmly secularist. What distinguishes the DSP from the CHP was Ecevit's conscious effort to appeal to moderate segments within the pro-Islamist camp. Such positioning together with a clear tone of populism in social and economic policy arena was effective in gathering support during the economic crisis years of early to late 1990's. Although both the DSP and CHP have been re-orienting their stands on religion by developing contacts with some religious communities, they have not been very successful in this respect. Both parties continue to represent bastions of secularism.

Centre-right: It has long been claimed that the ANAP and the DYP are artificially separated because of leadership struggles and that they both share the same ideological space. Both these parties have their historical roots in the DP of Adnan Menderes (1950's) and the Justice Party (Adalet Partisi- AP) of Süleyman Demirel (1960's and 1970's). These were both closed down following two military coups in 1960 and 1980 respectively. Despite ideological similarities, both the ANAP and the DYP have managed to maintain a distinct geographical base in the predominantly developed coastal provinces.[4] Both are pro-EU and pro-market in their economic policies. The DYP has an advantageous standing in its approach and linkages to the rural agrarian sectors compared to ANAP, which largely depended on newly urbanised segments of society. These two parties dominated the administration in the post-1980 period but failed to meet the expectations of the masses. Both have been hit by various corruption scandals that alienated them from the masses especially during the economic crisis periods.[5]

We included the GP of Cem Uzan in the centre-right category. This categorization may be controversial for the GP, since Uzan's campaign in 2002 sounded distinctly nationalist at times, mainly due to its populist policy stance and anti-western attitude in many policy areas. However, the GP's support remains heavily based on the same developed coastal regions from which ANAP and DYP, as well as the centre-left CHP, DSP and YTP also derive their support.[6] The GP remains heavily dominated by its leader Cem Uzan who is a prominent businessman with a blemished background. The Uzan family's allegedly corrupt business deals seem to have dominated their political agenda as well. Ever since their unsuccessful attempt to capture some seats in the Parliament and thus guarantee immunity for GP leadership, the party has effectively evaporated from the political scene. The Uzans' businesses have also been continuously hit by further corruption charges. The only legacy left by the GP is the fact that they were able to steal votes from the centrist parties of the incumbent coalition members especially from the DSP and ANAP. However, besides the geographic evidence on GP's electoral success we hope to provide further evidence concerning their electoral bases in our ensuing discussions below.

Extreme Right: The last decade of the twentieth century witnessed the rise of once marginal parties of the extreme-right to a dominant position in Turkish elections. First, in the 1994 municipal elections, the pro-Islamist RP captured the largest metropolitan centres. In less than two years, the RP became the largest party in a fragmented party system with only 21.4 percent of the vote. The RP's roots can be traced back to the MSP founded in 1973, following the MNP founded four years earlier. For most of the post-1960 period, electoral support for the pro-Islamist parties remained on the fringes of the system.[7] Never before the second half of the 1990s did the pro-Islamist tradition capture more than 12 percent of the popular vote alone.

In the aftermath of the 1995 general election, the pro-Islamist policy agenda found a significant reflection in the RP and DYP coalition (popularly called REFAHYOL). The challenge of the pro-Islamists to secularist Republican principles led to a series of reactions. It polarised secularists against the Islamists, Sunnis against Alevis and even widened the existing cleavages between the Turkish and the rising Kurdish nationalists. Tensions rose to a peak when the then ruling REFAHYOL coalition was openly challenged by the military representatives of the National Security Council (*Milli Güvenlik Kurulu*-MGK) in its meeting of the 28 February 1997. After nine hours of deliberations, the declaration of the MGK expressed uneasiness about attempts to harm and ultimately change the secular, Kemalist nationalist and democratic character of the Turkish constitution. Several precautionary measures, demanded by the military branch of the MGK, were submitted to the cabinet. These included demands for the regulation of Koran courses, social and economic activities of various Islamic brotherhoods (*tarikats*) and a halt to appointments that were seen as aimed towards building an Islamic cadre within the state bureaucracy. The RP leader Necmettin Erbakan tried to resist the military impositions, but could not obtain the necessary political support. Under pressure, he signed the MGK decisions, and the "28 February process" had formally begun.[8] It was subsequently ended with the early elections of April 1999, bringing to power a coalition of parties with a nationalist-secularist-liberal, as opposed to a religious, agenda.

In the mean time, the Constitutional Court closed down the RP in January 1998 on the grounds that the speeches of several party leaders were against the secular principles of the constitution. The Court also banned the former Prime Minister Erbakan and five other prominent members of the party from political activity for five years. By the end of April, the FP became the new address of almost all of the unbarred RP deputies. According to a 1995 amendment of the constitution, the FP could not claim any ties to RP. The Constitutional Court eventually closed down the FP in June 2001 on similar grounds to previous pro-Islamist parties. The SP was immediately founded by the FP leadership in July 2001. However, at the same time there occurred a severe cleavage of leadership in the ranks of the pro-Islamists and the old guard of the movement. The long-time leaders of the pro-Islamist movement who still followed Necmettin Erbakan's leadership remained in SP while the relatively younger generation founded a separate party of their own. The AKP was founded in August 2001 under the leadership of the ex-Istanbul mayor Tayyip Erdoğan, who, at the time, was banned from politics on the grounds of having inciting religious hatred, a number of years back. The AKP participated in the 2002 elections under Erdoğan's leadership but Erdoğan himself could not get elected to the TBMM because of his continuing ban. Only in March 2003, was Erdoğan able to get himself elected in a by-election from the South-eastern province of Siirt after a series of amendments to the existing legislation.

Pro-Islamist parties typically appeal only to Sunnis as opposed to Alevis and maintain good working relations with Islamist circles at large and various brotherhoods. Many of the pro-Islamist economic policy stands carry overtones of populism and state interventionism, especially in favour of the Anatolian small merchant and industrialist communities. On ethnic identity questions, the pro-Islamist parties have always been more able to appeal to Kurdish ethnicity on the basis of an all inclusive religious community (*millet*) concept. However, the nationalists have always used an anti-Kurdish rhetoric and policy stands to mobilize their electoral base.

The months leading to the 1999 general election witnessed the momentous capture of the leader of the separatist Kurdistan Workers' Party (*Partia Karkaren Kürdistan*-PKK). At the same time, public agenda was being shaped around discussions of increasing corruption scandals, mass demonstrations against the religiously sensitive ban of headscarves at universities, as well as the death of the ultra-nationalist leader Alparslan Türkeş. Türkeş's death eventually led to reshaping of the Nationalist Action Party (*Milliyetçi Hareket Partisi*-MHP) with a more centrist electoral appeal. The capture of the PKK leader Abdullah Öcalan and his trial, as well as the developments that led to NATO's military action in Kosovo, however, helped increase the nationalist fervour in the country. The DSP which had been in power for almost the previous two years prior to 1999, either as a coalition partner, or as a single minority governing party, greatly benefited from these developments. The DSP came out of the April 1999 election as the largest party but it was neither alone, nor was it the major benefactor from shifting electoral preferences. As expected, the DSP increased its vote share and became the largest party with 22.2 percent. The big surprise was that the MHP, which captured the second largest vote reaching nearly 18 percent, up by about 120 percent from its share in 1995.

The ethnic Turkish nationalist, anti-communist MHP was founded by one of the architects of the military coup of 1960 Alparslan Türkeş, who remained as its leader until his death in 1997. Türkeş was an active colonel in the coup of 1960 and a member of the ruling junta, the National Unity Committee (Milli Birlik Komitesi-MBK). He eventually got sidelined within the radical Group of 14 and got elected to the leadership of the Republican Peasant Nation Party (*Cumhuriyetçi Köylü Millet Partisi*-CKMP) in 1965, which was renamed in 1969 as the MHP. The MHP remained in the fringes of the Turkish party system from the very beginning, up until the 1999 election, gathering always below 9 percent of the vote in 6 elections it participated. However, in the mid-1970s it found two successive opportunities to participate in the Nationalist Front coalitions together with the AP and MSP wherein it was able to exert some nationalist influence over the hierarchy of Turkish bureaucracy and policy areas. However, ultimately the Nationalist Front (Milliyetçi Cephe-MC) governments were primarily responsible for rising urban terror and the eventual collapse of the centrist civilian establishment to provide domestic peace and order, which effectively prepared an invitation for the military to intervene for a third time in September 1980. The MHP was also closed down by the military regime of 1980 but eventually found its way back into the party system participating in the 1987 election as the Nationalist Work Party (*Milliyetçi Çalışma Partisi*-MÇP) obtaining 2.9 percent; once again its usual level of support. In 1991 it participated in the general elections in a pre-election coalition with the pro-Islamist RP, sharing eventually a total of about 17 percent of electoral support. The MHP was re-established in 1995 and participated in the 1995 elections alone and remained below 10 percent nationwide support threshold, and thus gained no seats in parliament. Despite concerted efforts to moderate their stands on domestic as well as foreign policy issues, the MHP remained openly anti-European and ethnic Turkish in its policy preferences. Muhsin Yazıcıoğlu's the Grand Unity Party (*Büyük Birlik Partisi*-BBP), whose pro-Islamist positions are stronger than those of MHP, is also included as a minor player in the nationalist camp.

Collapse of the Turkish Ideological Center in Perspective

The rapid rise of the AKP support in November 2002 election marks another step in the electoral collapse of centrist politics in the country. The left-leaning CHP is the only other party passing the 10 percent nationwide electoral support threshold to gain seats in the Parliament. The AKP received approximately 34 percent of the votes compared to 20 percent for the CHP. The remaining 46 percent of votes failed to gain representation in parliament due to the respective failure of their parties to gain support above the 10 percent electoral threshold. (See Table 1.1 above in chapter 1).

The incumbent government's coalition members suffered the heaviest losses. Compared to the 1999 election, the largest coalition partner, DSP shrunk down to 1.2 percent (See Figure 2.1). It may have set a world record for being the largest party in one election and losing almost all its support in the next one. Among the reasons for such a dramatic shrinking of electoral support comes first the major economic crisis that took place during the DSP's tenure.[9] Another reason was the poor organizational capacity of the DSP, which almost exclusively relied on the charisma of its legendary leader Bülent Ecevit. However, Ecevit's health was also deteriorating just prior to the general elections. This was a major issue used by his opponents within and outside of his party and was covered extensively in the media. Another major reason was the splits within the DSP which gave rise to yet another new party on the left of the Turkish ideological spectrum, the YTP, which was founded by two prominent members of the Ecevit cabinet: Hüsamettin Özkan the Minister of State and İsmail Cem the Minister of Foreign Affairs. For a short period of time, the then non-Parliamentarian Minister of Economic Affairs, Kemal Derviş courted with the YTP but eventually decided to join the CHP. The DSP projected an image of a party that did not look like it was going to gain any seats in parliament. As a consequence, voters seem to have shied away from DSP and were lured into voting for the likely left-wing survivor of the November 2002 election or the reactionary populist GP.

Among the other coalition partners, MHP lost 9.6 percentage points and shrunk down to its 1995 level of electoral support (See Figure 2.1). The junior partner of the coalition ANAP lost 8.1 percentage points. Hence, the coalition partners together lost about 39 percentage points of electoral support from the April 1999 elections. ANAP's electoral basis has been shrinking for nearly two decades ever since the early 1980s when it first came to power. ANAP had been in power until the 1991 general elections and afterwards was part of several coalitions. It effectively lost much of its constituency in the largest metropolitan centers and remained a dominant player only in small pockets of Anatolian provinces primarily in the Eastern Black Sea region where its leader was originally from. The ruling years and even in its aftermath during the coalition years where ANAP was in power, it continuously projected an image of an increasingly corrupt organization which contributed significantly to its melting electoral base.

The MHP's decline is more intriguing, since just about three years prior to the 2002 election it surprisingly rose to an imposing position in the party system by obtaining nearly 18 percent of the valid votes. Those were the times when the Bosnian crisis and the capture of the PKK leader Abdullah Öcalan fired up nationalist sentiments and thus helped mobilize masses towards a traditionally unflinching nationalist party. However, those were also the times when the legendary leader of the MHP Alparslan Türkeş' death created a sometimes uncivilized competition for the party's leadership. The first party congress after Türkeş' death had to be repeated due to violence that erupted during the election process of the new leader. The new leader Devlet Bahçeli was elected in a second party congress after the eventful first one and at the time of the 1999 election he never had a chance to consolidate his power in the rank and file. The unexpected rise of electoral support pushed him to an uneasy position to take part in a three party coalition with the DSP and ANAP. The DSP's charismatic leader Bülent Ecevit was known to be a long-time adversary of the *Grey Wolves*, which formed the heart of the party, but his aging composure reflected a more conciliatory image towards the nationalists at the time. More importantly however, the DSP-MHP-ANAP coalition had to deal with first, the 1999 earthquakes and then the economic crisis of 2001, which effectively imposed serious restrictions upon patronage distribution capabilities of the MHP ministers. Bahçeli's purely rational impulse was to appeal to the larger and, by definition, ideologically more centrist masses. Bahçeli hence aimed at consolidating MHP's partisan base during their tenure in the coalition government. The more emotional impulse was to provide a series of firm nationalist reactions, even those of a knee-jerk nature, if necessary to keep the *Grey Wolves* constituency happy and under control. Such a dilemma proved to be a difficult test for the MHP. In the aftermath of the August 1999 earthquake the MHP Minister of Health Osman Durmuş declared that Greek blood could not be used in the rescue operations. MHP ministers who had an economic policy-wise relevant portfolio dragged their feet to implement any privatization policy. As a consequence, the MHP could neither please its core constituency, nor could it enlarge upon it and was tarnished by poor economic performance during its tenure.

Having said this however, we should note that the MHP's performance in 2002 is not very poor compared to its long-term level of electoral support at the polls. In the first post-military coup election of 1961 the CMKP received about 13 percent of the vote. Afterwards, the MHP received between 3 to 6 percent until the 1987 election when it received about 3 percent of the valid votes. In 1995 it raised its support to about 8 percent and then to 18 percent in 1999. In 2002 the support level for the MHP declined to its 1995 level of about 8 percent. This however, is considerably higher than the MHP's pre-1980 level of support. What then are the characteristics of the new MHP constituency? Are they attitudinally considerably more nationalistic and patriotic than other parties in the system? Or are there other factors that better define the MHP constituency? We address these and other questions in Chapter seven below.

Figure 2.1 Electoral Support for Major Parties, 1950–2002

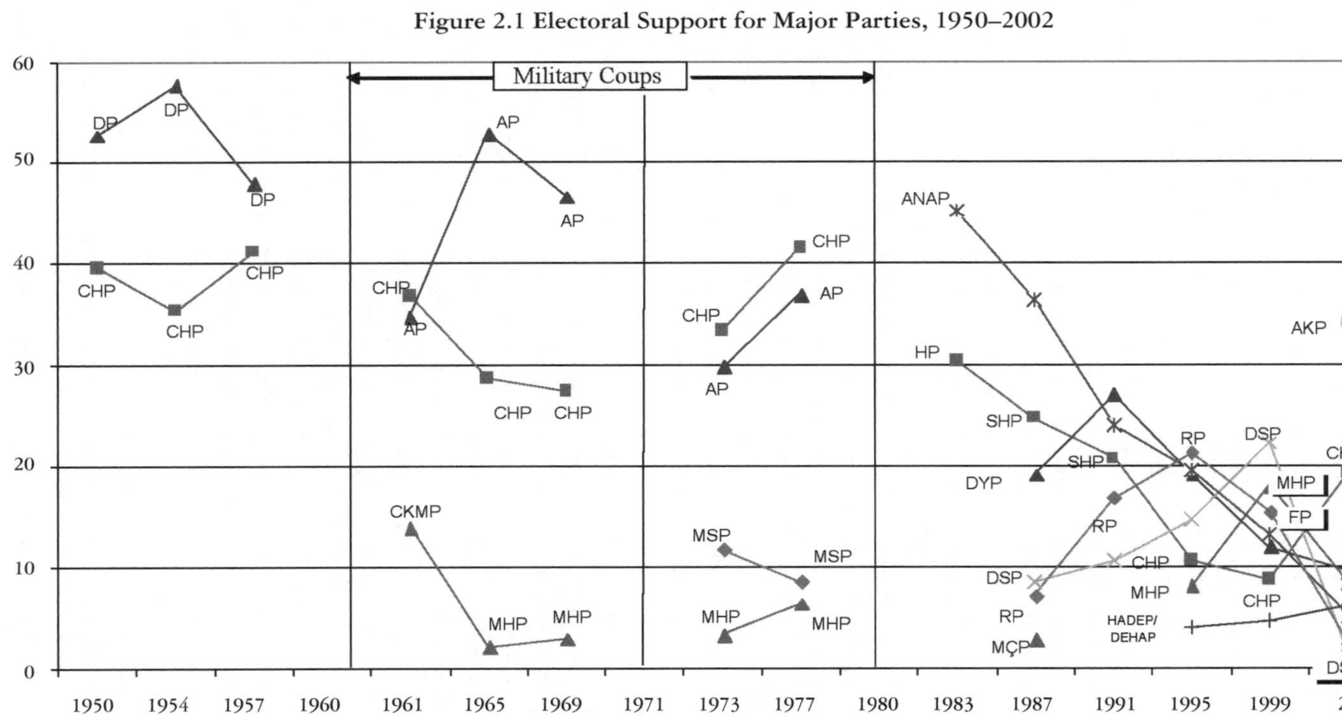

The two major opposition parties did not perform much better in November 2002 compared to their accomplishments in 1999. While the pro-Islamist SP suffered a loss of 12.9 percentage points, the DYP lost 2.5 percentage points. Besides the CHP and AKP and to a lesser degree the Kurdish DEHAP, all opposition parties incurred significant losses of electoral support. It is thus worthy of note that the collapse of the DSP-MHP-ANAP coalition did not help any one of the centrist opposition parties other than the CHP. In other words, besides the CHP's modest electoral gains all other parties that increased their support came from the margins of the Turkish ideological spectrum.

Figure 2.2 shows the progression of the collapse for the centre left and right parties. Prior to the 1980 coup, the centre right wing of the Turkish electoral scene has always gathered more than 40 percent of the votes while the centre-left being always smaller in size than the centre-right, with the exception of 1977 election, used to gather around 30 percent. In the aftermath of the 1980 coup, smaller parties on the margins of the ideological spectrum initially almost disappeared from the scene. This was mainly due to the military regime's limitations in the party system by vetoing pre-1980 leadership to participate in elections. The then newly imposed 10 percent nationwide vote threshold for representation in the Parliament was also responsible for poor performance of the smaller parties in the system. In 1986, under constant pressure from the public, a referendum was held to decide whether the pre-1980 leaders should be allowed to come back to the political arena. With a slight margin in favor of the lifting of the ban, an early election was held in 1987, which resulted in a major set back for the centre right parties that is, primarily the then ruling ANAP. Ever since, the centre-right group of parties has continuously lost support reaching an all time low at around 15 percent in 2002. Considering the fact that back in 1983 this group got nearly 70 percent and for most of the 1950s and 1960s it remained in excess of 50 percent electoral support as a group, this contraction is remarkable.

The centre-left's electoral support has oscillated around 30 percent for most of the post 1980 period. In fact, after the 1995 election wherein the centre-left received around 25 percent of the votes it resiliently bounced back up, again reaching about 30 percent in 1999. However, the following election of 2002 brought the lowest ever vote share for the centre-left with about 22 percent. What is striking is that for both the centre-left as well as centre-right, 2002 marks the lowest vote shares.

As a rule of thumb, it stands to reason that in elections, if one group of parties' share of the vote decreases, another groups' should correspondingly rise. This zero-sum nature of elections in the Turkish context brought the extreme-right wing parties to a dominant position for the first time ever. This time the extreme-right wing group of pro-Islamist and nationalist parties gathered about

Figure 2.2 Electoral Support Along Left-Right Ideological Spectrum, 1950–1999

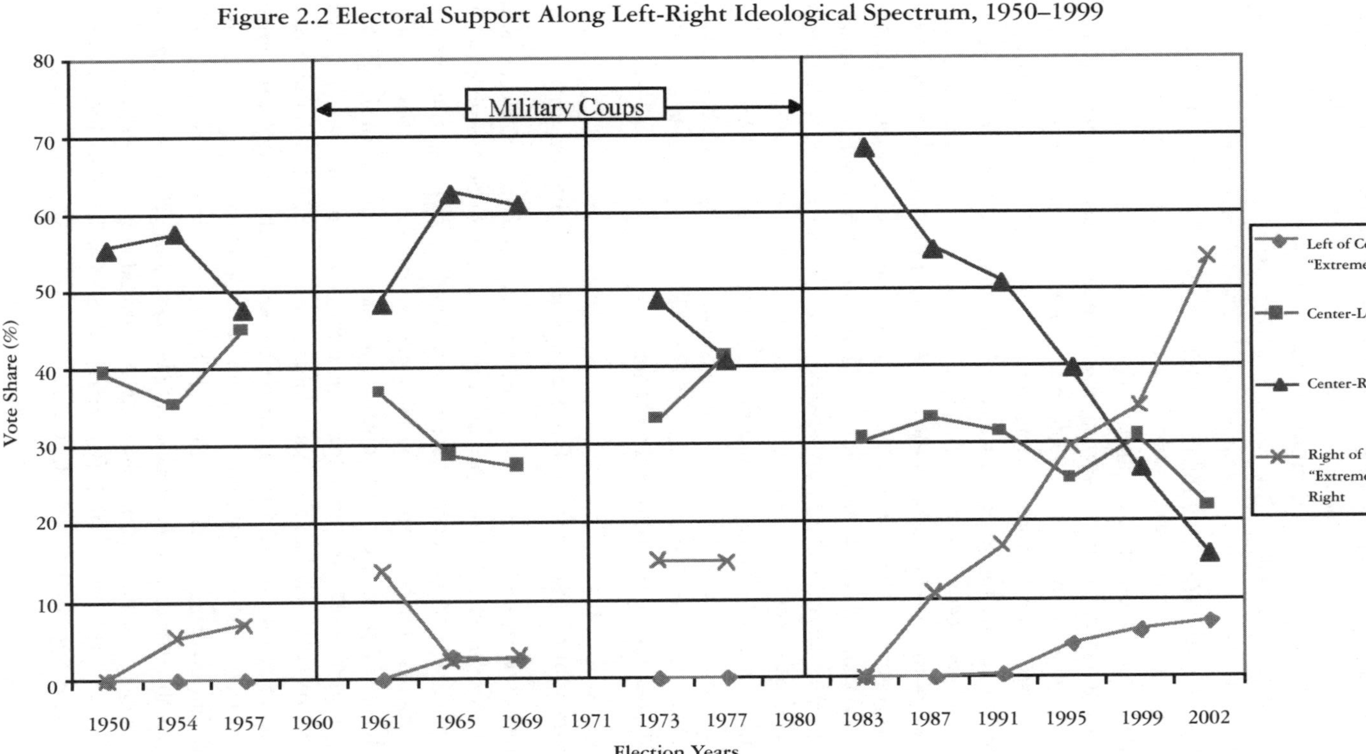

54 percent of votes to remain 32 percentage points above the second largest electoral support group of the centre-left wing parties. Two immediate questions to which we will seek answers below are as follows: Is the rise of the extreme-right end of the left-right ideological spectrum, a reflection of the underlying long-term shift of ideological preferences of the Turkish electorate that is here to stay, or is it a consequence of the short-term complexities of party competition that marks a temporary deviation that is to be counter-balanced in future elections? If this rise could be attributed to micro individual level ideological convictions that are positively predisposed towards rightwing policy stands, then the shift is more likely to be of a longer duration rather than a short run exceptional blimp in the ideological character of the electoral scene. If however, no accompanying micro individual level shift of ideological preferences can be found, then the whole nature of AKP's voters from an ideological perspective is open for debate. Could it be that the AKP in the aftermath of the 2002 election is the new ANAP of the Turkish electoral scene and thus represents the new centre-right for the Turkish electorate? If centrist ideological traits can be obtained for the AKP constituency, not only the nature of their tenure could be better understood, but also a longer term diagnosis of where this party could go and what it could undertake in its tenure and how long that tenure can be held could be much better analyzed. Accordingly, a major theme in our ensuing analyses in especially the chapter six below will be a discussion of the characteristics of the AKP constituency within the conventional left-right ideological spectrum.

Party system characteristics: Persistent Volatility and Fragmentation

Looking at the Turkish electoral scene after the November 2002 elections and trying to foresee what lies beyond, one need to bear in mind characteristics of the post-1980 Turkish party system in light of its roots in the pre-1980 developments. Three phenomena characterize the electoral nature of the Turkish party system. One is its continual instability reflected in significantly large groups of voters who shift from one party to another in two consecutive elections. As voters change their party of choice a larger and larger number of parties come into the field of competition. Given the constraining institutional arrangement of 10 percent nationwide level of support for gaining seats in the parliament, such a high level of fragmentation is surprising unless one takes the irreconcilable ideological cleavages and geographical regionalization of electoral support into account. A third salient feature of the Turkish party system is the continual differentiation of electoral preferences across the competing parties in different clusters of provinces.

Volatility

Since the first truly competitive general elections of 1950, on average, nearly 23 percent of the electorate changes its preferences from one party to another in successive elections (See Figure 2.3 below). In the early 1980s high volatility was primarily due to a changing menu of parties facing the electorate due to the closing and merging of different parties. However, for at least the last three elections – 1995, 1999 and especially in 2002 – we observe that the electorate shifts from one party to another for reasons other than the nonexistence of a previously available party. As underlined above, deterioration of leadership credibility, failing economic performances and an overall inability to respond to the demands and expectations of the voters at large are partially responsible for this continual shift in search of a better alternative among the available parties.

Another important reason behind especially the post-1980 coup period high electoral volatility is the disappearance of party identification (PID) primarily due to party closures of the military regime. Although we have no solid micro-individual level evidence for any degree of PID in earlier periods, the closure of all pre-coup political parties by the military regime impeded earlier tendencies of the electorate to associate itself primarily as a supporter of one of the parties seems to have disappeared during the last quarter of a century.[10]

Given the available election results and expectations concerning the impact of the then continuing economic crisis on party preferences, it should be hardly surprising that an even higher level of volatility compared to 1999 preferences took place in November 2002. As Table 2.2 shows, nearly half of the electorate has shifted from one party to another from the 1999 to the 2002 elections. If we divide the party system into four ideological groups – extreme left, center-left, center-right, and pro-Islamist and nationalist party groups – we observe that about 20 percent of the voters seem to have switched from one group to another between the 1999 and 2002 elections. Besides the CHP, and DEHAP, which inherited its predecessor HADEP's electoral tradition of representing Kurdish ethnicity in the country, there are no parties which gained on their 1999 vote level. The AKP and GP are the other two newly established parties that gathered significant electoral support. The GP was the dark horse of the November 2002 elections and relied on no previous electoral tradition. The AKP clearly had the RP/FP constituency as their target and competed with the SP for that base. In short, increasing volatility seems to benefit new right-of-the-center, in the case of AKP, and populist, in the case of the GP, parties.

In 2002 the pro-Islamist and nationalist group of parties peaked in electoral support reaching nearly 53 percent, an all-time high in Turkish politics. As such, this group is about 3.3 times larger than the center-right parties and about 2.5 times larger than the center-left parties. However, the real question is whether and when will the electoral support become consolidated and stabilized behind these new parties. If the past pattern continues, the next election is bound to create not only some deterioration of electoral support for the AKP but rather a major one creating yet another new right-of-center winner. Our analysis below addresses these questions concerning the character of different party constituencies at the micro-individual level of analysis. Who for instance did AKP voters in 2002 vote for in the previous election of 1999? Where in other words, do they come from? Are there limits in the minds of different party constituencies as to which party they could never vote for? If these boundaries are very soft and fluid, then grounds for continued volatility could easily be diagnosed.

Table 2.2. Party System Characteristics 1999–2002

	1999	2002
Volatility	20,15	50,91*
Fractionalization	85,15	81,44**
Ideological Volatility	12,70	20,00*
Effective Number of Parties	6,73	5,39
percent of vote unrepresented in the Parliament (percent)	18,32	45,33
Extreme-Left (EL)	6,02	7,27
Centre-Left (CL)	31,35	21,77
Centre-Right (CR)	26,77	16,13
Pro-Islamist&Nationalist (PIN)	34,85	53,37

* Highest (ideological) volatility ever in the Turkish party system. When FP is taken as the precursor of both SP and AKP the volatility drops down to 38 percent.

**Lowest fractionalization since 1991 elections.

Volatility index (V) is calculated by using i=1, . . . N parties in the following formula: $V=\{(1/2)\Sigma_N(|\text{Vote percent}_{i,t} - \text{Vote percent}_{i,t-1}|)\}$. The index lies between 0 and 1. V=1 represents a completely unstable system whereas V=0 represents one where all parties obtained the same vote shares as they did in the previous election. See Pedersen (1979).

Effective number of parties (ENP) = 1/(1-Fractionalization Index). The fractionalization index (F) is calculated by using election outcomes for i=1, . . . N parties in the following formula: $F=\{1-\Sigma_N (\text{Vote percent})^2\}$. F varies between 0 and 1. It reaches a minimum of zero when one party receives all of the popular vote. As the number of parties receiving relatively small electoral support increases the index will approach to one. See Rae (1967) on F. Laakso and Taagepera (1979), Taagepera and Shuggart (1989) on ENP.

Figure 2.3 Fragmentation and Volatility in Turkish General Elections, 1950–2002

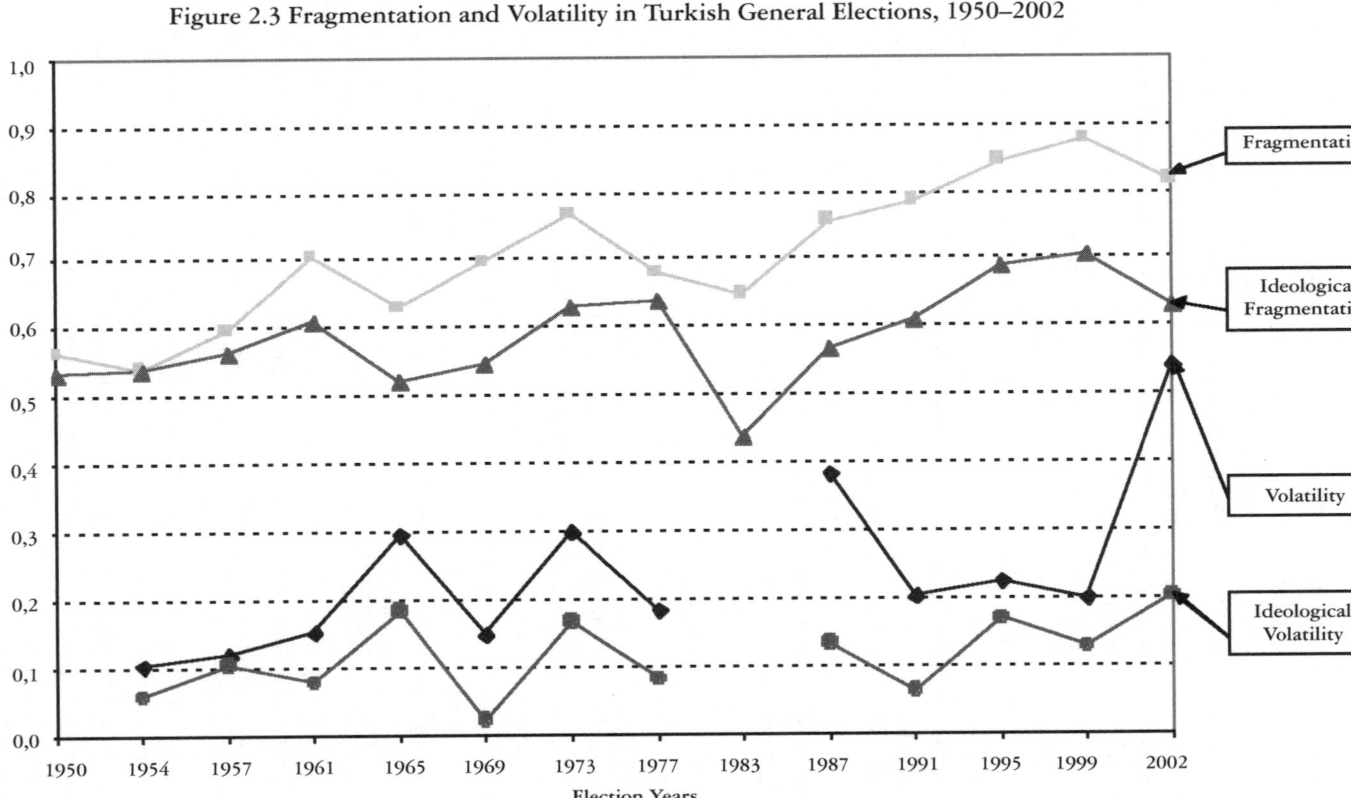

Fragmentation

Another puzzling characteristic of macro election results of the post-1980 period is the continuous and growing fragmentation in the party system. Until the November 2002 elections, despite the very limiting 10 percent nation-wide electoral support for getting representation in the parliament, more and more parties were able to attract voters' support in elections and ultimately winning representation. One aspect of fragmentation that is not reflected in the above index of fragmentation concerns the post-election splits in the parties. Factions that could not get 10 percent nation-wide support typically first get in on a party list and then become independents or create a smaller party of their own. Thus, larger centrist parties like ANAP, SHP/CHP or DYP could get representatives of smaller fractions into the parliament under an umbrella ticket. However, they simply could not accommodate their policy demands and ideological expectations for long and were unable to keep them under the same umbrella. One other reason for such splits is that the inner-party democratic character in such parties never did allow factions but rather pushed them out to become outsiders.

Besides fragmentation in the TBMM, increasing fragmentation in election preferences can also be seen. More and more parties were able to obtain vote shares within the range of 4 to 14 percent. In 1987 there were two parties within this range (DSP and RP) and one at around 3 percent (MÇP). In 1991 DSP reached about 10 percent and the RP-MHP coalition got about 17 percent. In 1995, CHP, DSP, HADEP and MHP were all within this range. Finally, in 1999, ANAP, CHP, DYP, HADEP and FP fell into this range while MHP and DSP were close with about 18 percent and 22 percent respectively. Looking back at the 1999 elections, it is clear that given the volatility of the electorate it was not possible that the party system could maintain such a high number of parties within such a close range of support. Coming into the 2002 elections however, we observe that only two parties get significantly above the 10 percent threshold while 5 parties (ANAP, DYP, MHP, GP and DEHAP) remaining between 4 to 10 percent, and DSP and SP getting about 2 percent each. In other words, while the electoral preferences remained very volatile, they also remained highly fragmented in 2002. Compared to 1999 and 1995, the party system is less fragmented. However, it is still more fragmented than the results of the 1991 election, or any one of the previous elections.

Many experts claimed that the electorate could have united the fragmented system behind one or two major parties in November 2002. This expectation would have been valid if there were no social, economic, ethnic, sectarian and regional differences in electoral preferences dominating the election results.

In a series of articles over the last decade it has been shown that Turkish general elections exhibit a clear pattern of geographic regionalization.[11] An important finding in this literature concerns the observation that there exists very little nationalization of electoral forces in the election results. For almost the past half a century, it has always been local and regional factors rather than national ones that shaped election results.[12] It would have been a real surprise if this general trend had changed in November 2002.[13] One major question, that we aim to address below, concerns the extent to which primordial and parochial cleavages shape party preferences of Turkish voters. To what extent have religiosity, ethnicity, urban-rural differences, socio-economic status been effective in differentiating party constituencies?

Patterns of geographical regionalization

Çarkoğlu's (2000, 2003), and Çarkoğlu and Avcı's (2002) evaluations of the provincial election results in summary show that Turkish provinces reflect three regions. One that covers the so-called "deep" East and Southeastern provinces; another covering the coastal provinces from the Eastern Black Sea down to the Eastern Mediterranean including the whole of Thrace and Aegean provinces; and lastly a large number of provinces that seem to have been squeezed in between these two regions. In terms of their socio-economic characteristics as well as political preferences, these three regions reveal a clear pattern as well. The East and Southeastern provinces are the least developed in all respects and have an ethnic reflection in their political preferences. Their clear preference for HADEP in the 1990s and DEHAP in the last election has its roots in the early 1950 and 1960s when this region also showed a distinct inclination for either the opposition parties or personalized minor parties. This is an important diagnosis. This diagnosis indicates that the electoral peculiarity of the "deep" East and Southeastern provinces is not a recent phenomenon. From the very beginning of the Turkish electoral system, these regions have had a peculiar feature.

The coastal provinces are typically the most developed and modern in their socio-economic backgrounds. Their political preferences are centrist. The provinces of the Anatolian plain fare relatively better in terms of socio-economic development compared to the "deep" Southeast but significantly worse off than the coastal regions. These provinces are the hotbeds of Turkish nationalist and pro-Islamist electoral support.[14] The results from the provinces indicate that a similar pattern is again observed in the last election. The distinct preference of the "deep" Southeast for DEHAP is again obvious but this time we observe a significant rise in its level as well as its spread across the provinces of the East and Southeast. The changing of electoral forces that in a sense challenge the system applies not only to the Kurdish electoral base but even more so for the pro-Islamist electoral base that seem to have advanced from the East into the West and the coastal regions. In a sense, the conservative preferences of the Anatolian steppes have expanded onto the coasts and Western provinces where we still observe some, but significantly shrunken, centrist-right or centrist-left support.

The election system that requires 10 percent nation-wide support to gain representation consistently kept 14 to 19 percent of the electorate unrepresented in the parliament since 1987. The largest share of the unrepresented votes in elections prior to the last one occurred in 1987 (19.8 percent) leaving the centrist DSP as well as right of the center MHP and RP out of the parliament. In 1991, the pre-election coalition between the RP and MHP kept the unrepresented votes at a minimum. However, in 1995 the two extreme ends of the Kurdish issue – that is the nationalist MHP and the ethnic Kurdish HADEP – remained out of the parliament, with total unrepresented votes reaching 14.4 percent. In 1999, the MHP got in and the CHP remained out of the parliament, which meant 19 percent of the votes did not get represented.

Given the fact that no large pre-election coalitions were formed before November 2002 and the persistent fragmentation in preferences, the unrepresented portion of electoral preferences in the National Assembly reached a peak of approximately 45 percent of the vote. What is remarkable about this large unrepresented segment is not only its sheer size but also its ideological nature. The AKP together with the independent MPs could quite conceivably make changes in the Constitution with little difficulty. However, the AKP's seat advantage in the Parliament does not translate into a vote majority in electoral support. Therefore, any time the AKP fails to obtain the CHP's cooperation in such changes, CHP and other opposition parties are justifiably going to question the legitimacy of such changes made by a party with only minority support and pressure the AKP to back down. In other words, the AKP's single party government needs to build a consensus in and also out of the Parliament in order to maintain its legitimacy as a government. The common observation that the AKP turned out to be a mild centrist party after all the excitement about its pro-Islamist roots, persistently ignores the electoral basis for such a cooperative stance in AKP government's policies. The fact that the AKP only commanded about one third of the popular votes in an election where participation was the lowest in the post-1980 era, may be the real reason behind this timid approach to policymaking, rather than a real change of character in their ideological orientations.

Among the parties that remain out of the Parliament, the ethnic Kurdish DEHAP has always suffered from the 10 percent nationwide representation threshold. As a predominantly regional party obtaining its support from the East and Southeastern provinces it nevertheless consistently increased its vote share over the last three elections (running under the HADEP banner in the first two). DEHAP has enlarged its support significantly and reached a larger vote share than ANAP, SP, DSP and the BBP. As such, it is now the sixth largest party in the system. But since HADEP and DEHAP's regionally concentrated electoral support is unrepresented in the Parliament this factor favors the parties that capture the second largest vote shares in those provinces. In 1995 and 1999 the pro-Islamist RP and FP benefited from HADEP being left out of the Parliament. In 2002 it was the AKP which on average gained less than half of the electoral support that DEHAP obtained in East and Southeastern provinces that benefited from this representational threshold. In short, regionalization in party support has implications not only for the way the representation system works but also for the way individual preferences are being molded. However, although we have recent evidence on the geographical shape of electoral support at the macro level we know next to nothing about the individual voter level reflections of regional differences in party choice.

Conclusion

Our short review above was aimed at highlighting the colorful ideological spectrum in the Turkish party system. The last decade has seen the collapse of the centre in favor of more extremist parties with an Islamist or nationalist agenda. Concomitant with such an ideological change was ever-increasing volatility and fragmentation in electoral preferences. Although the rise of Kurdish separatist movement in the 1990s brought the geographical divide in electoral preferences to the forefront of the electoral agenda in the country, there is evidence that such a peculiar cleavage in voters' preferences may be in the making from the very beginning of multi-party elections in the country.

As we approached the 2002 general elections there was little reason to believe that these overall patterns were likely to change. On face value however, these expectations were not justified since only two parties were able to gain seats in the parliament and thus fragmentation was down compared to earlier elections. However, in terms of changing party preferences, the 2002 elections has seen the highest rate of volatility. From the perspective of geographic divide in electoral preferences the previous patterns also continue to a large extent. Four peculiar features of the 2002 elections however remain. We have already underlined the first two of these features. The first concerns the low rate of participation and the second concerns the uncertain ideological nature of the winning AKP. We discuss the other two features concerning the peculiar context within which the November 2002 election took place in the next chapter. This peculiar context was shaped by a deep economic crisis and a series of fundamental reforms toward meeting the Copenhagen political criteria for membership of the EU. In the following chapter we briefly review the impact of the economic crisis and EU adjustment reforms on the political agenda of the country. Next we aim to clarify the nature of participation in the Turkish polity from a macro as well as micro individual perspective. Then we move on to the micro individual level analysis of the determinants of party preferences in November 2002.

3

CONTEXT OF POLITICAL PARTICIPATION: CONTINUAL ECONOMIC CRISIS AND POLITICS OF EU ADJUSTMENT

An important pattern that emerges from the aggregate data on Turkish elections is a high correlation between incumbent party's, or coalition's electoral support and the performance of the economy during its tenure. In other words, the worse (or better) the economy performs during inter-election periods, the greater the drop (or gain) in the electoral support for the party or coalition held responsible for this performance.[1] Given such attentiveness of the electorate on the prevailing economic conditions during an incumbent's tenure, it is not surprising that we also observe a great deal of effort on the part of the incumbents to manipulate the economic policy tools in such a way as to please their target constituencies. Reflections of these manipulations are typically observed in agricultural support prices, government employment and salary raises, delay of price increases in goods and services controlled by the public sector.[2] Typically, however, incumbents fail to stay in power and only upset the economic balances further.

Such distorted incentives are diagnosed all over world democracies. However, given the economic and social fragilities of the Turkish politico-economic system, political manipulations of economic policies have eventually led to a major collapse of the Turkish economy in early 2001. This happened against the backdrop of a series of major natural disasters. In fact, the collapse of the Turkish political centre that was in the making throughout the 1990s followed the tenure of the three party coalition of the DSP, MHP and ANAP which was plagued by crises. While some of these crises came with natural disasters, like the two massive earthquakes in August and November of 1999, the very coalition partners cast some others' seeds. The perceived ineffectiveness of the organisation of public relief efforts in the aftermath of the August 1999 earthquake not only enervated the grieving public, but also proved, once again, the inaptitude of public authorities to respond to the needs of the Turkish public. However, the parliamentary seat distribution, together with the inability of the civic anger to raise the pressure on the government, helped the coalition to survive the political after-shocks of the earthquake.

The impact of the financial crisis that hit the country first in November 2000 and next in February 2001 was much more severe on the political front. Political manipulations of fiscal policies leading to an unsustainable public debt were commonly diagnosed as the underlying reason for these crises, which resulted in unprecedented urban unemployment and a record depreciation of the Turkish lira against all foreign currencies. The crisis peaked on 21 February 2001 with an overnight devaluation of the Turkish lira by about 50 percent. By the end of the year, about 2.3 million people had lost their jobs and the economy had contracted in real terms by as much as 8.5 percent. Together with the August 1999 earthquake, the devastating impact of the economic crises has been reflected in the political arena in the form of alarmingly high alienation from the centrist political parties. The incumbent coalition partners were perceived as responsible for the economic crises and their clumsiness in responding to the earthquakes. Yet the centrist opposition was also attributed the blame for their perceived lack of credibility and willingness to cooperate with one another in order to respond to people in crisis.

A significant finding in all surveys of the winter and spring 2001 reported in newspapers is the large portion of the respondents (26.1 percent) who declared that they would not vote for any one of the existing parties and an equally surprising 10 percent who declared that they would cast an invalid protest vote.[3] The fact that in November 2002 general election turnout rate remained at 79 percent, lowest since 1977, points to the correctness of these diagnoses. In short, during the first part of 2001, about one third of the electorate was not undecided, but rather decided not to cast their votes for any one of the then existing parties. Recurrent crises and lack of accountability in the party system seemed to have pushed the Turkish electorate away from the available options in the party system. This alone was enough to bring uneasiness to the party system and thus possibilities of leadership changes, as well as the establishment of new parties under possibly fresh leadershi[4]

A key observation in the aftermath of the November 2000 and February 2001 economic crises is that politically motivated economic manipulation is primarily responsible for the ever-increasing public debt and its consequent crisis. Accordingly, the economic austerity program adopted in their aftermath aimed at limiting the ability of governments to engage in politically motivated policy manipulations. Nevertheless, intricate public bidding and spending arrangements that may take place before elections still kept political manipulation of the economy as a possibility. However, before the November 2002 election, the incumbent DSP-MHP-ANAP coalition seemed unable to deliver any significant amelioration in the economic conditions facing large electoral masses. Accordingly, the coalition's electoral support of about 54 percent in the aftermath of 1999 election shrank to about 15 percent in November 2002. This constitutes the largest drop in Turkish electoral history for an incumbent or coalition in two consecutive elections. We accordingly aim to diagnose below the extent to which economic evaluations of retrospective as well as prospective type are responsible for differentiating the party choice for or against the incumbents.

In order to fully assess the politico-economic context of the November 3, 2002 election we need to consider two historical developments that took shape simultaneously. One is the economic crisis and ruling coalition's ineptitude that created impatience and anger toward the Ankara establishment. The other is the surprising initiative taken by the outgoing Parliament to pass the legal adjustment package for EU membership candidacy before the elections. The outgoing government's willingness to bring the EU adjustments to the election agenda reflected a need to reshape the debate with an eye toward meeting the challenges of becoming a viable EU candidate.

The Economy and the Turkish Centrist Parties

Regarding the two-year-long economic crisis plaguing Turkey, the centrist parties, reluctant to make populist promises, lost their appeal. One major reason for the centrist parties to refrain from engaging into populist promises as often and as unscrupulously as their opponents, was the fact that they were in power. If they signaled any increase of populism, the World Bank and the IMF would immediately block the international financing of the running economic crisis, and within a matter of nearly hours, the economy would once again plunge into a new crisis. As such, the incumbent parties of the ruling coalition simply could not even portray a caring economic policy appealing towards the short-term needs of the suffering masses. No matter how incredible the promises of the AKP and GP might have been, they nevertheless signaled the masses that they would change the status quo and adopt more caring policies for the masses. The incumbent coalition partners could not credibly respond to such rhetoric simply because they had already had their chance and had not acted effectively. Even the challenging opposition parties such as the DYP, CHP and SP were unable to come up with believable alternatives that could attract the suffering masses. The CHP's inability to orchestrate a campaign challenge based on the economic issues was primarily a result of enduring leadership crisis among the elites. Besides elites' preoccupation with Byzantine struggles of leadership, the CHP, together with Tansu Çiller's DYP, lacked trustworthiness since they were in power just a few years ago, during the previous economic crisis, and thus were not seen by the masses as adept and potent parties that can deliver prosperity in a sensible and convincing way.

The SP's problem was slightly different in character than those of the CHP and DYP. SP was primarily in competition with the newly rising popularity of the new generation pro-Islamists of Tayyip Erdoğan and his friends. By clearly being identified with the old RP/FP pro-Islamist cadres in style and pro-Islamist rhetoric, an easy evaluation of their standing was also being made possible for the masses. This old generation pro-Islamists were able to come to power in the aftermath of December 1995 under the leadership of now banned Necmettin Erbakan and were simply unable to achieve anything other than political polarization during their tenure in coalition with the DYP. The February 28th process was a result of their uncooperative and provocative style. The main expectations of their core constituency however, seem to have been one of well-targeted patronage distribution rather than ideological fights with the secularist establishment in Ankara. Due to their low credibility in the eyes of not only the centrist masses, but also their own core constituency, the old generation pro-Islamists could not capitalize upon the economic collapse in the country.

Left-of-center parties also did not stand a better chance in this respect. Besides a few left-wing parties such as the Workers' Party (*İşçi Partisi*-İP) and the TKP a left-wing perspective in the economy could not be underlined during the campaign. These extremist perspectives were primarily nationalist in their orientation and were largely seen as adventurous and implausible given the foreign aid dependent and fragile Turkish economy. These parties' rhetoric towards the Kurdish minority was either xenophobically reactionary or too soft for larger masses of Turkish society. More importantly, these parties were in unison opposing Turkish membership in the EU and thus were not palatable for the centrist masses.

The centrist DYP's credibility was equally tarnished given the past performance of its leader Tansu Çiller in office when the 1994 economic crisis hit the country. The only potentially convincing party that could have used the economic alienation of the masses for building an electoral base was the CHP. However, the CHP also failed to deliver on this front despite, or perhaps because of the fact that it had on its ranks the widely visible Kemal Derviş who ran the economic program in the aftermath of the February 2001 economic crisis. In hindsight, the leadership struggles among the deeply divided left elites might have engulfed the naïve attempts of Derviş and his entourage, which at the on-set were very instrumental in pushing the country to an early election.

The fact that Kemal Derviş was running on CHP list and that CHP was unable to effectively use economic issues in a convincing way to attract votes is surprising if one also takes into account the media popularity of Derviş. In early summer 2002, the Turkish media was constantly pushing the electoral appeal of Derviş. However, as the summer progressed and the campaign began, the choices made by Derviş at critical junctures disillusioned many. First came his decision to part ways with the YTP, which he had originally encouraged enthusiastically to splinter away from the DSP as a new party. Despite his damage control efforts, in the minds of the Turkish voters this may have seemed too slick a move. After all, in the eyes of many laymen, Derviş had been involved in a failed attempt to eliminate the DSP and Bülent Ecevit from the political scene, trying to discredit him in an unprecedented campaign bordering on character assassination. The plan to capture the DSP leadership from within collapsed once the MHP leader Devlet Bahçeli accepted calls for early elections. Unprepared for such a move, the other coalition partners could only play along. After the election, Ecevit called this decision a "political suicide". Although it is hard to support this interpretation with solid data, it is nevertheless plausible to assert that in the eyes of Turkish public opinion, Derviş might have suffered for the maneuvers that created this situation. This was not because Ecevit still commanded some popularity, but rather because Derviş opted to play along the center-left establishment of CHP after having created expectations for a fresh new movement.

A second *faux pas* was Derviş' choice of running as a candidate under the CHP. Now that Derviş had broken away from the YTP, the mission was accomplished for the CHP leadership. YTP was not going to be a threat to split the left votes into two because of the potential popularity Derviş could have created for them. Hence, the CHP leadership did not particularly need him, or his obscure team. The CHP establishment also had to control Derviş and avoid having to deal with a popular shadow leader and his entourage within the party. Perhaps the only successful operation in this affair turned out to be this very control strategy of the CHP leadership. Derviş as a consequence was kept out of the limelight, not able to actively campaign on any significant issue and especially not being able to project a new alternative vision for the economy.[5]

In consequence, Derviş failed to attract significant newcomers to the CHP which continued to project an intellectually stagnant, unmovable status quo establishment. Derviş' genuine efforts to create unity in the Turkish left and transform it into a modern social democrat movement might have been too naïve strategically and devoid of much deep intellectual substance as well as popular bases of appeal. If this election was about the economic crisis, corruption and Ankara's clumsiness about helping the people, Derviş might not have had much to offer from the start. The financial panic might have ended nearly after 18 months of work by him and his team of economists, but much of the economy at the time had not felt any improvements yet. His image as a "World Bank man" could also not easily "sell" among an increasingly angry and alienated electorate. Considering the fact that even among the CHP elite his World Bank credential was not popular, made the whole job of running a new visionary economic agenda on his personality an almost impossible task. If the election was about the future of the economy, then Derviş needed to project a new fresh team of experienced specialists in the CHP lists, which he also could not provide. The lacking team and elite support base was also reflective of a narrow intellectual basis for a new social democratic agenda for the country that convincingly appealed to the masses.

The media might also have exaggerated Derviş's charisma. Old-style campaigning with mass meetings and hand-shaking might still be more important in Turkey than making a good impression on television interviewers. Moreover, Derviş projected a disillusioning, almost authoritarian pro-militaristic image in an interview he gave to Neşe Düzel in *Radikal* daily newspaper on October 21, 2002.[6] For those wanting a fresh left perspective on not only economic policy matters, but also on larger social issues, he simply seemed to be projecting an old *étatist* view. From civilian military relations to minority rights and democratization debates, it seemed that he had nothing novel and genuinely new to offer. Derviş might have had all the credentials for a successful savior of the Turkish economy but no real broader social vision for the potentially left leaning masses. After all, as we will elaborate in detail below, the Turkish electorate was for a long time steadily moving to the right of the ideological spectrum. The potential of the left to appeal to the left leaning centrists could have only be used if the economic suffering was brought to the center by a credible and likeable left leadership. Instead, such an easy campaign agenda was left to be exploited by the right-of-center in the party system.

Equally important was the lack of sincere argumentation by the left on the issue of democratization. The AKP however was playing a completely different tune to appeal to mass disillusionments in many different dimensions. As Tarhan Erdem aptly noted in an interview with Neşe Düzel, "Derviş (*and the*

CHP elite) chose to reconcile with the status quo (italics are ours)".[7] In contrast, AKP made a populist call for economic equality, while only scarcely using such controversial Islamist-related issues as the wearing of headscarves in schools.

In retrospect, the decision to go to early elections, DSP led coalition government's loss of credibility, and Ecevit's passing from the scene gave the AKP what it needed to win the majority in the National Assembly. Neither Derviş, nor the ex-foreign minister İsmail Cem, nor the old-time CHP insider Deniz Baykal could fill the vacuum from the left. Baykal's insistence on relying on his party's old guard ensured that the CHP would not be revitalized. Instead of being an alliance of young, dynamic agents of change in Turkey adopting democratic, egalitarian and progressive issue stands, the CHP became a faction of resistance to change.

The EU as a Salient Election Issue?

Another important observation concerns developments on the EU front. The most surprising development of Summer 2002 came with the unexpected passage of an impressive EU adjustment package from the Parliament. This package was passed after the Parliament had taken the decision to go for an early election. Even the most optimistic Europhiles were not expecting such a move. With a large number of resignations from the largest coalition partner DSP in Summer 2002 and the resulting YTP under the leadership of former Minister of Foreign Affairs İsmail Cem, the EU and related issues seem to have been pushed to the forefront of political debate in the country. At one point there were expectations that Cem and Derviş together would use the EU issues as a stepping-stone into riding the issue agenda of the country. However, other political party leaders have by that time only tangentially dealt with this issue in front of the electorate. Besides Cem, the ANAP leader Mesut Yılmaz stood in favor of this issue in his campaign. The MHP leadership openly questioned the worth of EU membership. At the time, ill-looking Ecevit did not seem to care about the EU issue or was simply unable to push behind any issue he believed in. Although publicly in favor of the EU membership, DYP leader Tansu Çiller seemed reluctant to push this topic perhaps considering backlash of the conservative constituencies in their competition with the AKP and MHP, AKP's core constituency was known to be skeptical about EU issues and thus the leadership was not willing to take the lead on this issue.[8] In short, if the EU issue were going to shape the electoral agenda in the next general elections, the political elites' willingness to raise the salience of the EU issues would be a major factor behind this development. If one believes that politicians only move by electoral incentives, then one would also claim that ANAP, more than anybody else, saw an electoral pay-off that no one dared to touch and took its chances by taking the initiative to pass critical pieces of legislation from the National Assembly before the election campaign actually started.

The EU-oriented legislation passed just before the election included abolishing the use of death penalty and opening the way for teaching and broadcasting in native languages other than Turkish (in principle allowing the use of Kurdish dialects in such activities). The EU adjustment package was seen by some as democratizing new regulations bringing the country closer to EU membership, while an opposing group portrayed these as one-sided concessions undermining Turkey's unity and independence. The parties in TBMM were clearly divided. MHP alone rejected all the legislation, while AKP opposed only the abolishing of the death penalty, knowing this vote would not impede the package's passing. ANAP was the new laws' main advocate, hoping it would lead to electoral support and the EU's agreement to advance Turkey's membership application.

ANAP's hopes that voters would reward it for acting on the EU issue however were not realized. It assumed and that the expectant EU institutions would also be pleased. The expected EU support that would push the positive economic expectations upward was also not realized since any action by the EU bureaucracy would only take place after the election. Similarly, public opinion was little affected since not only the measures would not be implemented until later, but also the salience of the EU in the minds of the voters was not as high as ANAP leadership had hoped. ANAP's campaign was not effective in pushing this issue since the party organization was falling apart on the expectation that it would not survive the 10 percent nationwide threshold. Many influential names resigned and joined AKP, MHP or became independent.

One issue that needs to be clarified before we move on to further analysis of electoral preferences still remains on our agenda. It concerns the question of whether or to what extent did the EU membership and related issues played a role in the November 2002 election. Our pre-election survey in October 2002, just prior to the November 3 elections and the post-election survey in January and February 2003, a few months after the election included questions that could help us determine the salience of EU membership and related issues. Table 3.1 shows the summary answers given to the most important problem Turkey faces in both the pre and the post-election surveys. These questions were asked in an open-ended format. Respondents could describe up to two most important problems on the agenda. Table 3.1 shows the collection of the answers given related to the most important as well as the second most important problem Turkey faces. We calculated the shares of problems among all answers given for both surveys.

Table 3.1 Most Important Problems of the Country

	Pre-election (%)	*Post-election (%)*
Unemployment	30	28
Economic instability and crisis	27	27
Inflation	20	19
Political instability-uncertainty	8	3
Education	4	3
Corruption-bribery	3	2
Health-social security	2	2
Conflict in Iraq-war	1	12
EU-Foreign policy	1	1
Others	4	3
Total	100	100

We observe that in both prior to the general election of November 2002 as well as in its aftermath, economic problems occupy the top three slots among answers. As expected, with the forming of AKP's single party government, political instability and uncertainty has significantly dropped in shares they occupy in the answers. With a war in the horizon in Iraq, nearly 12 percent of the respondents in the post-election survey placed war in Iraq as the most important problem facing the country, placing it on the fourth rank in the list. However, prior to the election, the Iraq war was not an important issue for the Turkish public. Education (4 percent), corruption-bribery (3 percent), health-social security (2 percent) were all placed above the war in Iraq.

Most significantly for our purposes, while the economic instability and crisis, unemployment and inflation topped the list, the EU and related foreign policy issues came to occupy the most important problem in the minds of only about 1 percent of the electorate. Despite the fact that in the aftermath of the election, the AKP leadership had worked on the issue of EU membership, no significant change is observed with respect to EU and related foreign policy issues in the aftermath of the elections. Hence we are led to believe that, despite the heated debates in early August and just prior to the Copenhagen summit in December 2002, the electorate continued to see EU and related foreign policy issues as of minor importance for the country.

In order to asses the degree to which respondents were able to evaluate the changes within the Copenhagen adjustment package passed in early August 2002, we asked whether or not they remembered the reforms that the EU adjustment package provided in both pre- as well as post-election surveys. Table 3.2 shows that before the elections, those who remember what the adjustment package was all about counted about 25 percent. About two to three months after the elections, on the other hand, those who remembered what the August package was about dropped to about 17 percent.

Table 3.2 Salience of the EU Issues

Do you remember the topics that the EU adjustment package passed from the parliament in August 3rd, 2002?

	Pre-election (%)	*Post-election* (%)
Remembers	25	17
Does not remember	74	82
No Answer	1	1

(Asked only to those who remember the topics) Could you tell us what these topics were?

	Pre-election (%)		*Post-election* (%)	
Abolishing the death penalty	73%	41	55%	20
Broadcasting and education in native languages		11		7
Human rights		14		21
Freedom of thought		4		4
Minority foundations		3		1
Other	27		45	

Those who said they remembered the contents and nature of this adjustment package were asked to list these reforms. The answers to this question were again obtained in an open-ended format. Whatever the respondents told the interviewers was noted. The answers show us that, while in the pre-election context, about 73 percent gave an acceptable answer concerning the amendments, in the post election survey, the acceptable answers dropped down to about 55 percent. In other words, about six months after the passage of the Copenhagen criteria adjustment package only about nine percent (55 percent of the 17 percent) of the electorate remembered what it really was about. Clearly, these answers show that only a small minority of the electorate did remember the August reform package in detail. The size of this minority became even smaller with the passage of time. Even the then-hotly debated issues of abolishing the death penalty and broadcasting/education in native languages other than Turkish were remembered by only about 5 percent (27.5 percent of the 17 percent) of the respondents in the aftermath of the elections – down from about 13 percent (51.8 percent of the 24.6 percent).

All of this suggests that the salience of the adjustment package for the electorate was quite low to begin with at the time of the election. With the passage of time, most voters seem to have forgotten about the content of these reforms. Obviously, voters could still hold views on EU reforms without having much information about them. Nevertheless, we observe that whatever views they possess on these reforms they still did not put the EU related issues at the top of their agenda.

One important reason for such an abrupt decline of attention on EU reforms and the persistently low salience of EU and related issues might be the failure of the political elite to push these issues forcefully in the public realm. In addition to the force with which these issues are used in election campaign, it may also be the case that whatever use there was of the EU issues in the election campaign this basically lacked consistency and coherence for the electorate to easily comprehend and evaluate them.[9]

Another reason for the decline of attention on and salience of EU related issues could be due to the emergence of major populist/nationalist threat from the GP and the MHP. While both parties' constituencies favored EU membership, their elite ideology was staunchly nationalist in the case of MHP or populist in the case of GP. Both parties were also highly anti-EU in their rhetoric and policy stands. Although both GP and MHP failed to mobilize sizeable constituencies against the EU, they nevertheless were successful in deterring the other major parties, especially the two likely winners (AKP and CHP) from being pro-active on the EU front (see Çarkoğlu, 2004, 35).

In short, the party campaigners in the AKP as well as CHP have most likely diagnosed that there were not much attention being paid to the EU issue and they were equally deterred from using the EU related issues for fear of being attacked by the nationalist as well as populist circles. As a result, the EU cause remained abandoned in the election campaigns. "[N]either CHP facing GP, nor AKP facing MHP in their core constituencies in coastal or central Anatolian provinces respectively, could afford to push EU related issues beyond the mere subtle linkage to various reform debates. In consequence, the anti-European front was not confronted publicly in any public debate and the two largest parties kept the EU issues at low salience. At the same time, the euro-skeptic front was conveniently kept divided into smaller party constituencies thus helping to waste their representation by keeping them out of the parliament for being below the ten percent threshold" (Çarkoğlu, 2003, 192). As a result, the EU issues did not exert a determining effect on the November 2002 election.

Threat from Irresponsible Populism

We have often referred to the impact of the GP in November 2002 on the centrist parties. Given the miserable economic state of affairs in the years prior to the election and the resultant alienation of the masses, a number of new parties took the stage and tried to appeal to the electorate on basically non-ideological and opportunistic populist rhetoric. One such emerging new party was Cem Uzan's GP, which few took seriously at first. When a polling result was published on September 30, however, GP seemed to be above the threshold and one of the few parties likely to gain seats.[10]

This situation revealed some of the problems in contemporary Turkish politics. The one-man show of Cem Uzan in GP's slick commercial show using his family's television and radio stations, as well as his cellular phone network could simply not be legally and politically counteracted. Many tenets of his campaign were in direct violation of the political campaign regulations, but no serious steps were taken to stop them. Uzan's speeches were full of exaggerated populist promises, including: increasing the number of provinces from 81 to 250; 200 square meters of state-owned land to be given to every family; cheap credits for every family to be paid back in 30 years; distribution of all school books for free; abolishing VAT Value Added Tax on foodstuffs; no tax on minimum wage and an overall reduction of taxes; and higher support prices for agriculture. Some of these points – like no taxes on minimum wage – were shared by the MHP and DYP. Uzan's promise of a university for every province was matched by DYP and even surpassed by promising new ones in provinces that already had one university. It seems however, that once this bidding game started, others – especially DYP's Tansu Çiller – followed suit with her own version of populism, like promising a tractor for every farmer and shifting the state banks for agriculture and small merchants to farmers and small merchants. Obviously, the appeal of populism was more irresistible to the opposition than for the incumbent coalition partners that were effectively being disciplined on economic grounds by primarily the international financial circles.

Such an irresponsible populism and anti-establishment rhetoric resembles the experiences of Ross Perot in the United States and Sylvio Berlusconi in Italy. Uzan, and to some degree Erdoğan, turned their campaign speeches into expressions of detestation and loathing against the not only the then ruling government but also the whole establishment. For Erdoğan this establishment included mostly western and secularist minded intellectual circles together with state bureaucracy and its partners in the business community. For Uzan it included his competitors in the media and their associates in the power circles of Istanbul business community. Obviously, none of Uzan's promises could be realized within the austerity program. But this type of campaigning was meant to convince voters that leaders cared about them and intended to do something about their suffering. A sophisticated argument about the lack of resources to achieve such goals would not influence many. The people wanted change, blamed the establishment, and sought to express their anger. Uzan, and in some ways the AKP, seems to have given them exactly what they wanted. We aim to show below the impact of this apparent disgust with the government and the establishment in shaping voters' preferences (see Chapter 6 and 7 below).

Conclusion

The November 2002 election brought to power a very different group of leaders and, for the first time since 1991, a single-party government. While AKP's core constituency was skeptical about EU membership, the new rulers began with an impressive tour of European capitals and a push for a starting date on negotiations regarding Turkish membership. Similarly, they seemed to move forward on supporting a solution to the Cyprus issue. In three years of their tenure in office they seem to have accomplished most of what they set out for themselves. Turkey got a starting date for EU membership negotiations in December 2004 and eventually started the negotiations in October 3rd 2005. Before the December 2004 decision the complicated Cyprus issue took a significant turn primarily due to initiatives taken by the AKP government and the Turkish side of the island approved the Annan Plan while the Greek side refused it in April 2004. This seems to have given the upper hand to the Turkish side on the Cyprus conflict. However, such an interpretation could easily be opposed by a pessimistic one stating that the actual start of EU negotiations without reaching a real solution on the island actually leaves Turkey vulnerable to veto threats of the Greek administration during the negotiation phase and thus renders a solution on the island more difficult unless Turkey accepts certain concessions that are very risky from a domestic politics perspective. Both the implementation of the Copenhagen criteria adjustment packages, as well as the resolution of the Cyprus issue are likely to spark chauvinist if not nationalist reactions within the country that could effectively push the AKP back to an isolationist pro-Islamist corner especially approaching the general elections in 2007. Especially after the no votes in the European Constitution referendums in France and the Netherlands, and the rise of the Turkey skeptic right-wing parties in France and Germany, rise in nationalism in Turkey is not a very far-fetched scenario.

We maintain that such scenarios could easily be multiplied if no serious analysis of the AKP constituency is available. We aim therefore to provide such an analysis to render evaluation of such scenarios more plausible and convincing. Only then, we could be more comfortable in judging whether the present two-party dominance in the party system is viable and sustainable. Only then, we could evaluate the likelihood of AKP continuing to dominate the electoral scene and thus truly becoming a centrist right-wing party and convincingly inheriting the DP-AP tradition in Turkish politics. Only then, we could comfortably evaluate whether high volatility and fragmentation period in Turkish electoral system has finally come to an end. Consequently, we could convincingly diagnose the truly transforming impact of the EU membership adjustment on Turkish politics. Our analyses in the ensuing chapters will thus focus on determinants of vote choice for AK However, in so doing we also aim at underlining the distinguishing characteristics of other major competitors of the AKP in terms of demographics, ideological stands and issue preferences. Among these ideological predispositions in general and particularly the impact of religiosity together with evaluations of the voters concerning the economic performance of the incumbent government in the November 2002 election occupy a peculiarly important place.

The decade preceding the November 2002 election witnessed an unmistakable collapse of the center in Turkish party system. Accompanied with high levels of fragmentation and volatility in the system, the once dominant centrist parties of the 1990s were reduced to insignificant players in the aftermath of November 2002 election. Chapter six below presents a detailed analysis of the long-term trends in left-right ideological predispositions and an assessment of the character of the AKP and other parties in a changing ideological environment.

Our overarching theoretical interest in analyzing the November 2002 election concerns the nature of political participation in the country. We therefore start our analysis in chapter four first by focusing on the macro-geographic characteristics of electoral participation in Turkey. Then we move to micro-individual level analysis of our survey data in chapter five and focus on not only the conventional but also the unconventional political participation patterns in Turkey in comparison to western democracies. We conclude with a short overview and assessment of the patterns in political participation in general and the Turkish electoral behavior in particular.

4

ANALYZING POLITICAL PARTICIPATION AT MACRO LEVEL OF ANALYSIS

Every election is in one way or another peculiar. That is what makes electoral politics a continually dynamic and fluid phenomenon that begs the attention of systematic analyses. Such analyses though, underline not only short run temporal spikes of peculiar impacts upon electoral developments, but they also indicate longer term regularities and patterns that shape the nature of electoral choices in a given polity. The November 2002 general election in Turkey has also taken shape under quite peculiar circumstances. Having contextualized the election of November 2002 with its competing parties, personalities of the elites and the issues being debated in the campaign, we now set out to diagnose patterns in the way Turks have participated in elections for the last nearly six decades.

We follow in this quest an often used methodological focus of contrasts. We first concentrate on the macro-level patterns in electoral participation. We use the provincial geographic data to diagnose the patterns and trends in participation rates in Turkish general elections. Next, we move on to a deeper micro-individual level analysis of the determinants of various conventional as well as unconventional political participation behaviors.

Political Participation: The conventional vs. the unconventional

Actions aimed at influencing political decisions through impacting on the election or selection of political authorities take three different forms. In every society where mass politics has emerged, some form of mechanism that recruits the masses into the political process has been invented and implemented. Plebiscites in totalitarian and authoritarian regimes, national and local elections, referendums, recall and initiative have all been devised as structures that provide channels of expression of the "popular will". All such machinations purport to provide legitimate and official channels of expression of the choices of the voters. They also serve the political authorities in many ways. Whether it is the results of a plebiscite, where only one and officially approved list of a party or candidates appear on the ballot, or it is a competitive national election, where many genuinely different political party lists or candidates compete, the political authorities consider and publicly announce their results to be the "people's choice". Consequently, they provide legitimate grounds for the authorities, approved through mass support, in taking binding decisions for the societies over which they have jurisdiction. Through participation in such acts of mass approval or disapproval, the people take part in the ritual of authorizing the right of the political incumbents of authority positions to govern. Finally, when repeated over time, such conventions provide an opportunity to socialize large masses of people into the political regime that governs the country. Such widely shared political rituals and practices tend to become conventional channels of electoral expression and influence. They impact on the character of the regime, and represented support, or lack of, to the existing political order and the political authorities in government. Such acts of political participation have been depicted as *conventional participation* (Barnes and Kaase, 1979, 84–85). The most ostentatious form of such conventional acts of participation is simply taking part in the ritual of voting or abstaining from such action. However, *conventional* acts of political participation are not simply identical with taking part in voting. Membership and taking part in political party activities from selection of candidates or sponsoring them to campaign activities or donations, raising public awareness, involving in public debates and deliberations to seeking solutions for communal or national problems and issues, and writing letters and petitions to legislators, cabinet ministers, prime ministers, or presidents have been officially approved, legitimate, legal and publicly accepted forms of political actions. They can and from time to time do influence political decisions. It is thus warranted to assume that all such acts constitute conventional acts of political participation.

In this day and age it is relatively easy to notice that not all acts of political participation flow through conventional channels and structures. Indeed, most forms of political influence that makes the headlines in every major daily paper since the ominous developments of September 11, 2001 have been mostly what may be considered as "*unconventional*" forms of political action (Barnes and Kaase, 1979, 66). However bizarre, bloody, and violent they may be, such acts also aim at influencing binding decisions that political authorities take. There seems to be a thread that runs through all such acts.

They all protest some policy, decision or policy outcome of governments. They also are not sensitive to using legitimate channels, mechanisms and rituals of political influence. Indeed, they seem to be "anti-establishment", "anti-regime", and even "anti-system" in content. They often tend to condemn not only a certain political decision, but may travel further and condemn the government or the very form of government and the political elites as an entire socio-political stratum, and the socio-economic and legal structures, which produced the decision or policy in question. A suicide bomber is not just protesting a decision of a foreign or domestic government, but also the entire political regime and the system of government that produced a decision or policy, which is presumed to inflict an unjust, thus illegitimate sanction upon a person, community, or nation. Therefore, *unconventional* political participation again takes legitimacy of political decisions and policies into perspective, though this time it is the presumed lack of legitimacy that seems to be defining the act in question. Legitimate channels and modes of influence are presumed not to be effective or efficient enough to bring an end to unjust practices in question. The severity of violation and undermining of a sense of justice and fairness call for bizarre and shocking acts to raise the awareness of people, impress them and their political masters, and pressure them to halt their unjust and unfair political practices and decisions. Stoppage of traffic on the main roads, occupation of government or corporate buildings, wildcat strikes, non-peaceful demonstrations, throwing stones or cakes at political authorities, hanging members of pressure groups from buildings, and chaining oneself to the gates of nuclear power stations, constitute some examples of the gamut of protest behavior, which in part, define unconventional political participation. Such acts often precipitate legal action by the political authorities and often run counter to the laws of the land. They often cause discomfort, and they intend to shock and impress people of the severity of a certain practice, such as pollution, which if unperturbed causes grave dangers to life on our planet. They are also carried out to bring the plight of a religious or ethnic community to the limelight of international public opinion. The Basque, Chechen, Irish, Kurdish, Palestinian, Tamil and many other ethnic nationalists, Catholic, Druze, Jewish, Shiite, Sikh, Sunni, Greek Orthodox, Protestant and many other religious evangelists have emerged to use disparate forms of, and often violent protests to put what they consider to be the plight of their communities on the national and international agendas.

A careful examination of acts of political influence also indicate that not all unconventional acts occur against a government or to protest a political practice, decision, and policy. Some equally unconventional, illegitimate, illegal, and violent acts occur in support of government policies, in the name of protecting a socio-political order, a religious privilege or practice, an ethnic community, or a political system. Such acts occur to repress those acts of protest that are carried out to reverse policies, decisions, or undermine political regimes and systems. Rallies organized to break up protest marches, wildcat strikes, peaceful demonstrations or political meetings occur in almost every country as well. Repressive acts of participation are also a form of unconventional political participation (Barnes and Kaase, 1979, 87), for they also fail to be sensitized to legal and legitimate rules of the political game of a system. They often tend to employ brute force and produce violence, which is not condoned by the masses and the political elites alone. However, legally elected governments and legal political organizations, such as political parties and associations occasionally resort to such methods to intimidate what they consider to be threatening forces or grave opposition.

Consequently, political participation consists of forms of conventional and unconventional actions of influence. The latter also occurs in two different forms of protest and repressive participation. In this and the following chapter, we will examine all three forms of political participation. Below we first provide a short overview of the literature on Turkey and then move on to the analysis of perhaps the most studied conventional acts of political participation, that is, the very act of voting with the help of geographic provincial election results in Turkey for diagnosing macro patterns therein.

Models of Political Participation in Turkey

Studies of political participation in Turkey, with any kind of rigor, date back to the 1950s. However, between the early 1950's and the late 1960's most studies focused on voting statistics, used aggregate data, and followed an atheoretical approach to political participation. A major deviation from the norm of the time was the study published by Daniel Lerner. Lerner seemed to suggest a causal chain that explained voting participation. The survey data he used were collected from a series of Middle Eastern countries and Turkey in the late 1940s. Lerner (1958) argues that industrialization and urbanization set loose a socio-psychological process into motion. The rural masses realize job opportunities and improved welfare of urban centers, which propel them toward the cities. Once they arrive in the cities, they are further motivated to learn how to read and write and follow the news in the media. They discover that literacy is a necessity in the urban lifestyle and written culture of the city. Job opportunities, market developments, international trends and events could only be followed properly, if one is literate enough to follow the news in the print media. Literacy tends to motivate mass media exposure, which Lerner suggested, ignites an interest in the affairs of government, which in turn, leads one to develop an inclination to support a party at the polls, with the hope that it ascends to power. The gist of the argument that Lerner propounded was that industrialization led to urbanization, which in turn precipitated horizontal social mobility, and promoted literacy and mass media exposure, and thus developed the participatory culture and structures of modern society (1958, 60).

No national survey took place in Turkey, which would provide some insight into political participation until the mid 1970s. However, in the meantime, several rural studies were conducted, which unearthed some facts about political participation of the rural population. Most notable among them was the one carried out under the leading role of Frederick W. Frey. They were conducted in 1962 and a series of publications were made out of these studies between 1963 and 1976[1]. These studies underlined the important role played by socio-economic development in determining political participation in the rural areas of Turkey. Attitudinal factors were not systematically analyzed in these studies, however, some evidence that national identity and political efficacy played some role in the determination of conventional participation emerged (Özbudun, 1975, 40–44). It also became clear that controlling the critical political resource of landownership failed to explain much in the variance of conventional participation (ibid., 48). However, anthropological studies did indicate the importance of patronage mechanisms in political party activities and canvassing of the vote (Kudat, 1975, 61–87, and Sayarı, 1975, 121–133). In a seminal study of a *gecekondu* settlement (shantytown) in metropolitan Istanbul, where recently settled peasants lived, Karpat was able to find that patronage relationships played a major role in determining conventional participation (1975, 103). Patron-client relations, which grew out of uneven distribution of political resources, such as wealth and literacy, seemed to have created patronage networks among regional, confessional, ethnic, and other communities, who provided pools of votes for the local notables in the rural areas, and urban thugs, who controlled such desired resources as land, housing, and jobs.

In the meantime new publications began to appear and corroborate some of the earlier findings, and cast doubt on others. It was Deniz Baykal who, contrary to Lerner's proposition, pointed out that the urban environment is not necessarily supportive of conventional political participation (1970, 73). Baykal's study, published in 1970, used aggregate voting statistics and other aggregate socio-economic and cultural data, and unearthed a negative correlation between urbanization and conventional political participation in Turkey (1970, 73). His other findings seemed to cohere with the earlier findings in Turkey and abroad on the positive correlations between income, occupation, education, and sex roles, as independent variables, and conventional political participation (voting participation) as the dependent variables (1970, 32–70). Nevertheless, Baykal's study stopped short of suggesting any alternative model of political participation.

A more sophisticated effort at building something like a model to explain political participation in Turkey was conducted in an edited volume by Engin Akarlı and Gabriel Ben-Dor (1975). The main thesis of that study was built around the earlier proposed "Center-Periphery" hypothesis of Şerif Mardin, as an explanation of Turkish politics (Mardin, 1973). Mardin argues that Ottoman modernization created a deeply divided cultural milieu between the powerful Center of the Ottoman society, which is constructed of the ruling elite of the Ottoman society, who constituted a culturally homogeneous community, and the rest of the society, which was no less than a heterogeneous majority. He further suggested that Republican Turkey inherited and re-constructed its own center and periphery. The cultural values around which the Center was constructed was now somewhat different from its Ottoman past; however, the Periphery managed to stay the same mix of ethnic and religious communities, usually at odds with each other and the Center (state).

Ayşe Kutad's chapter is a synopsis of her earlier, anthropological studies of Eastern Anatolia, while Sabri Sayarı's work focused on the use of patronage as a tool of promoting populist policies and politics (ibid., 61–87, and 121–133). Both authors focused on the role of the rural power structure in organizing and mobilizing the peasants as voting blocs by the powerful local notables, who enjoy strong linkages with different party machines. Ergun Özbudun's chapter in the same book provides empirical analysis of the voting data (33–60) to further analyze how socio-economic development and power, measured as land ownership, are related to voting participation in the Turkish villages. Özbudun used Frederick W. Frey's earlier study (1963) of the Turkish villages and traced the voting records of those villages about which Frey had collected data to test the explanatory power of some attitudinal variables on political participation. He had unearthed some positive relationship between national identification and political efficacy, and voting participation. Özbudun, using voting participation as a measure of political participation was able to find moderate to weak relationships between socio-economic development and political participation (1975, 40–44).

Social Mobilization and Political Participation

Ergun Özbudun continued to work on the role of socio-economic change and political participation and in a volume published, he proposed a model of conventional political participation in Turkey. Özbudun (1975) contended that voting participation and electoral behavior in Turkey were mainly the outcome of the vicissitudes of rapid social mobilization that was taking place in Turkey since 1950. The post World War II era in Turkey witnessed a major drive towards modernization of agriculture and a similar attempt at industrialization through state and private initiatives in a capitalist economy. The mechanization of Turkish agriculture paved the way for increasing efficiency and huge surges of yields of agricultural production, on the one hand, and a huge dislocation of surplus agricultural labor, on the other. The budding industry of larger cities of the country provided a natural attraction for the excess and unemployed labor in rural areas. Consequently, rural migrants started to arrive at the cities in increasing numbers. Hence, a concomitant rise of urban population began to occur in the 1950's, and robustly continued into the 1960's and beyond. Under the influence of industrialization and urbanization literacy, mass communication, circulation of the daily newspapers, purchases of transistor radios, and eventually TV sets and VCRs began to increase. Through the 1960's and the early 1970's larger numbers of Turkish surplus labor found their way into Western Germany and other European countries in pursuit of jobs. The images of post-industrial life-styles presented through and by the media and the personal experiences in Germany and elsewhere in Europe began to make major changes in the definition of welfare, life-style, and "images of good life". The expectations and attitudes of the Turkish rural and recently urbanized masses began to show dramatic changes.

Özbudun incorporated Karl Deutsch's (1961) theoretical insight into the process of modernization and its political consequences. He seemed to argue that industrialization and urbanization created new social and psychological realties, which precipitated new forms of political participation (1976, 84–96). However, there was a major caveat in Özbudun's study. His operationalization of political participation comprised of voting participation alone. Therefore, it did not even cover the whole gamut of conventional political participation in Turkey. Indeed, in an article published in 1981 Kalaycıoğlu and Turan demonstrated that in Turkey political participation consisted of three dimensions of contacting political authorities and political discussions, political campaigning, and voting participation (1981, 127 – 133). Another constraint of Özbudun's 1976 study was his dependence upon aggregate statistics. His analyses had to depend upon ecological correlations, and thus regional, rural-urban and major city voting patterns were analyzed vis-à-vis the role played by socio-economic development and land distribution statistics (Özbudun, 1976: 97–213). However, Özbudun pointed to some anomalies in voting records, which tended to give the impression that there had been widespread "mobilized voting" of the female voters in the past. Those female voters who seemed to have had no or very little education failed to show signs of "autonomous voters" participating on their own volition and deciding only on the basis of their own political attitudes (Özbudun, 1976, 96).

However, an earlier study published in 1971 had unearthed the fact that villages in Eastern Anatolia voted in haphazard fashions (Nuhrat: 219–244). Nuhrat had discovered that such behavior occurred in villages, which were dominated by powerful landlords (patrons) who owned all real estate in and around the villages in question. Özbudun also seems not to have found much evidence supporting such "mobilized voting" in rural areas where land distributions indicated large holdings owned by a single family or person (Özbudun, 1976, 163–167). However, Özbudun discovered the same pattern of higher voting participation in villages than in the cities, as had Baykal five years earlier (ibid., 168). He then went on to analyze the effects of rural socio-economic development and unearthed that the poorer the villages became, the more they tended to participate in the elections, which Özbudun believed was another indication of "mobilized voting", which confirmed earlier findings of Nuhrat (ibid., 169, and Nuhrat, 1971).

Finally, Özbudun unearthed that it was the rural migrants into the major cities, who tended to abstain from voting participation the most (1976, 204), which he interpreted as the decline of "mobilized voting" in the cities. His argument was that the rural settlers were emancipated from the grip of the landlords, and left alone with their low level of literacy and lack of integration into the city culture, and lacked the motivation to take part in the electoral process (ibid., 203–204).

Geographic Bases of Political Participation in Recent Turkish Elections

A long-term account of electoral participation patterns in Turkey can only be conducted with the use of geographical data. Survey based micro-individual level data simply does not exist for the earlier periods of Turkish elections. Even for the most recent elections a conceptually coherent election study does not exist. We therefore start our analysis of electoral participation by underlining its geographic nature. Our focus in the ensuing sections is to first provide a macro-level depiction of electoral developments in the country with the use of party system indicators. We then move on to describe and analyze the nature of election outcomes, especially the nature of participation rates across Turkish provinces during the multi-party election period since 1950, focusing especially on the post-1980 period.

Aggregate election data have been scantly used in Turkish voting studies, especially from a long-term perspective.[2] However, as Çarkoğlu and Avcı (2002) demonstrated, a long-term analysis of geographical consistency of electoral preferences can be used to diagnose emerging patterns in ideological structure of voter preferences.

Below, the focus is on the temporal geographical consistency of electoral preferences over the 1950–2002 period. Geographic differences in participation rates and bases of support for major parties in the system are identified according to a commonly adopted centre-periphery paradigm in Turkish politics to answer certain basic questions concerning the nature of the still unfolding electoral geography within the centre-periphery paradigm. What are the discernible characteristics of the emerging electoral geography of participation in Turkey for the last five decades? How homogeneously do Turks turnout and cast their votes in general elections across different provinces? What are the socio-economic bases of turnout in the party system across different provinces and regions of the country?

Below a short discussion of the conceptual framework that form the basis of the ensuing analyses is given and its implications for a geographical analysis of electoral dynamics are underlined. Following a description of the data and methodology used in the ensuing analyses the findings are presented and implications for further analyses in a comparative perspective are discussed.

Center vs. Periphery in Turkish Electoral Geography

The centre-periphery framework is based on Mardin's (1973) interpretation of socio-political history of Ottoman Turks.[3] According to Mardin Turkish politics is built around a strong and coherent state apparatus run by a distinct group of elites composed primarily by the military and bureaucracy. The *center* is confronted by a heterogeneous and often hostile *periphery* composed mainly of the peasantry, small farmers and artisans. The *center* is built around Kemalist secular principles. It urges a state-run nationalist modernization program. The largely parochial *periphery* reflects hostile sentiments toward the centralist and mostly undemocratic, hierarchical and coercive modernization project of the center and includes regional, religious and ethnic groups, often with conflicting interests and political strategies. Mardin's formulation of the center-periphery cleavages refers primarily to a cultural duality. However, in what follows we maintain that it also provides a basis for understanding behavioral patterns in individual vote choice as well as providing clues as to the nature of geographical regularities in election outcomes across places of residence.

Predominantly rural Turkey of the 1950s with its mostly isolated villages, limited mass education, transportation and communication facilities was perhaps more fitting for the center-periphery framework. Over the past five decades significant advances were made on all dimensions of development that may be taken as a reflection of an integration of the periphery with the center. "Typical villagers of earlier decades, who lived in closed communities and had little contact with outsiders, are fast disappearing. Rather the typical villager is more likely to have relatives or former neighbors in the big cities of Turkey or Europe" (Toprak, 1996, 94). However, despite a more open Turkish society, which had largely been integrated through a widened access to communication and transportation, the extent of the transformation into a modern social order is not so clear.

Esmer (1999) provides some clues as to the extent of differentiation between the value systems of the *center* and the *periphery*. The level of trust in different institutions is slightly lower for the higher educated representatives of the center than those relatively lower educated respondents (p.49) of the periphery. More significant differences are observed in respondents' evaluations of the shortcomings of democracy.[4] In the rural areas, respondents seem to be much more supportive of a "powerful" leader and military rule. Similarly, while the highly educated representatives of the center seem to believe in the legitimacy of the democratic system in the country, among the peripheral representatives, the legitimacy of the democratic system is considerably lower. More striking is the huge differences between the center and the periphery representatives' overall levels of tolerance in social relations. Esmer's (1999, 88–90) overall tolerance index shows that the less educated representatives of the periphery are significantly less tolerant than the higher educated center.

On the political front there is ample evidence of the continuity of center-periphery cleavage. Kalaycıoğlu's (1994a, 422) analysis of the data gathered in the 1990 Turkish Values Survey reveals "the continued importance of the conflict between the values of the center versus the values of the periphery" which has come to be signified by religiosity. Besides religiosity in determining party choice, other typical variables reflecting peripheral traits such as ethnicity and place of residence are also found to be significant in voting decisions of Turkish voters (Kalaycıoğlu, 1999, 64–66; Çarkoğlu and Toprak, 2000, 117–118).

The continual reference to the center-periphery conceptual framework in the Turkish electoral literature is in stark contrast to the lack of much effort in the original article on specificities of the -by then more than two decades old-multiparty system. Mardin was more preoccupied with depicting a general historical and sociological framework rather than dealing with the electoral events of his time. When these were helpful in depicting exemplary developments within the conceptual discussions, they were used conveniently. However, the dynamics of party competition that molded and divided the electorate into different parties on the same side of the ensuing center-periphery cleavage were left untouched as a problematic conceptual issue. As a result, the empirical extensions of the center-periphery framework tended to depict a rather homogenous picture of the two sides of the cleavage. However, neither the center, nor the periphery, was monolithic homogenous entities. Their over all characteristics seemed to adhere to the depictions of Mardin; but their party specific idiosyncrasies were largely left to be uncovered by the ensuing discussions. In our ensuing analyses below, we aim to fill this gap in the literature from only a limited angle. We aim to show that participation in elections in the multi-party election period of 1950–2002 geographic patterns of varying intensity of participation played a significant role in shaping the electoral forces.[5]

Although recent studies have identified the dynamics of change in the Turkish party system, geographical bases of rising electoral cleavages in the form of secularist vs. pro-Islamist, or Turkish vs. Kurdish nationalist movements did not attract much attention. A long-term account of these changes from a geographical perspective is also not available.[6] However, from the very beginning, the literature on Turkish electoral behaviour has continuously noted significant political as well as socio-economic cleavages that seem to shape mass political preferences. The early analyses with a geographical orientation towards electoral results by Magnarella (1967), Tachau (1973) and Özbudun and Tachau (1975) underline peculiarities of the Turkish Eastern and South-eastern provinces as well as particular geographical strongholds of different parties. Combining the descriptive electoral geography with provincial development indicators also proved to have some explanatory power in accounting for variation in electoral outcomes across Turkish provinces.[7]

Çarkoğlu and Avcı's (2002) analysis of Turkish electoral geography with a long-term perspective focusing on the 1950–1999 multi-party elections period complemented by the geographical analyses of the last two general elections in 1999 and 2002 reveal several patterns.[8] There is a qualified support for the continuing relevance of the centre-periphery framework in Turkish electoral politics. Distribution of party votes across provinces reveals a clear distinction of centrist as opposed to peripheral bases of support. However, both centrist as well as peripheral electoral forces are quite heterogeneous. On the peripheral constituencies pro-Islamist, nationalist as well as ethnic Kurdish vote appear to have distinct regions of support. While the least developed southeast and eastern Anatolian regions where Kurdish ethnicity is intensely present show a distinct pattern of support for Kurdish ethnic parties especially in the 1990s, the central Anatolian provinces form the support basis for nationalist and pro-Islamist parties. Centrist parties are typically dominant in socio-economically developed western and coastal provinces. In the most recent elections there is continuing electoral fluidity while fragmentation of partisan support has declined only in the 2002 election. Peripheral forces have expanded over the last decade at the expense of primarily the centre-right.

Below we present a more in depth analysis of the patterns of electoral participation that gave rise to the above outlined trends in electoral support for parties in a geographical perspective. As a starting point for the ensuing analyses we take the character of the center-periphery framework, which provides the basis for expectations about the geographical reflection of cleavages that shape very basis of Turkish electoral behavior that is the rate at which people tend to participate in elections across provinces. From a geographical perspective, we expect that relatively more modern provinces where the Republican ideological penetration through secular and developmentalist state policies of the last eight decades will be differentiated from the rest of the country. As illustrated by earlier studies, as the share of rural population and the share of agriculture in provincial economic activity increases, so does the electoral support for peripheral tradition at the expense of the centrist parties. Especially, the east and south-eastern provinces where this penetration has been minimal, and where the bulk of Kurdish population lives, are expected to also form a separate group. The rise of ethnic identity in the eastern and south-eastern provinces over the last two decades has contributed to this trend. However, even in the earlier decades of the multi-party period the roots of this ethnic cleavage, apparent in differentiated party preferences across these provinces, are observable. However, while the extent to which ideological, and thus to a limited degree, the partisan differentiation across these provinces are quite clear with their reflections on the centre-periphery cleavages within the party system over the years, we have limited guidelines for the way participation rates should be shaped across the various geographies of the country. We expect that the under-developed regions of the country to be under the influence of the parochial ties and thus evidence of mobilised voting should be evident therein. Accordingly, we expect a relatively higher rate of participation rate as the rural population share across provinces increases. Translating this expectation into the centre-periphery framework of Mardin, we see that the peripheral forces across the Anatolian provinces are expected to be associated with higher rates of participation than those that are expected to be closer to the centrist politics a la Mardin.

Analysis of Turnout Rates

In our analyses we take the State Institute of Statistics' classification of provinces into Statistical Regional Unit Classification. This classification divides the country into three regional levels. The details of this classification are presented in Table 4.1 below. In the first level of classification 12 province clusters are formed. This classification is quite different from the conventional geographic regions. Istanbul alone forms the first region according to the State Institute of Statistics' classification. The Central Anatolian provinces are separated into two newly created regions and as a result the second province cluster of Level 1, the Western Analtolia region, comprises of Konya and Karaman together with Ankara and the Central Anatolia region comprises of the Kırıkkale sub-region (Kırıkkale, Aksaray, Niğde, Nevşehir, Kırşehir) and the Kayseri sub-region (Kayseri, Sivas, Yozgat). Similarly the Marmara region is divided into West (Tekirdağ, Edirne, Kırklareli comprising the Tekirdağ sub-region and Balıkesir, Çanakkale comprising the Balıkesir sub-region) and East Marmara (Bursa, Eskişehir, Bilecik as comprising the Bursa sub-region and Kocaeli, Sakarya, Düzce, Bolu, Yalova as comprising the Kocaeli sub-region) regions.

Figure 4.1 shows the 12 regions of Level 1 on the map of Turkey. These new clusters of provinces exhibit a subdivision of the conventional geographical regions into sub-regions on the basis of geographical proximity and socio-economic development levels. In the ensuing analyses we use the Level 1 classification with a single modification. We grouped the metropolitan provinces of İstanbul, Ankara and İzmir as a single cluster of Metropolitan provinces and left the rest of the classification intact.

In our ensuing analyses we use a dummy variable regression model to depict statistically significant variations across the 12 regions described above for the whole multi-party election period of 1950–2002. Our model is specified as follows:

$$TR_i = \alpha + \Sigma \beta_j D_{ij} + u_i \qquad 3.1$$

where TR is the provincial turnout rate and the D_j refers to the regional dummy variables which take the value of 1 for the provinces of the jth region and 0 otherwise. We use the metropolitan provinces as our reference group and thus α captures the mean estimated turnout rate in İstanbul, Ankara and İzmir. β_j gives the estimated difference between the metropolitan provinces and the region j. When a given region's dummy variable turns out to be statistically insignificant it means that for that particular region the estimated turnout rate is about the same as the metropolitan provinces used as our reference category.

The same equation is estimated for all 14 elections and the results are summarized in Figure 4.2 below. However, before going into the regional

Table 4.1 Statistical Regional Unit Classification

	Level 1	Level 2	Level 3
1	İstanbul	İstanbul Sub-region	İstanbul
2	Western Anatolia	Ankara Sub-region Konya Sub-region	Ankara Konya, Karaman
3	Eastern Marmara	Bursa Sub-region Kocaeli Sub-region	Bursa, Eskişehir, Bilecik Kocaeli, Sakarya, Düzce, Bolu, Yalova
4	Aegean	İzmir Sub-region Aydın Sub-region Manisa Sub-region	İzmir Aydın, Denizli, Muğla Manisa, Afyon, Kütahya, Uşak
5	Western Marmara	Tekirdağ Sub-region Balıkesir Sub-region	Tekirdağ, Edirne, Kırklareli Balıkesir, Çanakkale
6	Mediterranean	Antalya Sub-region Adana Sub-region Hatay Sub-region	Antalya, Isparta, Burdur Adana, Mersin Hatay, Kahramanmaraş, Osmaniye
7	Western Black Sea	Zonguldak Sub-region Kastamonu Sub-region Samsun Sub-region	Zonguldak, Karabük, Bartın Kastamonu, Çankırı, Sinop Samsun, Tokat, Çorum, Amasya
8	Centre Anatolia	Kırıkkale Sub-region Kayseri Sub-region	Kırıkkale, Aksaray, Niğde, Nevşehir, Kırşehir Kayseri, Sivas, Yozgat
9	Eastern Black Sea	Trabzon Sub-region	Trabzon, Ordu, Giresun, Rize, Artvin, Gümüşhane
10	Southeastern Anatolia	Gaziantep Sub-region Şanlıurfa Sub-region Mardin Sub-region	Gaziantep, Adıyaman, Kilis Şanlıurfa, Diyarbakır Mardin, Batman, Şırnak, Siirt
11	Centre-east Anatolia	Malatya Sub-region Van Sub-region	Malatya, Elazığ, Bingöl, Tunceli Van, Muş, Bitlis, Hakkari
12	Northeast Anatolia	Erzurum Sub-region Ağrı Sub-region	Erzurum, Erzincan, Bayburt Ağrı, Kars, Iğdır, Ardahan

Figure 4.1 Statistical Regional Unit Classifications

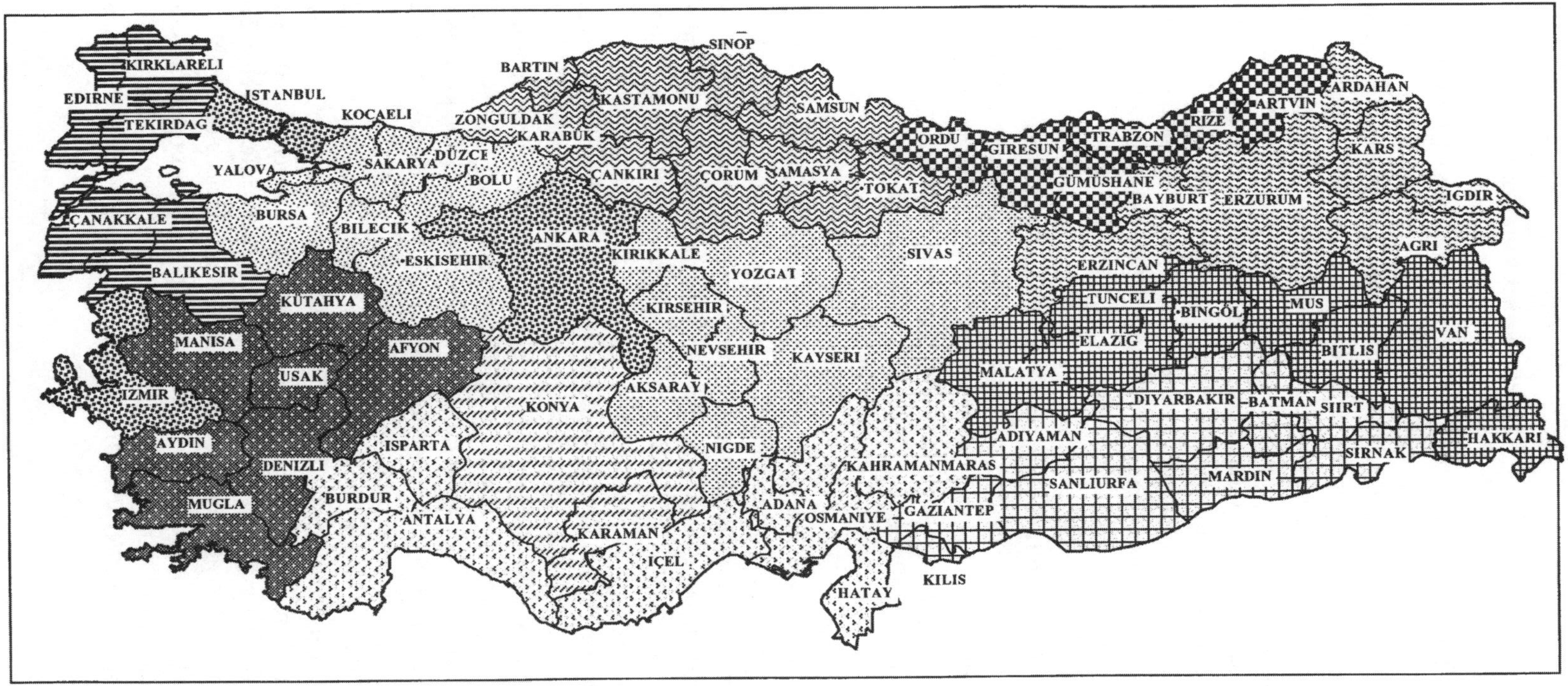

differentiation of turnout rates some trends in the overall nationwide turnout rates shown on the same figure are worth stressing. The first two general elections of the multi-party era show the highest turnout rates of about 89 percent. Following the 1954 election, turnout rates have fallen considerably reaching an all time low of about 64 percent in 1969. While the two elections in the 1970's exhibited higher rates of participation, with the introduction of compulsory voting in the 1982 election law, turnout rates reached unprecedented levels of about 92 to 93 percent in 1983 and 1987 respectively. With the normalization of electoral politics following the referendum of 1987 in the 1990s the turnout rates seem stabilized around 85 percent. In the 2002 elections turnout rate dropped below 80 percent for the first time in the post-1980 period.

Unfortunately we are not in a position to account for province to province variation in turnout rates, with explanatory variables other than the regional dummy variables reflecting provincial socio-economic development levels (for example due to lack of data especially in the early elections). However, even by using solely the regional dummy variables we are in a position to explain more than 30 percent of the total variation in turnout rates except for the two consecutive elections in 1995 and 1999.

When we look at the regional variation in election turnout and trends therein, several patterns emerge. The three metropolitan provinces İstanbul, Ankara and İzmir have the lowest turnout rates in elections prior to 1980. If we take these provinces as representatives of centrist electoral tendencies, this is very much in line with our expectations. However, with the introduction of compulsory voting in the post-1980 period and increasing turnout rates as a consequence, we observe that this pattern has changed. In post-1980 elections relatively less developed regions tend to have turnout rates lower than the national average, while the Aegean provinces other than İzmir consistently have the highest rates. Starting with the 1991 elections, when a distinct Kurdish electoral constituency started to take shape North Eastern and South Eastern provinces displayed the lowest turnout rates. As a result the relatively less developed provinces to the east of Sivas tend to have lower turnout rates compared to relatively more developed provinces of the western coastal provinces.

Making sense of these provincial participation rates on the basis of regions is cumbersome. In order to simplify the analysis a summary periodic measure of consistent pattern across provinces needs to be developed. To accomplish this task a factor analysis of provincial election returns is used. The technique allows one to concentrate on correlations between elections over provinces (T-mode analysis).[9] Factor analysis permits the researcher to reduce an unmanageably large matrix of correlations to a smaller matrix of similarities between each observed election and a limited number of mathematically derived factors or

Figure 4.2 Turnout Rate Across Geographic Regions

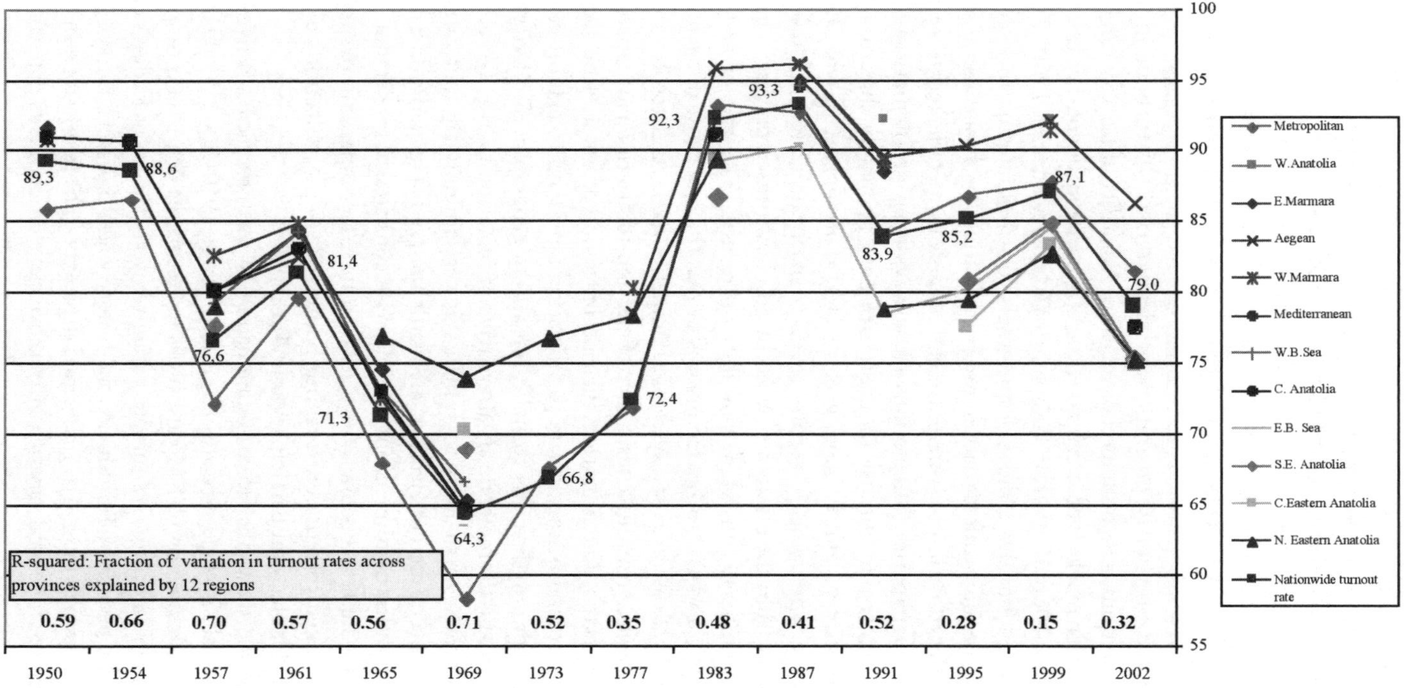

Only statistically significant regional differences are shown.

dimensions. "The factors, or dimensions, can then be interpreted as identifying the most distinctive and representative separate election patterns discernible for the study period as a whole" (Shelley et al. 1996, 282).

T-mode factor analysis is used in a similar fashion to Archer and Taylor (1981), Archer et al. (1986) and Shelley et al. (1996), to reveal electoral participation epochs by conducting factor analysis of turnout rates across provinces over all elections.[10]

As noted previously, an important characteristic of turnout in Turkish general elections is its high level of volatility. Volatility of turnout can be taken as a reflection of a lack of "electoral epoch" (Archer and Taylor, 1981; Campbell et al. 1960, 1966; Key, 1959; Pomper, 1967; Schattschneider, 1960). However, as our ensuing analyses show, despite high volatility rates in Turkish general elections, periodic differentiation into participation epochs are also apparent.

The identification of different electoral epochs as reflected in consistent rates of participation in elections has always been problematic and relied predominantly on the use of aggregate data primarily due to a lack of adequate survey data. Following Key's (1955) argument, in what he called critical elections, voting results reveal a sharp alteration of pre-existing cleavages within the electorate, whereby scholars focused on sharp changes in the geographical consistency of election results. The rise of new issues, charismatic leaders or other factors was seen as the root cause of reshuffling of partisan loyalties in party systems (Pomper, 1967). As a result of all such developments, changing consistency of election-to-election participation rates is also expected. Our question then becomes one of identifying periods in Turkish electoral history where participation rates tend to exhibit consistent patterns, not only levels of turnout, but also in geographic similarity.

Within this framework an alternative application of the T-mode factor analysis proves particularly useful. In this version, only turnout rates across provinces over different elections are factor analyzed. The derived factors then represent different dimensions of time-wise consistency in electoral participation (See Table 4.2 below). Any breaks in these factor patterns over the years are then taken to represent turning points, or simply reflections of critical elections for electoral participation in Turkey.

Figure 4.3 shows the factor-loading pattern of the three factors derived from a varimax analysis of provincial turnout rates across 1950–2002 period. A factor loading in this version of T-Mode analysis represents the degree of correspondence of a geographical pattern of turnout for a given year. The factor loadings obtained reveal three periods in Turkish electoral history where provincial turnout rates are similar across provinces. The first period depicted by the first factor that captures 39.3 percent of the total variation in 14 provincial election results differentiates the post-1980 elections from the earlier elections. The pre-1980 elections are then

Table 4.2 Dimensions of Participation

	1983–2002	*1965–1977*	*1950–1961*	*Communalities*
1950	0,14	–0,12	**0,87**	0,79
1954	–0,12	0,19	**0,84**	0,76
1957	0,36	0,38	**0,55**	0,57
1961	0,51	0,44	**0,59**	0,80
1965	0,03	**0,78**	0,23	0,66
1969	–0,25	**0,88**	0,12	0,84
1973	–0,25	**0,83**	–0,08	0,76
1977	**0,57**	**0,53**	0,08	0,61
1983	**0,84**	–0,02	0,13	0,73
1987	**0,85**	–0,01	0,15	0,75
1991	**0,86**	–0,02	0,09	0,75
1995	**0,91**	–0,13	0,04	0,85
1999	**0,90**	–0,22	0,11	0,86
2002	**0,91**	–0,07	–0,03	0,83
Percent of Variance	*39,3*	*20,0*	*16,1*	*75,3*

Extraction Method: Principal Component Analysis.
Rotation Method: Varimax with Kaiser Normalization.
Rotation converged in 4 iterations. Missing values are replaced with mean

divided into two periods. The second factor represents the four elections between 1965 and 1977 and the third corresponds to the first four elections between 1950 and 1961. It should be noted that both 1977 and 1961 elections show provincial turnout patterns that highly load on more than a single factor indicating that these elections exhibit transitory stages rather than representing clear periodic traits.

To summarize the patterns observed in these three periodic dimensions of turnout patterns across provinces factor loadings across the provinces were cluster analyzed to form province clusters that were similar to one another within each cluster, while cross cluster differences were maximized (See Table 4.3 below). The eight province clusters obtained show provinces that are similar to one another in the turnout periods identified by the three factors derived.

Table 4.3 shows that the 27 provinces in Cluster 1 rank average in all three periods. In other words these are the provinces that conform to the turnout pattern for the whole country as grasped by the latent factor derived for thee periods derived. We see that besides the newly established provinces of the late 1980's and 1990's (Ardahan, Iğdır, Batman, Siirt, Şırnak in the East and Bartın and Karabük of the Western Black Sea) there is a corridor of provinces starting from Çankırı and Ankara and going all the way south to the Mediterranean

Figure 4.3 Dimensions of Participations, 1950–2002

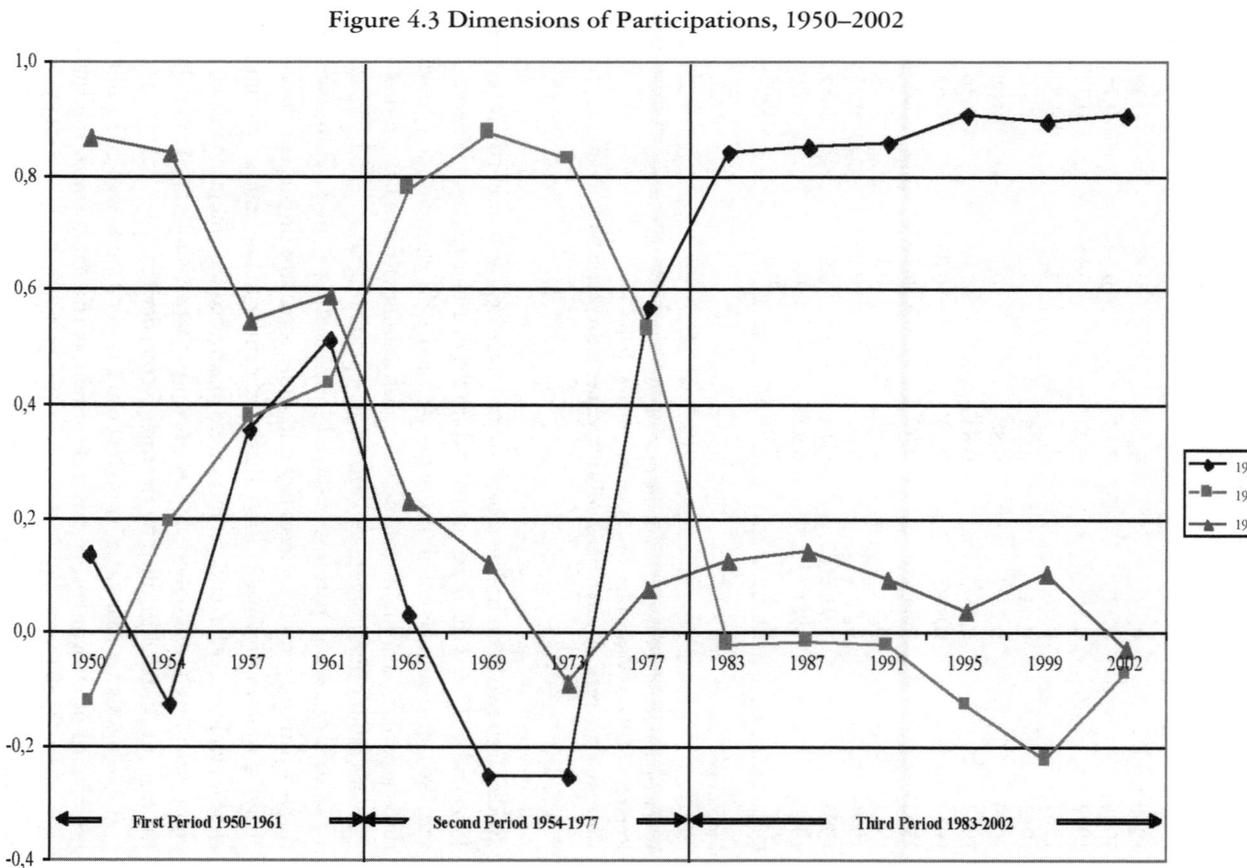

coast of Antalya, İçel and Hatay covering Kayseri, Kahramanmaraş and Adıyaman. İzmir on the Aegean coast, Sinop and Giresun on the Black Sea coast and Kocaeli in the Marmara region fit this overall temporal pattern. Bitlis, Mardin, Muş and Van of the East and Southeastern regions in Cluster 2 have a higher loading, thus turnout rates for the distinct period of 1965–1977 while being of average turnout pattern for the other two periods. The seven provinces of Cluster 3 have lower turnout pattern grasped by the 1965–1977, period while obtaining a higher than average turnout pattern in the post-1980 elections. Besides Kastamonu of the Black Sea coast, these are all provinces of the inner Aegean region including Konya of the central Anatolia. The nine provinces in Cluster 4 have distinctly higher than average turnout patterns for the 1950–1961 period, while scoring a higher turnout pattern for the 1965–1977 period and remaining below average for the post 1980 period. Starting from Samsun on the Black Sea region this cluster covers provinces in its south going as far as Sivas and Yozgat. Besides Adana and Gaziantep in the south Bingöl and Ağrı of Eastern Anatolia are also parts of this cluster. The eleven provinces in Cluster 5 have distinctly lower turnout patterns for the post-1980 period, while staying about average turnout pattern for the previous two periods. These provinces range from Rize on the Black Sea coast and cover provinces in its south and east going all the way down to the Syrian border of Şanlıurfa. Hakkari stands out as a single distinct province that deviated from the turnout patterns observed in all periods identified. Hakkari remained well below the average turnout pattern for the 1950–1961 period, while scoring significantly higher turnout rates for the periods that followed. The eighteen provinces in Cluster 7 score significantly higher turnout rates from the pattern observed in post-1980 period while remaining about average in previous periods. These are predominantly coastal Aegean and Marmara region provinces starting from Bolu and Eskişehir in Western Central Anatolia and excluding İstanbul, Kocaeli, Yalova and Düzce. The four provinces in Cluster 8 show lower than average patterns obtained for all three periods.

Figures 4.4 to 4.6 pictorially summarize the temporal patterns in turnout rates on the map of Turkey. We divide the factor scores into three. Those provinces that obtain less than –0.3 are grouped into "low", those between –0.3 and +0.3 are grouped into "average" and those above +0.3 are grouped into "high" for all three of the temporal dimensions identified. We see in Figure 4.4 that "high" turnout provinces in the first period form a region that runs in the east from Ağrı and Kars to Erzurum, Erzincan into Sivas. Similarly, they occupy provinces from Sinop and Samsun on the Black Sea coast down to Kırşehir and Nevşehir all the way down to İçel, Adana and Hatay on the Mediterranean coast. Besides Eskişehir and Bilecik as a small pocket in west central Anatolia to Kırklareli, Edirne and Tekirdağ in the

Table 4.3 Clusters of Provinces across Temporal Dimensions of Participation, 1950–2002

	1	*2*	*3*	*4*	*5*	*6*	*7*	*8*
Participation 1983–2002	–0,15	–0,46	1,21	–0,48	–1,50	1,08	1,15	–0,89
Participation 1965–1977	–0,18	2,32	–1,25	0,64	–0,23	3,43	0,18	–1,43
Participation 1950–1961	–0,05	–0,27	–0,40	1,32	0,00	–5,22	0,34	–1,88
# of Cases in each Cluster	*27*	*4*	*7*	*9*	*11*	*1*	*18*	*4*
1	ADIYAMAN	BİTLİS	AFYON	ADANA	DİYARBAKIR	HAKKARİ	AYDIN	ARTVİN
2	ANKARA	MARDİN	BURDUR	AĞRI	ERZİNCAN		BALIKESİR	ELAZIĞ
3	ANTALYA	MUŞ	DENİZLİ	AMASYA	ERZURUM		BİLECİK	İSTANBUL
4	ÇANKIRI	VAN	KASTAMONU	BİNGÖL	GÜMÜŞHANE		BOLU	TRABZON
5	GİRESUN		KONYA	GAZİANTEP	KARS		BURSA	
6	HATAY		KÜTAHYA	SAMSUN	MALATYA		ÇANAKKALE	
7	İÇEL		UŞAK	SİVAS	ORDU		ÇORUM	
8	İZMİR			TOKAT	RİZE		EDİRNE	
9	KAYSERİ			YOZGAT	TUNCELİ		ESKİŞEHİR	
10	KIRŞEHİR				Ş.URFA		ISPARTA	
11	KOCAELİ				BAYBURT		KIRKLARELİ	
12	K.MARAŞ						MANİSA	
13	NİĞDE						MUĞLA	
14	SİİRT						NEVŞEHİR	
15	SİNOP						SAKARYA	
16	AKSARAY						TEKİRDAĞ	
17	KIRIKKALE						ZONGULDAK	
18	BATMAN						KARAMAN	
19	ŞIRNAK							
20	BARTIN							
21	ARDAHAN							
22	IĞDIR							
23	KARABÜK							
24	KİLİS							
25	YALOVA							
26	OSMANİYE							
27	DÜZCE							

Figure 4.4 Province Clusters 1950–1961

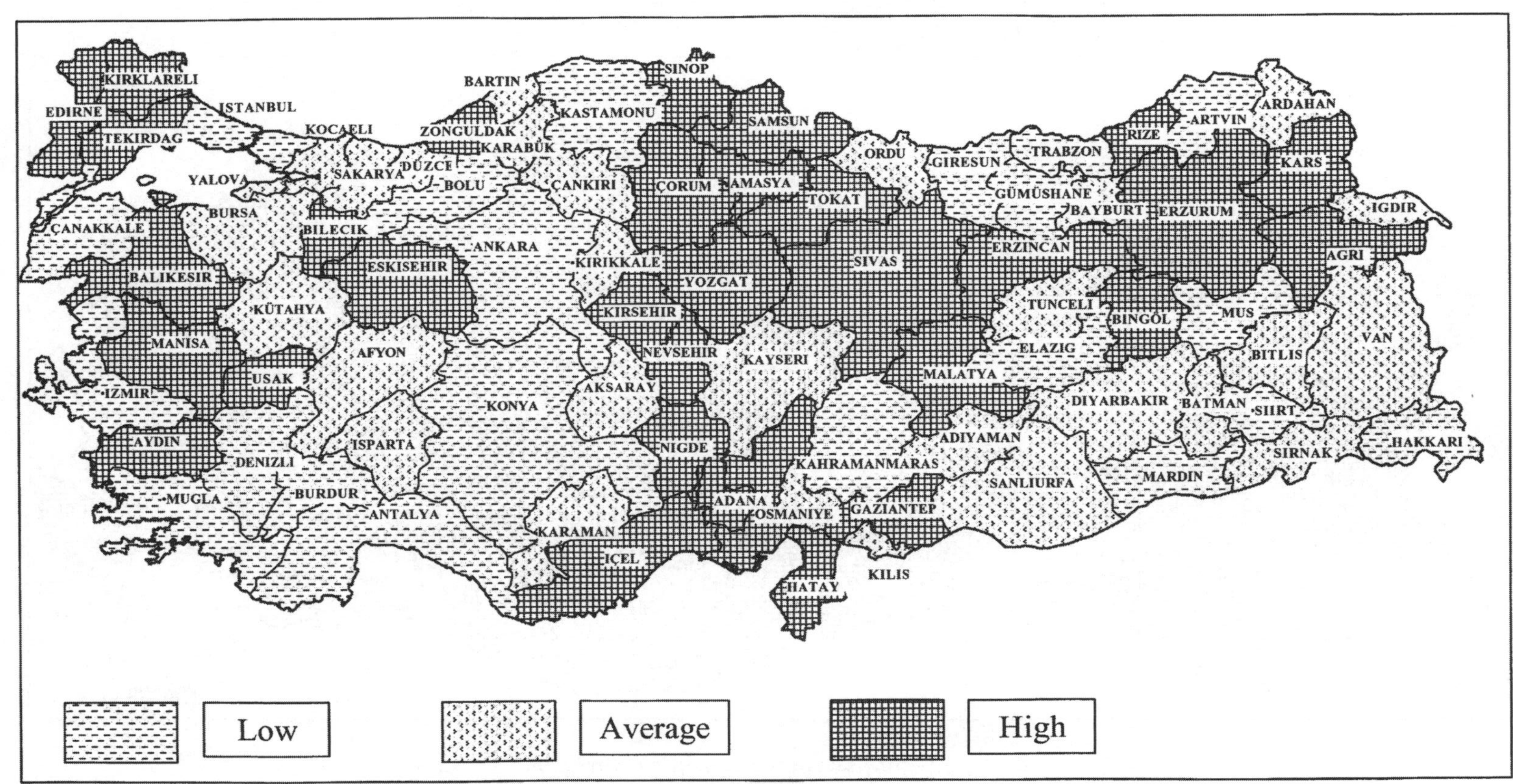

Figure 4.5 Province Clusters 1965–1977

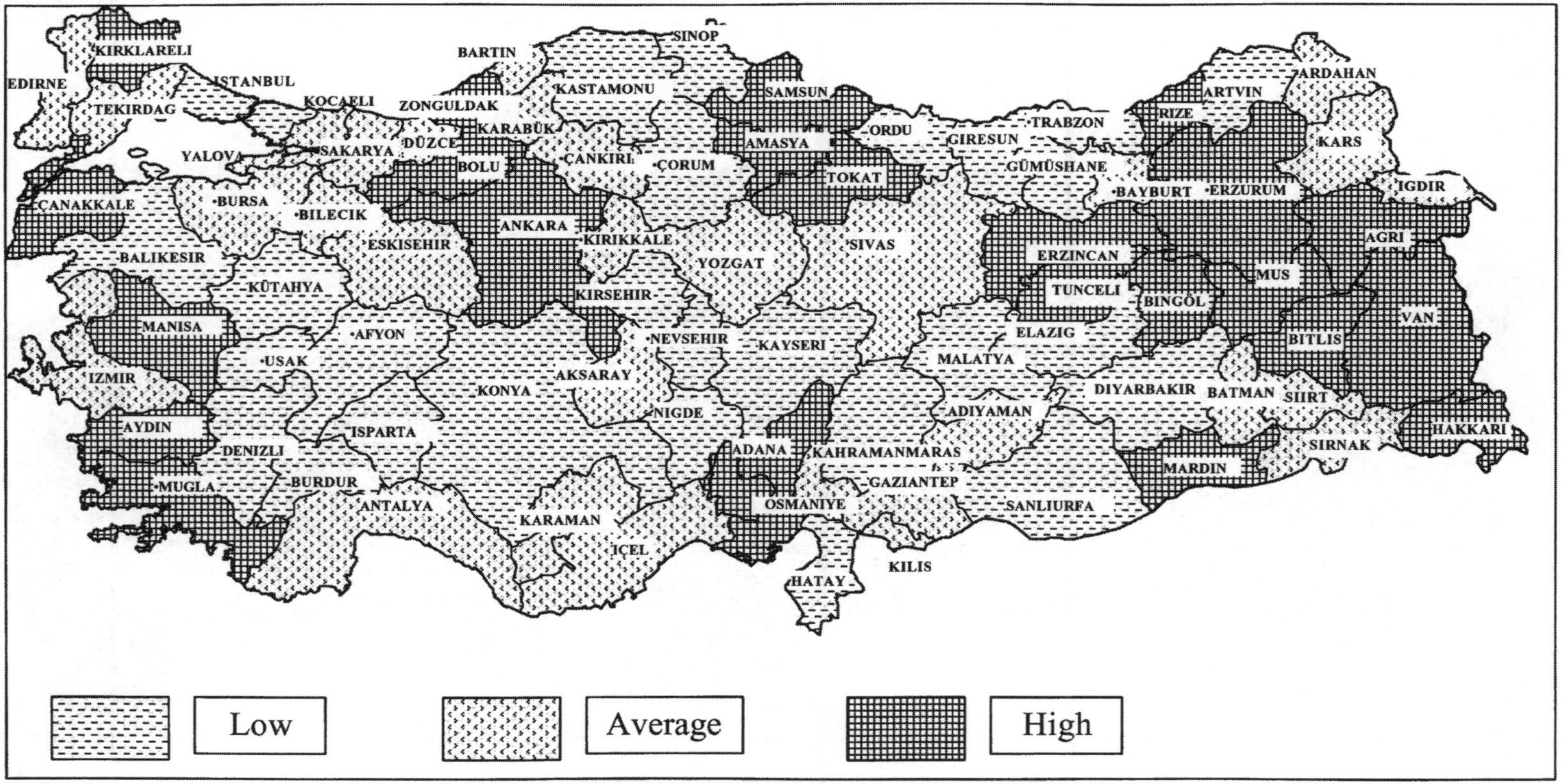

Figure 4.6 Province Clusters 1983–2002

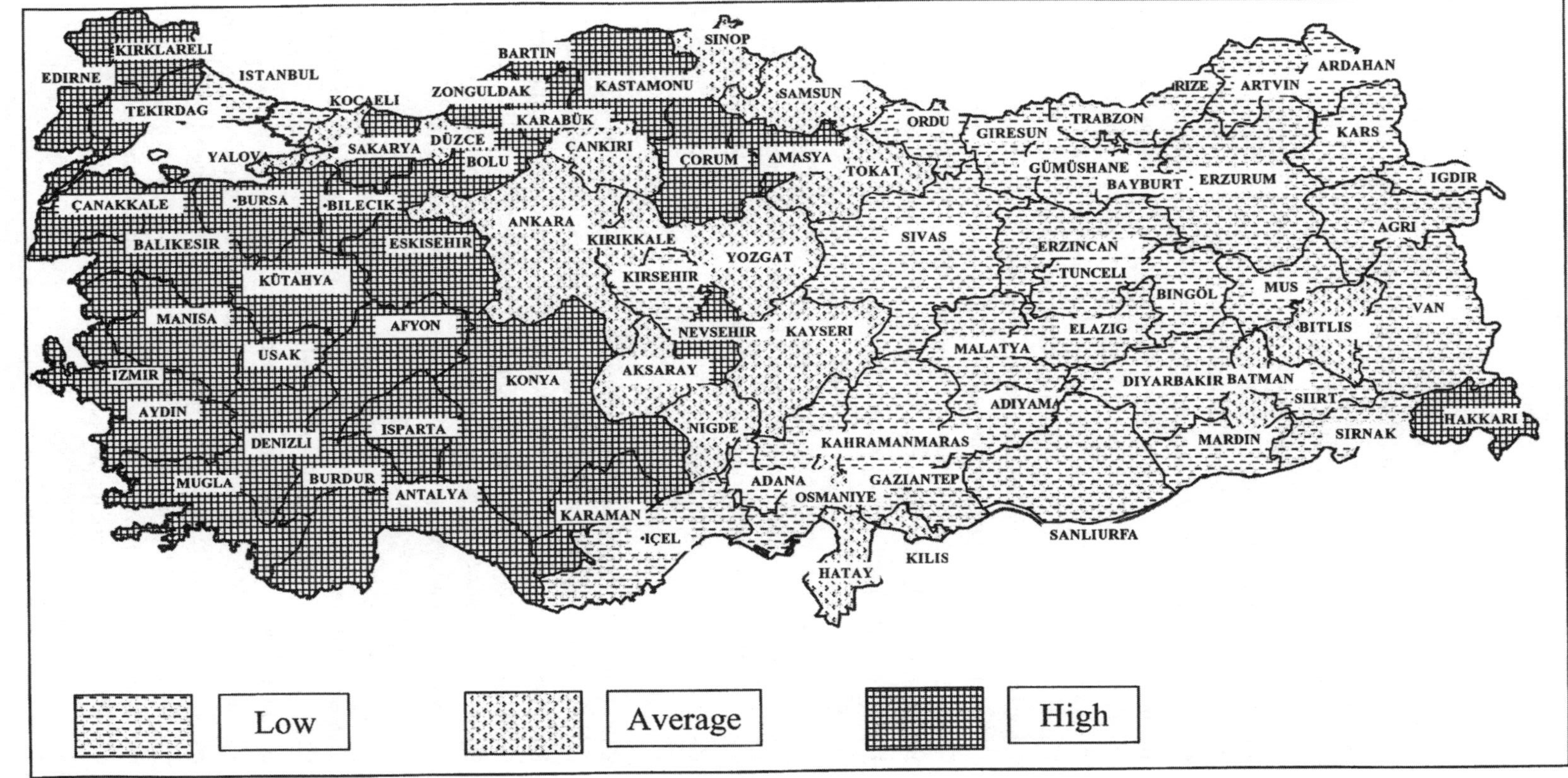

Marmara region down to Balıkesir Manisa, Uşak and Aydın in the Aegean region. Most of the South-Eastern Anatolian region provinces score "average" for the 1950–1961 period and the central Anatolia and western Mediterranean region provinces remain "low" for this period.

When we move into 1965–1977 period (see Figure 4.6), Eastern Anatolian provinces from Hakkari, Van and Ağrı to Erzurum and Rize in the north to Erzincan and Tunceli in the west score above average. Samsun, Amasya and Tokat form a pocket of "high" turnout provinces on the Black Sea coast and Çanakkale, Manisa, Aydın and Muğla form a similar "high" turnout region in the Aegean region. Adana, Zonguldak, Bolu, Ankara and Kırklareli are small islands of "high" turnout provinces. From İstanbul and Balıkesir in the West down to inner Aegean provinces of Kütahya, Uşak, Afyon, Denizli to Central Anatolian Konya, Niğde, Kayseri toward east Malatya, Elazığ, Diyarbakır and Şanlıurfa in the southeast we see "low" turnout provinces.

For the post-1980 period the pattern of turnout is much clearer. We have a "high" turnout province region in the west starting with Amasya, Çorum and Kastamonu on the Black Sea region down to Eskişehir, Konya and Antalya (see Figure 4.7). All provinces except İstanbul and Kocaeli are then in this region of "high" turnout. "Low" turnout region starts with İçel in the Mediterranean coast and spans nearly all provinces to the east of Gaziantep, Kahramanmaraş, Sivas and Ordu. Notable exceptions are Hakkari with an above average turnout and Batman and Bitlis scoring about the average turnout for this period.

Conclusion

Our analysis of provincial turnout rates reveals first of all that there are periodic patterns that impede us from evaluating participation rates in elections in a homogeneous manner. There are three distinct periodic dimensions in Turkish turnout rates across provinces. For the first four elections of 1950 to 1961 and the following four elections during 1965–1977 period the relatively low socio-economic development regions of the central and eastern Anatolia region rank relatively "high" in their turnout rates compared to most of the rest of the country. However, in the six elections of the post-1980 period we see clearly that east and south-eastern Anatolia regions of the least developed provinces score "low" in their turnout rates relative to the rest of the country. In short, besides periodic variation in turnout rates a clear geographical differentiation is also significant. This is very much in line with our expectations concerning party choice as well. Accordingly, we will be using the same geographical regions depicted above in our micro-individual level party choice analyses. We now turn to micro-individual level analysis of conventional as well as unconventional political participation patterns.

5

ANALYZING POLITICAL PARTICIPATION AT THE INDIVIDUAL LEVEL OF ANALYSIS

As we have noted in our introductory chapter, some village and "*gecekondu*" studies focusing on the character of political participation had used survey methodology in the 1960's and the 1970's. However, it was a major nation-wide survey conducted in 1974 under the auspices of the University of Iowa that provided the first opportunity to collect data at the level of the individual. Socio-economic and attitudinal data collected from a national sample of more than 2000 individual voters included rural and city dwellers, women and men, rich and poor and thus provided the first opportunity to test a set of hypotheses, which had been impossible to properly test with aggregate data.

Kalaycıoğlu (1983) reports the findings of a comparative study of Kenya, South Korea, and Turkey, based upon a causal analysis of socio-economic, cultural and psychological determinants of conventional political participation. This study was able to differentiate between the effects of political resources and attitudes, and assess the relative role of each political resource and attitude in determining conventional political participation. One major finding of the study was that gender seemed to play a far more important role in determining political actions in Turkey, and also comparatively than had been earlier proven to be. The game of political influence happened to be exclusive to the male members of Turkish society in the 1970's. However formal education also seemed to be playing a critical role, independent of Socio-economic Status (SES) in determining political participation. The gender discrepancy seemed therefore to dwindle among those men and women who were well educated (see Kalaycıoğlu, 1983, 454). It was once more unearthed that SES played no significant role in determining political participation in Turkey.

Kalaycıoğlu (1983, 456) corroborated earlier claims made by Baykal and Özbudun that the size of urban settlement was negatively related with conventional political participation. People tended to participate less in politics in the urban centers of the country. Kalaycıoğlu explained this finding with reference to the "decline-of-the-community" hypothesis of Verba, Nie, and Kim (1978, 270–271), on the one hand, and the strength of mobilized voting in rural areas, on the other. What the study seemed to show was that there were two contradictory influences of urban settlements on political participation. One was the direct effect of urbanization on political participation, which was negative, and the other, a positive indirect effect. Indeed, just as Lerner had earlier argued, urbanization seemed to motivate literacy and mass media exposure; however that influence on political participation was far lower than its direct negative impact. The intimidating influences of living in a large urban center, what Verba et. al. (1978) called the "decline-of the-community" effect, were much more significant than the motivation that the urban life-style provided for the inhabitants to participate in politics.

Finally, political attitudes seemed to be critical in determining political participation. They seemed to function as a psychological precondition to motivate acts of political influence by individual citizens in Turkey. Political participation seemed to be nurtured in a social context where cultural characteristics and psychological characteristics played a more important role than status variables, in specific social classes or SES in Turkey. Hence, political influence did not seem to be a simple function of social status in Turkish society. The role that economic variables played in determining political participation was not tested in Kalaycıoğlu's causal models. Secondly, his analysis was confined to conventional political participation, and failed to include protest and repressive potentials in Turkish society.

In the 1990s, Kalaycıoğlu tried to remedy the second caveat of his earlier study. In an article published in 1997, Kalaycıoğlu analyzed the role of political resources and political attitudes on unconventional political participation in Turkey. He proposed to explain protest behavior in terms of political opportunities, resources and motives of the individual actor (1997, 53). He then went on to incorporate gender, place of residence, and satisfaction with one's life as exogenous variables, and formal education, religiosity, political interest, and political efficacy as endogenous variables of a causal model that accounted for protest potential in Turkey. The findings of the path analysis revealed that formal education played a relatively minor role in determining protest potential, and so did political efficacy. However, political interest and religiosity seemed to be playing more significant role in the determination of protest potential in Turkey. Interestingly enough, religiosity seemed to decrease protest potential, though political interest increased it (ibid., 63). Men seemed to be more inclined to participate in protest activity, while age seemed to play no role in influencing protest potential in Turkey. Finally, what used to be treated as a grand variable in earlier research, urbanization, seemed not to play any significant role in determining protest potential in Turkey (ibid., 65). The causal model specified in that study seemed to demonstrate a relatively large capacity to explain protest potential in comparison to similar models used in Austria, Germany, the Netherlands, the U.K, and the U.S. (ibid., 68).

When both studies are considered together, political motives and/or attitudes emerge as the most important determinant of both conventional and unconventional political participation in Turkey during the second half of the twentieth century.

An Individual Level Model

In chapter four we argued that political participation can be defined as the actions of the citizens voluntarily and consciously carried out to influence the political decisions made by the authorities, which can take three different forms. They can be designed and implemented within what the authorities and the majority of citizens may consider as legitimate and in the legal realm of political interface between the rulers and the ruled. Such acts of political participation are referred to as *conventional* acts of political participation. A second form of *unconventional* political participation is focused on protest behavior without taking legitimacy or legality into consideration. The third type of political participation consists of acts that are intended to suppress criticisms and protests of the established political order, government, or the authorities. They are usually referred to as repressive forms participation. Hence, not all forms of political behavior can be considered as political participation. Only those forms of political behavior, which are carried out by the volition of the citizen, to which one attributes a political meaning can be considered as acts of political participation[1].

The above-mentioned perspective suggests that political participation consists of acts, which are the outcome of some mental process, which prepares one to act when certain conditions are met. When one perceives a threat to one's interests, beliefs, faith, and values, or when one observes a chance of impacting on the election of a candidate to public office, then we would expect the person in question to try to wield some influence on the political decision-making process. In short, political participation is an outcome of one's beliefs, values, and attitudes, which we are inclined to refer to as ***political motives***.

Although motives are necessary for political participation, they cannot in themselves be fully responsible for political participation. In order to wield any influence on political decisions, the citizens need to mobilize some ***political resources*** at their disposal[2] . These may range from wealth or health to organizational membership, or knowledge of the legal system. Unless such resources are efficiently and effectively used, it is hard to assume that either one can burst into action to influence political decisions or the authorities in question can ever be influenced.

It would still be hard to imagine that a citizen can attempt to influence the selection of the political authorities, or their political decisions even if one has the necessary political resources and the motives to mobilize the resources. One would still need an opportunity to wield the political resources at one's disposal, once one has the motives that orient him/her toward the political decision-making process. If these opportunities get to be systematically supplied in the form of regularly held national or local elections, political rallies, election campaigns and so on, one would find ample chances to attempt to influence political decisions. The overall arrangements of a political system in providing those opportunities of influence constitute a system, which we are inclined to call the ***opportunity structure*** of a country. Opportunity structures are determined by the political regime of the country. If pluralist, the citizens can find ample opportunities to wield their impact on the selection of the authorities and the political decisions they make without fear, and intimidation. Otherwise, the opportunity structures are going to provide scant and sporadic chances for acts of political participation to occur. Indeed, in monistic (i.e., totalitarian regimes) opportunity structures participation in politics is tantamount to heroism. However, mobilized political acts could be quite welcome in such opportunity structures. There are still examples of mass political action under authoritarian / totalitarian regimes, which attest to the mass mobilization capabilities of governments, rather than voluntary political activism and attentiveness of the citizens.

Consequently, we argue that if the motives, political resources, and the political opportunity structures reinforce each other to provide for voluntary action to influence political decisions, the individual citizens will find it to their self-interest to indulge in political action. Otherwise, political participation should not be expected to occur at all.

Political Motives

An individual citizen can be motivated to participate in politics when s/he has a credible expectation that his/her actions will bear results. It is hard to imagine that a citizen can move to alter a political decision, if s/he believes that such action will be ignored by the authorities, or worse, that his/her life may be at risk. A feeling of political efficacy is a critical motive in kindling political participation. Similarly, being informed about politics, and keeping a keen interest in developments within the realm of politics also matter. A prior understanding of what is at stake will be necessary for one to consider acting at all. Without being informed about political events and happenings, one cannot reasonably be expected to act. Keen interest in politics helps a citizen to systematically follow the news and keep up with political developments. Interested, informed and efficacious citizens will be ideally situated to act to influence political decisions.

Political Resources

It is the political resources that one acquires over the years, mainly through the process of political socialization that instigate the above-mentioned political motives. Among them, the nature of settlement in which one lives (urban/rural), gender, lengthy exposure to formal education, and organizational affiliation seem to play a major role in determining whether one develops political motives, or not (Marsh and Kaase, 1979, 101). Political resources also seem to matter in determining the very substance of the political attitudes one develops (Ibid., 112; Kalaycıoğlu, 1997, 55). How intensely one feels politically efficacious, interested and informed about politics are often determined by one's education, peer relations, and family background within which one develops one's political self. The interactions between political resources and motives determine the shape and content of acts of political participation in a context shaped by the opportunity structure.

Political Opportunity Structure

Political opportunities provided for one to participate in politics also influence one's political motives. If one perceives limited chances of any real change in the political elite upon the influence of individual citizens, the opportunity structure fails to contribute to a feeling of political efficacy. Furthermore, if the opportunities provided by the regime intimidate those from contesting the political authorities, irrespective of resources and motives one has, one would be disinclined to engage in any action to influence political decisions. On the contrary, if the opportunity structure in which one is embedded provide for wide variety of chances for one to take action to influence political decisions without any intimidation or fear, then one can be inclined to engage in acts of political participation. The constitution, related statute laws, and regulations draw the contours of the opportunity structure. However, the cultural context, customs and folkloric understandings of authority, the interactions between the ruled and the rulers, and the perceived role of central authority (government) in everyday lives of citizens define the distinctive nature of the opportunity structure in question. Therefore, opportunity structure can be both persistent and alterable over time. Constitutions and statutes regulating political interactions change, on the one hand, and so do the cultural orientations, and customs, on the other. What seemed to be an opportunity structure that discourages political participation at some point in time may become an opportunity structure that encourages political participation at some other time. Such changes often lead to some similar variation in the frequency and scope of acts of political participation.

The Changing Political Opportunity Structure in Turkey

The opportunity structure of the Turkish political system has been in flux. In the interwar period (1923–1940) the Turkish pragmatic single party system had no room for legitimate political opposition. Although people were encouraged to participate in the elections, the elections were more or less plebiscites. Hence, we can talk more of political mobilization of the masses, than conventional political participation. Protest participation occurred but at severe risk for those involved. Such acts were equated with rebellion, and a variety of rebellious acts also took place in the interwar period, as well. Government initiated and mobilized acts of participation left little room, if any for the acts of repressive participation to materialize. Turkey remained out of the World War II and avoided further human capital losses that it inherited from long war years prior to the foundation of the young republic in 1923. While the world was burning during the war years Turkey did receive quite an important series of influences from the fascist as well as the communist opponents. Yet no party seem to have gathered behind it a mass gathering since neither the cultural nor the institutional environment at during the one-party regime were amenable to any kind of significant participatory behavior.

The 1945–1960 era of two-party pluralism brought about the first competitive, free and fair elections in the Republican era, in 1950. It provided a greater opportunity for mass political participation compared to the one-party era however, there were strict boundaries on political activism in the 1950s. Communism and socialism were definitely outlawed and often declared as the public enemy number one. However, Islamic revivalism enjoyed an era of tolerance under the DP rule. Furthermore, strict applications of censorship of the press and the media continued relentlessly.

The years between 1961 and 1980 came under the influence of the liberal 1961 Constitution, and multi-party pluralism, which led to multiplication of political parties in the National Assembly, coalition governments, a plentitude of socio-economic, and political voluntary associations, and a vigorous and free press. Socialist, social democratic, national socialist, religious parties and political organizations sprouted and took root during this period. The opportunities for being involved in acts of political influence opened up in Turkey. Conventional participation increased with leaps and bounds. Not only voting, but also such acts of participation as contacting, campaigning, and debating increased both in variety and frequency (Kalaycıoğlu and Turan, 1981, 123–35; Kalaycıoğlu, 1983, 85–113). Similar increases in protest behavior, and concomitantly in repressive behavior occurred at the same time. The load of mass political participation became so awesome for the political system that it failed to cope with it. As the streets of the country degenerated into a battleground of the fighting political forces, the legitimacy of political participation eroded in the eyes of the political authorities. The vigorous context of associational activities, the active free press, the participant citizen, and the coalition governments began to be increasingly identified with lack of stability in the country.

Consequently, when the great need of law and order was addressed in the 1982 Constitution, all sorts of restrictions were imposed upon political activism, associability, party formation, and electoral competition. Once more, the political opportunity structure became highly constrained in the aftermath of 1983, when Turkey went back to multi-party politics. The 1982 Constitution and the related statute laws defining the characteristics of the regime pick and choose from among the acts of political participation to promote and sanction. They encourage voting participation, (participation in the elections have even become mandatory), however, participation in political organizations were banned for students, state employees, and academics. Political parties were also restricted in their choice of structural models. They could not establish youth, and women's associations, and also village level organizations. Consequently, civil initiatives, civil society activism, and associability were ebbed to a new low in Turkey (Kalaycıoğlu, 1995, 43–69; Kalaycıoğlu, 1998, 111–35). An image of political participation that defines the role of a "good citizen" as someone, who votes in local and general elections, but otherwise stays aloof to politics was projected in the 1982 Constitution. Consequently, the image of an opportunity structure, which equates voting with conventional participation, and discourages any other form of political participation emerged in the 1980s and continued in the 1990s.

The outcome of dramatic change from an authoritarian to a liberal format in the opportunity structure from 1923 to 1980 took a sharp turn towards a constrained pluralist format once again in 1982. However, in terms of its intended consequences the 1982 Constitution has been successful in increasing voting participation. In comparison to the pre-1980 period of Turkey, and to other political systems with competitive elections, Turkish voting participation rates seem to be quite high in the post-1983 period. The stipulation of the Elections Act that voting participation is mandatory for all eligible voters has caused an initial increase in the voting turnout throughout the 1980's and the 1990's.

Resources and Motives as Sources of Political Participation in Turkey

Place of residence, age, gender, religion, and formal education come to play a role as resources which precipitate acts of political participation, when the opportunity structure permits them to interact with the political motives. Political efficacy, political interest, and overall perception of satisfaction / dissatisfaction with life, motivate people to expend energy to influence political authorities. However, we have grounds to assume that such motives are also partly determined by political resources (Kalaycıoğlu, 1997, 54–55). Consequently, we can draw up causal linkages between a series of resources and perceptions acting as exogenous factors influencing and determining political motives and through them political participation (Kalaycıoğlu, 1983, 343–442, and Kalaycıoğlu, 1997, 54–7).

Age, gender, place of residence, and satisfaction / dissatisfaction with life, constitute factors that are exogenous to the development of other motives and the influence of opportunities on the occurrence of acts of political participation (Kalaycıoğlu, 1997, 54–5). The young and male urbanites seem to find a greater chance to exploit the opportunities provided to them to take part in the political life of Turkey. Satisfaction /dissatisfaction with life is an autonomous source of supportive / conventional or aggressive / unconventional acts of participation (Kalaycıoğlu, 1997, 55).

Place of residence and gender often play some role in determining the length of time one attends school. By and large formal education plays a crucial role in one's socialization, which prepares a citizen for political life (Marsh, Kaase, 1979, 112). Not only conventional, but also protest participation seems to be critically influenced by formal education. A host of political attitudes and orientations are thus directly influenced by the formal educational influences of the individual. Most critically, religiosity, political efficacy and political interest have been observed to be influenced by the length and nature of formal education (Kalaycıoğlu, 1997). Lengthy secular education often leads to low levels of religiosity, and heightened feelings of political efficacy and increases in interest in politics. No education and religious education inculcates an increasing emphasis on religion in one's socio-political life. Lack of education also undermines political efficacy and interest in politics. No formal educational background seems to promote a feeling of powerlessness and disinterestedness in the broader realms of political life.

In light of the above-mentioned analysis a causal model of political participation can be formulated. We would like to suggest that both conventional participation and protest behavior are observed to be positively correlated (Marsh and Kaase, 1979, 87–131). We are inclined to suggest that the following causal model should be expected to wield similar explanatory power for both conventional and unconventional participation (see Figure 5.1).

In the following three different tests of the model for three different types of political participation, dependent variables will be conducted. We will operate with the assumption that the same sets of independent variables play similar roles in determining conventional participation, and both forms of unconventional participation of protest and repression potentials.

The Data Set

The data used in the following analyses were collected in a representative national survey conducted in the two weeks of October 2002, before the November 3, 2002 national election in Turkey. The details of the survey sampling and the field experience can be found in the Appendix. The findings presented below will also utilize, where appropriate, the data collected in the national surveys through the Turkish Values Studies of 1990 and 1997 as part of the World Values surveys, which were conducted by a team of researchers under the leadership of Ronald Inglehart of the University of Michigan. The findings from the data set of the 1990 study have already been published elsewhere (see Kalaycıoğlu, 1997, 51–70).

Figure 5.1 A General Model of Political Participation

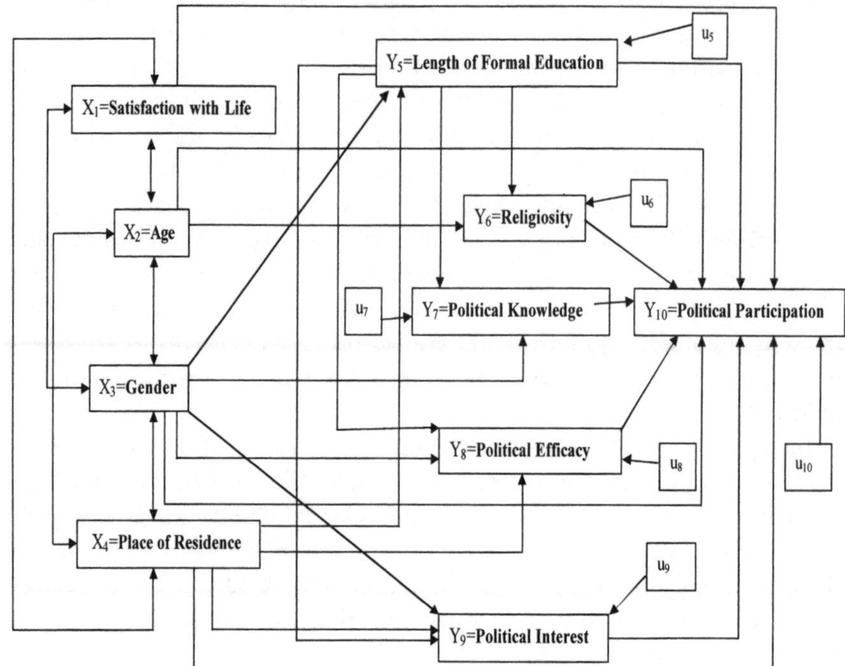

Simultaneous Equations:

$$Y_{10} = p_{101} X_1 + p_{102} X_2 + p_{103} X_3 + p_{104} X_4 + p_{105} Y_5 + p_{106} Y_6 + p_{107} Y_7 + p_{108} Y_8 + p_{109} Y_9 + p_{10u10} u_{10}.$$

$$Y_9 = p_{93} X_3 + p_{94} X_4 + p_{95} Y_5 + p_{9u9} u_9.$$

$$Y_8 = p_{83} X_3 + p_{84} X_4 + p_{85} Y_5 + p_{8u8} u_8.$$

$$Y_7 = p_{73} X_3 + p_{74} X_4 + p_{75} Y_5 + p_{7u7} u_7.$$

$$Y_6 = p_{62} X_2 + p_{65} Y_5 + p_{6u6} u_6.$$

$$Y_5 = p_{53} X_3 + p_{54} X_4 + p_{5u5} u_5.$$

Sources: Kalaycıoğlu, 1983, 387–407; Kalaycıoğlu, 1997, 57.

Operationalization of the Variables

The Dependent Variables

Conventional Participation: In the causal model outlined in Figure 5.1, political participation is measured as protest potential, which is defined as readiness to take part in acts of protest. Conventional participation is operationalized by means of a factor analyzing the responses registered by the interviewees to a set of questions on the voting records, contacts with bureaucracy and the deputies of the TGNA, taking part in communal discussion regarding public problems, issues and campaign activities (see Tables 5.1 and 5.2). Responses to each item in Tables 5.1 and 5.2 were ranked in descending order from taking part to not taking any part in the above-mentioned list of activities. The items listed in Tables 5.1 and 5.2 were subjected to a factor analysis with the purpose of classifying them into dimensions of conventional political participation. The factor solution of the items in questions as presented in Table 5.3 indicate that there are three distinct and linearly independent dimensions of voting, contacting, discussion and campaigning, which seem to occur in such an intertwined manner that the two activities cannot be discriminated against through a varimax factor solution (see Table 5.3 for more detail).

Table 5.1: Conventional Political Participation (Frequency Distribution-%)*

Item	No	Yes	DK/NA	Total
Will vote on November 3 2002	5,3	92,8	1,9	100
Appeals to Deputies of National Assembly	95,0	5,0	0,0	100
Appeals to Government in Ankara	97,4	2,6	0,0	100
Appeals to Provincial Governor	96,6	3,4	0,0	100
Appeals to sub-provincial Governor	95,5	4,5	0,0	100
Appeals to City Mayor	91,1	8,9	0,0	100
Takes part in communal discussion to solve a public issue	83,8	16,2	0,0	100
Tries to persuade others to vote for a certain party or candidate	70,0	27,8	2,2	100
Distributed political pamphlets and other party propaganda in the campaign	92,5	7,5	0,0	100
Took part in the campaign rally, meeting or demonstration of a political party or candidate	83,6	16,4	0,0	100
Campaign contribution to the accounts of a party or candidate	97,1	2,9	0,0	100

*N=1984, **DK/NA: Don't know/No answer

Table 5.2: Conventional Political Participation
Number of Times Voted in National Elections
ever since the voter became eligible to vote

Item	N	%
Never took part in any national election	304	15,3
One general election only	142	0,7
Two general elections	90	4,5
Three or more general elections	186	9,4
Every general election	1231	62
DK/NA	31	1,6
Total	1984	100

**DK/NA: Don't know/No answer

Table 5.3: Conventional Political Participation-Factor Analysis Results

Rotated Component Matrix (a)

Items	Component		
	Discussion/ Campaigning	Contacting	Voting
Distributed political pamphlets and other propaganda material in the campaign	**0,82**	0,01	–0,06
Participated in the campaign rally, meeting or demonstration of a political party or candidate	**0,77**	0,00	–0,01
Campaign contribution to the accounts of a party or candidate	**0,68**	0,00	–0,01
Tried to persuade another voter to vote for a certain party or candidate	**0,51**	0,00	0,17
Take part in communal discussion to solve a public issue	**0,44**	0,17	0,14
Appeal to the Government in Ankara	0,01	**0,71**	–0,08
Appeal to the Deputies of the Grand National Assembly	0,01	**0,64**	–0,10
Appeal to the Governor of Province	0,00	**0,64**	–0,08
Appeal to the Governor of Sub-district	–0,01	**0,62**	0,15
Appeal to the Mayor's Office	0,13	**0,60**	0,16
Will vote on November 3, 2002	0,01	–0,06	**0,75**
Number of elections participated after qualifying as a voter	0,00	0,01	**0,71**

*Extraction Method: Principal Component Analysis. Rotation Method: Varimax with Kaiser Normalization.
Rotation converged in 4 iterations.

In full conjunction with the earlier studies on conventional political participation (Kalaycıoğlu and Turan, 1981, and Kalaycıoğlu 1983), in Turkey conventional political participation contains three separate dimensions of discussion and campaigning, contacting and voting participation. Among those three dimensions the voters seems to be most active in voting participation and less active in all the rest. Taking part in persuasion and campaigning activities and even engaging in discussion with the intent of bringing about a solution to a public problem and issue seem to be much more practiced than contacting activities. Among the political authorities the elected officials and most distinctly the local officials seem to be more frequently appealed to seek solutions for problems encountered in life. The voters seem to be least inclined to seek contact with the agents of the state, even when they serve at the provincial or provincial district (*ilçe*) levels.

Protest Potential

Protest potential is operationalized by means of factor analyzing the responses registered by the interviewees to the following set of questions:

> "Have you ever taken part, or would you consider taking part in any of the activities listed below?
>
> 1. Petitioning (*Toplu Dilekçe*)
> 2. Participation in boycotts
> 3. Participation in legal demonstrations
> 4. Participation in wildcat strikes
> 5. Occupation of buildings or offices"

The responses given to each of the above-listed questions ranged between "participated," "would consider participating," or "never consider participating." The first category was assigned a numeral value of '3', the second category was assigned '2', and the last category was assigned the value of '1'. The individual frequency distributions per variable mentioned above are presented in the following table (see Table 5. 4). The missing cases were omitted from further analysis. Then, the above-mentioned five variables were subjected to a principal components analysis and they all loaded on the principal (single) factor (see Table 5.5). The factor scores were then calculated from the principal factor loadings of the principal factor solution presented in Table 5.5.

Table 5.4: Protest Potential

Potential Action	Takes part in Petitioning	Takes part in Boycott	Takes part in Legal Demonstrations	Takes part in Wildcat Strikes	Takes part in Occupation of Builldings
Never takes place (1)	68,7	81,4	77,3	90,5	93,4
May take place (2)	20,9	12,1	16,6	4,8	2,7
Took place (3)	6,6	3,2	3,3	1,2	0,6
DK/NA	3,8	3,3	2,8	3,5	3,3
Total	100	100	100	100	100

N=1984

Table 5.5 Protest Potential: Factor Analysis

*Component Matrix**

Items	Component Protest Potential
Petitioning	0,75
Takes part in boycott	0,84
Takes part in Legal Demonstration	0,83
Takes part in Wildcat Strike	0,79
Takes part in Occupation of Building or Place of Work	0,66

*Extraction Method: Principal Component Analysis.
1 component extracted.

Repression Potential

Repression potential is operationalized by means of factor analyzing the responses registered by the interviewees to the following set of questions:

> "Have you ever taken part, or would you consider taking part in any of the activities listed below?
>
> Break a non-legal strike
> Break up legal demonstration, rally or meeting
> Oust those who occupy a building or place of work"

The responses given to each of the above-listed questions ranged between "participated," "would consider participating," or "never consider participating." The first category was assigned a numeral value of '3', the second category was assigned '2', and the last category was assigned the value of '1' (see Table 5.6). The above-mentioned three variables were subjected to a principal components analysis and they all loaded on the principal (single) factor (see Table 5.7). The factor scores were then calculated from the principal factor loadings of the principal factor solution presented in Table 5.7.

Table 5.6: Repression Potential

Potential Action	Takes part in Breaking up Legal Demonstrations	Takes part in Breaking up Non-legal Strikes	Takes part in ousting those who Occupy Buildings
Never takes place (1)	91,8	92,7	88,8
May take place (2)	3,9	3,1	6,6
Took place (3)	0,8	0,7	0,7
DK/NA	3,3	3,5	3,9
Total Percentage	100	100	100

N=1984; DK/NA: Don't know/No answer

Table 5.7 Repression Potential

*Component Matrix**

Item	Component Repression Potential
Take part in an act of breaking a strike	0,869
Take part in an act of breaking up a legal demonstration, rally, or meeting	0,892
Take part in an act to oust protestors who occupy a building or place of work	0,87

*Extraction Method: Principal Component Analysis.
1 component extracted.

The Independent Variables

Gender is operationalized by assigning '1' to female and '2' to male respondents in the sample. Age is measured by subtracting the birth dates registered by each respondent from the year 1997. Place of residence is operationalized by assigning the numeral '2' to city dwellers and '1' to the inhabitants of the rural settlements. The scale of education employed in this paper is designed to measure the length of exposure to formal, secular education in Turkey. Those who attend religious schools are thus assigned the numeral value of '-1', those with no schooling '0', those with elementary to post graduate school experience were assigned numeral values that ranged between '1' and '8'.

Attitudinal variables were operationalized by means of calculation of factor scores that corresponded to satisfaction with life, political interest, political efficacy, and the two dimensions of religiosity, which we refer to as religious belief and religious traditionalism, through principal components of factor analysis. The five factors extracted from the factor analysis run were subjected to a varimax rotation, so that each dimension (variable) would be linearly independent of each other (see Table 5.8). Therefore, in the following regression analysis we have managed to avoid a concern with multi-collinearity, for those independent variables included in the preceding factor clustering exercise. The procedure used in operationalizing the attitudinal variables in this paper is the same as my previous analysis of protest potential in Turkey (Kalaycıoğlu, 1997, 60–61).

Findings

The results of the path analyses conducted with the 2002 survey data from Turkey indicate that the general model of political participation is relevant for conventional and protest participation, but fails to account for the variance in repression potential (see Figures 5.2 through 5.4). Conventional political participation and protest potential seem to be the end result of the interaction between the distribution of political resources and motives. It seems as if having political resources play a critical role in determining the political interest and political efficacy one feels, which in turn stimulates one to take part in either conventional or protest participation (see Figures 4.2 and 4.3). However, repression potential seems to be quite different from either conventional or protest participation. Repression potential seems to be most dependent upon age, or most specifically on being relatively young. No political resource other than age or any political motive, incorporated in the general model here, seems to play any role in causing voters to take part or refrain from engaging in repressive acts of participation. Consequently, we tend to conclude that repressive acts of political participation in Turkey are mostly the work of "mobilized youth". We will turn to a more thorough analysis of repressive participation later on in this chapter.

Table 5.8: Political Motives

*Rotated Component Matrix**

Items	Component		
	Political Knowledge	Political Interest	Political Efficacy
Knows the name of the minister in charge of the economy who was invited to run the austerity program from his job at the World Bank	**0,68**	0,07	0,07
Knows when the Cyprus intervention took place	**0,66**	0,29	–0,09
The name of the party and its leader that are reputed to lead according to the pollsters	**0,63**	–0,07	0,20
Know important issues of the campaign	**0,43**	**0,42**	–0,08
Knows when the EU accepted Turkey as an eligible candidate for full membership	**0,40**	0,29	–0,14
How interested with Politics	0,16	**0,82**	0,13
Interested in the ongoing election campaigns	0,00	**0,81**	0,23
Follow government activities	0,25	**0,47**	0,16
How important that a certain party wins for your household income to increase	–0,04	0,06	**0,80**
How much of an impact will your vote have on the outcome of Nov. 3, 2002 elections	0,06	0,08	**0,77**
Party that can bring a major solution to a pressing problem exits	0,07	0,19	**0,59**

*Extraction Method: Principal Component Analysis. Rotation Method: Varimax with Kaiser Normalization.
Rotation converged in 6 iterations.

Conventional Participation

Findings indicate that religiosity, political interest, and length of secular formal education play a major role in determining political participation (see Figure 5.2). Political motives make a relatively big impact on taking part in conventional acts of political participation. Political interest emerges as the most important political motive, followed by political efficacy and being politically informed, in determining taking part. Conventional political participation seems to be a mode that is least attractive to the youth. It seems as if, as the voters get older they tend to take part in conventional acts of political participation. The young either do not have the time or they do not find conventional acts of participation meaningful. They seem to show more eagerness to take part in more direct and potentially risky, and even violent, acts of political participation (see Figures 5.3 and 5.4).

Among the variables considered, the length of formal secular education seems to be an intervening variable. It seems to exert a heavy influence on most political motives that precipitate acts of political participation. However, education per se does not seem to motivate any form or mode of political participation, including conventional participation.

We also observe that women are less inclined to take part in unconventional forms of political participation than men. Gender seems not to play any significant role in precipitating conventional acts of political participation. Conventional participation does not seem to be a men's game any longer in Turkey.

Urbanization still seems to undermine conventional political participation in Turkey. It seems as if the "decline-of-the-community model" of political participation found in the 1970's in Turkey still seems to be operating with the same effect and validity (Verba, Nie, Kim (1978) as adapted to the Turkish case see Kalaycıoğlu, 1983, 412–413). Similarly, the indirect effect of urbanization on conventional participation through formal education still seems to be positive and yet relatively bigger than the direct effect of urbanization on conventional participation.

We have unearthed that the direct impact of satisfaction with life on conventional participation is negative. Those who seem to be satisfied with life do not seem to be inclined to take part in conventional acts of political participation. Political participation still seems to be perceived as a way of registering one's grievances and complaints, or plead for help. Hence, the satisfied do not seem to bother to show their support in the democratic system and participate in politics through conventional channels of participation.

Religiosity does not seem to motivate people to take part in conventional acts of political participation either. In opposition to popular belief that religious groups and communities have become more involved in political action, our findings indicate that overall religiosity plays no role in determining conventional political participation.

Figure 5.2 A Causal Model of Political Participation
(Conventional Political Participation-Turkey 2002)

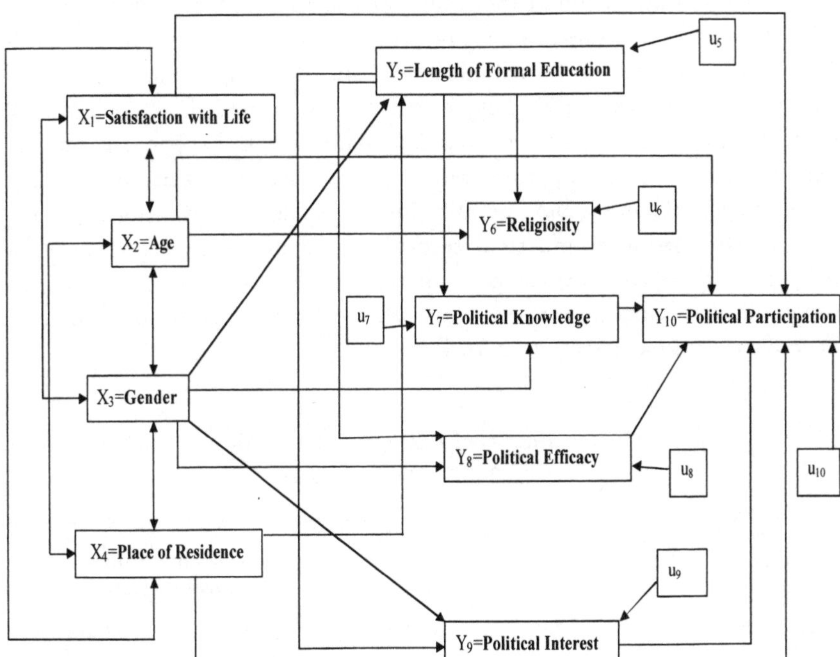

<u>Simultaneous Equations</u>:

$Y_{10} = -0{,}06\ X_1 + 0{,}24\ X_2 - 0{,}00^*\ X_3 - 0{,}08\ X_4 + 0{,}00^* Y_5 - 0{,}00^* Y_6 + 0{,}12\ Y_7 + 0{,}15\ Y_8 + 0{,}27\ Y_9 + 0{,}90\ u_{10.}$

(N=1573, R=0,43).

$Y_9 = 0{,}13\ X_3 + 0{,}02^*\ X_4 + 0{,}25\ Y_5 + 0{,}97\ u_8.$

$Y_8 = 0{,}06\ X_3 - 0{,}02^*\ X_4 - 0{,}08\ Y_5 + 0{,}97\ u_7.$

$Y_7 = 0{,}34\ X_3 - 0{,}02^*\ X_4 + 0{,}31\ Y_5 + 0{,}86\ u_7.$

$Y_6 = 0{,}09\ X_2 - 0{,}30\ Y_5 + 0{,}94\ u_6.$

$Y_5 = 0{,}30\ X_3 + 0{,}31\ X_4 + 0{,}95\ u_5.$

Note: Only those paths that are empirically determined to exist are shown in the preceding causal model.
* Statistically not significant at p < .05 level.

Earlier studies from the pre-1980 era indicate that a similar model has considerable amount of explanatory power in Turkey (Kalaycıoğlu, 1983, 343–446). A comparison of the results of a study conducted in the 1970's with the above-mentioned study is presented in the following table (see Table 5.9). Age, urbanization, formal education, and all political motives seem to act in the same way in Turkey in 2002, as they had done so in 1974. Consequently, it is warranted to conclude that conventional participation has been and still is a form of participation that the older voters turn to in Turkey. Urbanization has an ongoing debilitating influence on conventional participation, though other political resources and motives precipitated by urbanization fuel conventional participation in the Turkish cities. Finally, one can argue that political motives have been the most important determinants of conventional participation in Turkey.

Table 5. 9: Determinants of Political Participation in Turkey (1974, 2002) (Direct Effects)

Variables	Conventional Political Participation 1974	2002
Gender	0,19	0,00
Age	0,12	0,22
Residence (Urban/Rural)	–0,09	–0,08
Satisfaction w/ Life	n. a.	–0,05
Formal Secular Education	0,00	0,00
Occupational Status	0,00	n. a.
SES (Interviewer Estimate)	0,07	n. a.
SES (Education +Occupational Prestige)	0	n. a.
Mass Media Exposure	0	n. a.
Organizational Membership	0,24	n. a.
Political Knowledge	n. a.	0,12
Political Efficacy	0,10	0,15
Political Interest	0,20	0,27
Religiosity	n. a.	0,01*
Number of Cases	2068	1573
R	0,56	0,43
R^2	0,31	0,18

Sources: Kalaycıoğlu, 1983, 351; Participation Survey 2002.
* Statistically not significant at $p < .05$ level of significance. n.a.=Not applicable.
Table entries are direct influences by path coefficients, unless they are otherwise designated.

Protest Potential

When the same model is applied to protest potential in Turkey it performs almost as well as the conventional participation model (see Figure 5.3). Young male voters seem to be more inclined to take part in protest behavior. Urbanization per se seems to be providing fertile ground for protest participation. Consequently, protest potential seems to be concentrated in the declining communities of the Turkish cities and it is young males who are more ready to take the relatively more risky or less approved road to participation. Protest seems to be a more of a male game.

Interestingly enough religiosity seems to have a sizable and dampening effect on protest potential. Religiosity in the way it develops in Turkish society does not seem to be fuelling protest behavior. Radical Islamic groups have always existed in Turkish society, yet they have always been marginal to Turkish politics. Mainstream political Islam has vied for power through conventional channels of political participation since the 1960s. In fact, the political parties and interest groups espousing Sunni Islamic values have been extremely successful in obtaining power in the Turkish Grand National Assembly since the 1970s and in the cabinets of various Prime Ministers since 1973. Consequently, there seems to be greater proclivity to penetrate the legitimate channels of influence through canvassing the vote and mobilizing voters at the polls, than engage in acts of protest. Such acts of protest seem to be perpetrated by those who feel politically less efficacious than those who commit conventional acts of participation. Protest behavior in Turkey seems to be enacted out of desperation, and by those who do not seem to have much chance of having their say with the political authorities. Religiosity does not seem to condone such acts, which seem to be perceived as rebellious behavior. We should also add that some forms of protest behavior contain a relatively high risk of being hurt or incarcerated. If the pious voters get their way through the ballot box, why should they feel the need to take part in acts of protest, where severe political, legal, and even lethal risks are involved?

Political motives still play a major role in determining the protest potential of the individual voters. However, as noted above political efficacy seems to play a relatively little role among the political motives incorporated into our model. This should be taken as a sign of relative lack of power or perception of the relative ineffectiveness of the act of protest in which the voter takes part. Nevertheless, the individual takes part in such acts as building occupation or wildcat strikes, for he or she seems to have the impression that conventional acts do not suffice in getting what s/he deserves. However, we have also unearthed that participation in protests requires to be informed about politics and to have a deep interest in political life. Those who lack interest and information about politics do not seem to take part in any form of participation in Turkey, whether it is conventional or not (see Figures 4.2 and 4.3).

The causal model used here seems to have slightly less explanatory power than the same model used in the previous studies in 1990 and 1997 (see Table 4.10). The direct influence of formal secular education on protest potential seems to have been completely eroded. However, formal secular education still plays a critical role in determining political motives, which in turn, play a major role in determining protest potential.

Table 5.10 Determinants of Political Participation in Turkey

	Protest Potential		
Independent Variables	1990	1997	2002
Gender	0,08	0,10	0,10
Age	–0,03*	–0,05	–0,06
Residence (Urban/Rural)	n. a.	n. a.	0,06
Satisfaction w/ Life	n. a.	n. a.	0,00
Formal Secular Education	0,15	0,21	0,00
Occupational Status	n. a.	n. a.	0,14
Political Knowledge	–0,09	–0,15	0,07
Political Efficacy	0,15	0,28	0,17
Political Interest	–0,15	–0,36	–0,18
Religiosity			
Number of Cases	980	1248	1579
R	0,47	0,64	0,37
R^2	0,23	0,41	0,14

Sources: Kalaycıoğlu, 1997, 62; Turkish Values Survey of 1996/7, Participation Survey 2002.
* statistically not significant at $p < .05$ level of significance. n.a.=Not applicable.
Table entries are direct influences by path coefficients, unless they are otherwise designated.

The role played by religiosity and political interest seemed also to have become less pronounced over the years in determining protest potential in Turkey (see Table 5.10). The main reason for such a diminished influence of some of the critical variables as measured in 2002 seemed to be the decreased variance in the dependent variable. The Maoist Kurdish terror movement called the Partiya Karkeren Kurdistan (PKK) had become less influential after its leader Abdullah Öcalan was captured in 1999. Similarly, in the aftermath

Figure 5.3 A General Model of Political Participation (Protest Potential-Turkey 2002)

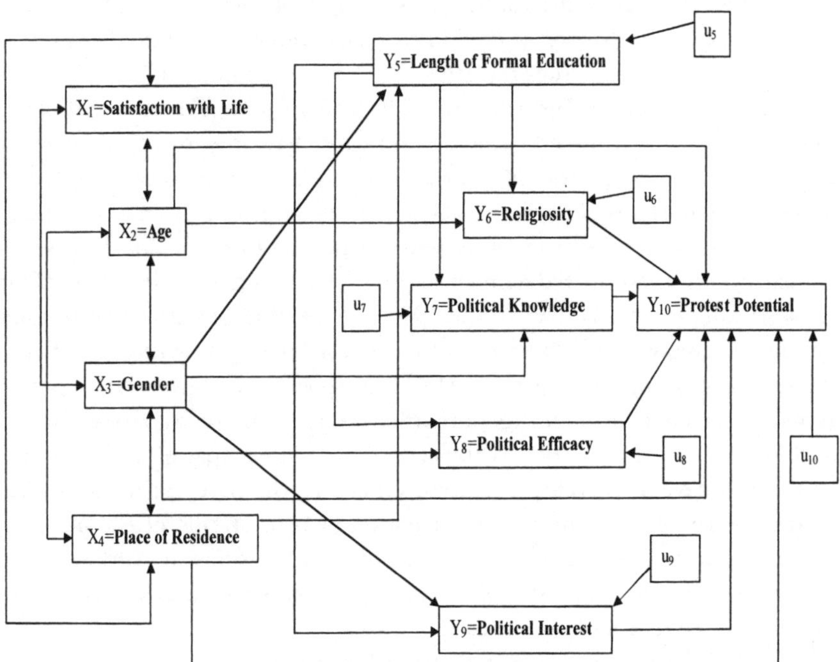

Simultaneous Equations:

$Y_{10} = -0{,}00^* X_1 - 0{,}06 X_2 + 0{,}10 X_3 + 0{,}06 X_4 + 0{,}00^* Y_5 - 0{,}18 Y_6 + 0{,}14 Y_7 + 0{,}07 Y_8 + 0{,}17 Y_9 + 0{,}93 u_{10.}$

(n=1579, R= ,38).

$Y_9 = 0{,}13 X_3 + 0{,}02^* X_4 + 0{,}25 Y_5 + 0{,}97 u_8.$

$Y_8 = 0{,}06 X_3 - 0{,}02^* X_4 - 0{,}08 Y_5 + 0{,}97 u_7.$

$Y_7 = 0{,}34 X_3 - 0{,}02^* X_4 + 0{,}31 Y_5 + 0{,}86 u_7.$

$Y_6 = 0{,}09 X_2 - 0{,}30 Y_5 + 0{,}94 u_6.$

$Y_5 = 0{,}30 X_3 + 0{,}31 X_4 + 0{,}95 u_5.$

Note: Only those paths that are empirically determined to exist are shown in the preceding causal model.

* Statistically not significant at $p < .05$ level.

of September 11, 2001 religious groups bent upon wreaking havoc in the country have somewhat subsided, in particular after the forceful submission of the Hizbullah terror network in Turkey in 2001 (see Table 5.11). In fact, spatiotemporal comparison of the Turkish data seems to indicate that protest potential has decreased from the 1990's to 2002 (see Table 5.11).

A comparison of the Turkish data with similar findings from consolidated democracies of Europe and the US indicate that only in terms of legal demonstrations and petitioning Turkey used to lag behind in the 1990s (see Table 5.11). In terms of boycotts, wildcat strikes and occupation of buildings the Turkish participation rates had been low, but not the lowest in comparison to consolidated democracies in the 1990s (see Table 5.11). What is interesting to note is that, in the 1990s such acts of protest as petitioning and legal demonstrations that might have been tolerated by the authorities, did not seem to occur frequently. However, those acts which seemed not to have much chance of being perceived as legitimate by the political authorities, such as boycotts, wildcat strikes, and occupation of buildings, seemed to have attracted more involvement in the past. As noted above, protest behavior took the form of negation or contestation of the political system, rather than legal objections to political decisions, in Turkey. Once anti-system movements lost their attraction, protest potential seems to have rapidly eroded in Turkey in the early 2000s.

Nevertheless, protest potential in Turkey seems to be determined by a coterie of such factors as political resources, (such as youthfulness, and urbanization lifestyle, education) and motives (such as political interest and being informed about politics), within the context of a pluralist opportunity structure (see Figure 5.3, and Table 5.12). Table 5.12 indicates that similar factors are also at play in the consolidated democracies of Europe and North America, as well as in Turkey, in determining protest potentials of the individuals voters (see Table 5.12). An examination of the multiple correlation (R) and determination (R^2) coefficients in Table 4.12 indicates that the explanatory power of comparable models of unconventional political participation in consolidated democracies and Turkey are also quite similar. It seems as if the causal model employed in this study, which purports to explain protest potential as a consequence of political opportunities, resources and motives seem to have relatively general applicability among democracies.

Repression Potential

The causal model we have employed in our analysis fails to provide any meaningful explanation to the determination of repression potential in Turkey (see Fig. 5.4). We would also like to emphasize that repression potential is

Table 5.11: Comparative Protest Potential in Consolidated Democracies and Turkey
(Percentage of those who recall participation in the corresponding acts)

	Unconventional Acts of Political Participation				
	Petitioning	Boycotts	Legal Demon-strations	Strikes	Occupation of Buildings
Austria	45,5	4,8	9,8	1	0,7
Belgium	44,5	8,3	21,2	5,7	3,6
Britain	74,5	13,2	13,6	9,6	2,4
Denmark	50,3	10,2	27	16,7	2
France	51,4	11,3	31,2	9,4	7,2
Germany (West)	55,1	9,2	19,5	2,1	1
Iceland	46,6	**21,1**	**23,4**	0,1	*1,3*
India	22,4	15,2	15,3	5,4	0,7
Italy	44,2	10	34,1	**5,6**	7
Netherlands	50,1	8,4	25	2,5	3,1
Portugal	24,8	3,5	19,2	3,1	1,4
Spain	17,5	4,7	21,2	5,7	2,4
Sweden	69,9	15,8	21,8	2,9	0,2
USA	70,1	17,4	15,1	4,4	1,8
Turkey (1990)	12,8	5,2	5,3	1,4	1,2
Turkey (1997)	13,5	6,3	6,1	2	0,5
Turkey (2002)	6,6	3,2	3,3	1,2	0,6

Sources: World Values Survey (1989–91) and Turkish Values Surveys (1990, and 1996/7). The figures in bold are the highest percentages per column and the figures in italics are the lowest.

even more scant than protest potential in Turkey. Similarly, the amount of variance to be explained in the dependent variable (repression potential) is so small that the model under examination produces a multiple correlation coefficient (Pearson's product moment correlation, R) of 0,10, which is barely significant in the statistical sense of the word. Indeed, political resources and motives incorporated in the model fail to explain more than one per cent of the variance in the dependent variable (repression potential) (see Figure 5.4). The only slight exception seems to be age. Repression potential exists among the young, though gender, urbanization, satisfaction with life, education, and political motives fail to provide any meaningful explanation as to why it occurs.

Table 5.12 Multiple Regression Analysis of Protest Potential Scales

	France	U.K.	U.S.A.	Germany	Turkey 1990	Turkey 1996	Turkey 2002
Age	–0,28	–0,29	–0,29	–0,25	– ,01*	–0,05	–0,08
Sex/Gender	0,18	0,21	0,16	0,14	0,09	0,12	0,13
Education	0,26	0,13	0,26	0,14	0,34	0,38	0,03
Strength of party identification	0,23	0,11	0,06	0,08	0,00*	0,12	0,13
Political Efficacy	n.a	0,13	0,10	0,22	0,11	–0,10	0,08
Policy Dissatisfaction	0,11	0,16	0,15	0,07	–0,09	–0,12	0,14**
R 0,58	0,5	0,56	0,50	0,41	0,50	0,39	
R^2 0,34	0,25	0,31	0,25	0,16	0,25	0,16	

	The Netherlands	U.K.	U.S.A.	Germany	Austria	Turkey 1990	Turkey 1996	Turkey 2002
Age	–0,19	–0,28	–0,33	–0,25	–0,16	–0,04	–0,02*	–0,09
Sex/Gender	–0,09	–0,12	–0,04	–0,09	–0,11	–0,08	–0,13	0,11
Education	0,15	0,10	0,20	0,18	0,16	0,21	0,30	0,04
Religiousness	0,17	0,03	0,12	0,12	0,07	n.a.	n.a	–0,21
Religious Belief	n.a	n.a	n.a	n.a	n.a	–0,19	–0,30	n. a.
Religious Traditionalism	n.a	n.a	n.a	n.a	n.a	0,13	–0,15	n. a.
Trade Union Membership	–0,03	–0,09	–0,04	–0,06	–0,03	–0,18	0,18	–0,13
Occupational Prestige	0,01	0,06	0,04	0,01	0,09	0,09	n.a	n. a.
R 0,39	0,41	0,48	0,42	0,34	0,47	0,49	0,35	
R^2 0,15	0,16	0,23	0,18	0,12	0,22	0,24	0,12	

Sources: Marsh and Kaase, 1979, 131; Dalton, 1988, 69–70; Kalaycıoğlu, 1997, 67–68, Political Participation Survey, 2002.
(*) Statistically not significant at ,05 level of significance.
All table entries are standardized partial regression coefficients, except 'R' and 'R^2', which are the Pearson product-moment multiple correlation coefficients and determination coefficients for those independent variables and the dependent variable in the upper rows of each part of the Table. The last two columns of the Table on Turkey are our calculations from the Turkish Values Survey of 1990 and 1996/7. For more details see (Kalaycıoğlu, 1997, 68).
(**) Measured as economic dissatisfaction

Under the circumstances we are inclined to conclude that repression potential occurs as "mobilized behavior", in which powerful patrons provide the incentives for their youthful clients to take part in acts to undermine legal demonstrations, party meetings, and the like. Unfortunately, we do not have any variables that tap such incentives in out data set. The only two independent variables that seemed to have shown some correlation with repression potential, other than age are chauvinism and unemployment. They hint that the repression potential seems to exist among the likes of soccer hooligans and the young lumpen-proletariat. They seem to be prone to mobilization, without being much informed about politics, or lacking political efficacy or interest. With the right kind of incentives and with the prodding of relevant patrons they seem to burst into repressive behavior. However, we should caution the reader that both chauvinism and unemployment have statistically significant but also weak correlations with repression potential in Turkey. Consequently, we are inclined to go so far as to note that repression potential is more a product of "mobilized political behavior" than the other acts of conventional and protest participation.

Conjectures and Conclusions

Political participation in Turkey has incorporated a widening variety of acts over the years. Such acts of conventional political participation as voting, campaigning, debating, discussing and deliberating political issues with the intent of finding solutions for them, contacting political authorities have been employed by a large segment of the voting age population in the multi-party era. Protest potential, culminating in unconventional acts of participation in politics, has shown a trend for increasing frequency and variety over the years. Petitions, boycotts, legal demonstrations, and wildcat strikes have all been on the increase throughout the 1990s, while such potentially violent acts as occupation of buildings are on the decrease.

Acts of political participation seem to be as frequently carried out in Turkey as in most consolidated democracies. Furthermore, the factors that seem to engender acts of political participation in Turkey seem to be quite similar to those factors that precipitate such acts in most consolidated democracies. In both Turkey and consolidated democracies conventional political participation and protest potential seem to be an outcome of political resources used by those actors who are motivated to act in a pluralist opportunity structure, which enables citizens (or groups of citizens), to respond to and exert pressure on government.

Figure 5.4 A General Model of Political Participation (Repression Potential-Turkey 2002)

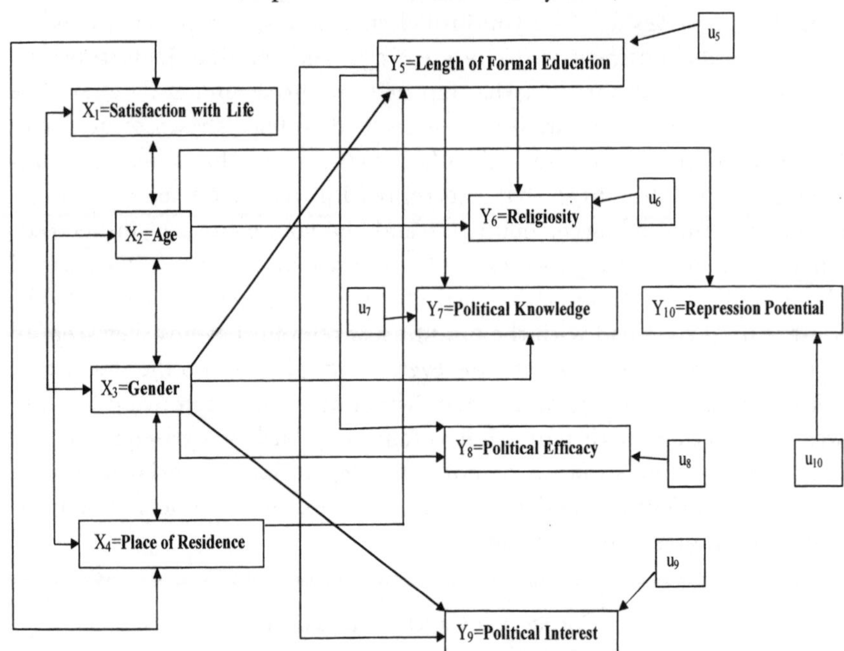

Simultaneous Equations:

$$Y_{10} = -0{,}02^{*} X_1 - 0{,}06\ X_2 + 0{,}03^{*} X_3 + 0{,}04\ X_4 - 0{,}02^{*}Y_5 - 0{,}02^{*} Y_6 + 0{,}05^{*}Y_7 + 0{,}04^{*} Y_8 + 0{,}04^{*} Y_9 + 0{,}95\ u_{10.}$$

(n=1600, R= ,10).

$$Y_9 = 0{,}13\ X_3 + 0{,}02^{*} X_4 + 0{,}25\ Y_5 + 0{,}97\ u_8.$$

$$Y_8 = 0{,}06\ X_3 - 0{,}02^{*} X_4 - 0{,}08\ Y_5 + 0{,}97\ u_7.$$

$$Y_7 = 0{,}34\ X_3 - 0{,}02^{*} X_4 + 0{,}31\ Y_5 + 0\ {,}86\ u_7.$$

$$Y_6 = 0{,}09\ X_2 - 0{,}30\ Y_5 + 0{,}94\ u_6.$$

$$Y_5 = 0{,}30\ X_3 + 0{,}31\ X_4 + 0{,}95\ u_5.$$

Note: Only those paths that are empirically determined to exist are shown in the preceding causal model.
* Statistically not significant at $p < .05$ level.

Turkey seems to be experiencing a phenomenon of conventional political participation and protest potential, which is similar to consolidated democracies of the European Union and the US. Nevertheless, certain restrictions persist in the opportunity structure of Turkey, which discourages its citizens from being involved in unconventional acts of political participation. The sluggish performance of the TBMM in promulgating the necessary changes in statute laws, which would introduce the 1995 amendments of the 1982 Constitution in the laws, restricts the scope and magnitude of political participation in the country. A less restrictive opportunity structure is likely to provide more latitude for protest behavior in Turkey. A similar surge in involvement in party politics by the youth and women of the country is a likely outcome with a change in the statute laws. Such a development will also lead to a wider involvement of the masses in conventional forms of political participation as well. The current bottleneck to further increases in the magnitude, scope, and variety of both conventional and protest participation seems to be produced by the opportunity structure of the country, more than any other factor at work.

Consequently, we are inclined to argue that in terms of political motives and the application of political resources to pressure governments and influence political decisions Turkish citizens seem to have accumulated a relatively high level of consciousness, skills and knowledge. They seem to use such skills proficiently and effectively. Hence, such a citizenry enabled the functioning of a vigorous multi-party system in Turkey. A culture of pluralism has gained considerable amount of ground, however, the political regime of the country, and most specifically its constitution stands out as the greatest impediment for the consolidation of a more pluralist context.

Finally, we would like to note that repression potential seems to occur in Turkey infrequently and through the actions of patrons who mobilize otherwise politically uninformed and uninterested youth to serve their political objectives. In the past Turkey had suffered from such acts of repression. For example, on May 1, 1977 a May Day parade was subject to such a repressive act, which left hundreds injured and many dead. In the 1970s, Turkey went through a period of heightened protest and repressive participation. It seemed as if those who were more involved in protest participation were motivated by social democratic, socialist, and Marxist-Leninist ideas and ideals. Those who reacted to them and tried to repress such protest activities seemed to have emerged from among the ranks of anti-communist ultra-nationalists. In the early 2000's both of these groups of ideologies and related movements seems to have mellowed. They seem to have vied for power through the conventional channels of political participation.

The social democrats have fared well in the polls and so have the anti-communist ultra-nationalists. They both managed to get into several coalition governments and simultaneously showed less inclination to fight their differences out in the streets. Consequently, repression potential seems to have subsided even more than protest potential.

The recent rapprochement with the European Union also appears to have provided greater legitimacy to conventional channels of participation in a democratic regime (opportunity structure). The war against terror that the United States has declared since September 11, 2001 also appears to have increased the risks of protest behavior and repressive acts, and most specifically those that seem to be motivated by religion have become quite risky. The attitudes toward unconventional political participation which emanated from religion swiftly increased in Turkey during 1997, when a radical Sunni Muslim party (the Welfare Party) lost power after being pressured by a coalition of secular forces led by the military in June 1997. There was a sudden upsurge in unconventional participation of the religious activists from 1997 up until the 1999 general elections. However, the religious protest and repressive acts failed to garner votes for the religious parties propagating enhanced role of Islam in the public realm in Turkey in the April 18, 1999 elections. Soon after this event, occurred the attacks on the Twin Towers in New York City and the Pentagon in the United States on September 11, 2001. The attitudes toward religious protest and repressive participation changed dramatically in the US and the EU member countries. Under the influence of such international and domestic changes in the opportunity structure both protest and repression potentials seem to have eroded in Turkey.

6

VOTING IN ELECTIONS: CONTINUITY AND CHANGE IN NOVEMBER 2002

As noted earlier, lack of continuity, persistent high volatility and ever increasing fragmentation of electoral preferences can all be linked to recurrent military regimes and their impact on the institutional structure of the Turkish electoral scene. In this chapter we aim at taking this observation as a given and focus instead on the reflections of such dynamic change on the ideological, attitudinal, and political behavioural patterns in the Turkish polity using our data from the November 2002 pre-election survey complemented in some instances with other sources of data.

Continuity and Change along Left-Right Ideological Dimension

Our ensuing micro individual based survey analyses are anchored into the macro electoral patterns through the relatively frequently asked questions of party and self-placements along the conventional left-right (L-R) ideological scale over the last nearly two decades. Ergüder (1980–1), Ergüder, Esmer and Kalaycıoğlu (1991), Esmer (1999) and Çarkoğlu and Toprak (2000) all diagnose that while the majority of the Turkish voters locate themselves at the very centre of the left-right ideological spectrum, over time, a significant portion have shifted from the centre to the right of the spectrum. These centrist voters can be labelled as independents that seem unable or unwilling to identify with any political party. The fact that their numbers have been declining over the last decade while the number of those who locate themselves at the right end of the spectrum keeps increasing is a micro individual level indicator for the changing nature of political cleavages in the country. One potential explanation for this phenomenon is the rapid population growth, which caused an influx of new voters in large numbers in the post-1980 era. The recent lowering of the voting age to 18 added significantly to this dynamism and fluidity of the electorate. At the beginning of the new millennium, the majority of Turkish voters are under the age of thirty. Most have spent their adolescence in the depoliticised 1980s. Their parents and peers have not been able to provide them with a stable model of party identification. The ban of the 1980 military regime over the leadership of the pre-coup political parties for taking part in politics had left the older generation of voters in suspense and confusion as to which party stood for what. Hence, the military regimes have effectively disrupted the political socialisation of the new influx of voters into the party affiliation of their political role models.[1]

In our pre-election study of electoral preferences, the respondents were provided with a conventional one-to-ten L-R ideology scale and asked to place themselves as well as each of the major parties in the system on this scale.[2] In a temporal assessment of these self-placements, the continual shift to the right end of the spectrum becomes quite clear. We clearly see that starting from 1990 those individuals at the very center of the ideological spectrum that comprised about 43.5 percent of the respondents at the time start to decline. In 1996, the centrist positions comprised 32.6 percent and in 2002 32.2 percent. Table 6.1 also shows that from 1990 to 2002 the left-of-center and centrist positions have shrunken, while the right-of-center has grown in size. Although it is hard to time precisely the shift in ideological orientations, it seems that the biggest change occurred in the mid-1990s, when the country was being torn between Kurdish ethnic separatism and the rise of the pro-Islamist movement (Kalaycıoğlu, 1999:71–72). Almost concurrently with deadly and increasingly costly ethnic separatist activities in the southeastern Anatolia, were regional conflicts in the Balkans (the war in Bosnia and Kosovo) and the Caucuses, which both had significant links to nationalist sentiments in the country and these opportunities were conveniently exploited by the politicians to stir up sensitivities. What is striking in the data from the 2002 election is that this shift to the right is still continuing; although it appears to have slowed down. However, in 2002, while only 15 percent of the electorate was on the left of center, nearly 43 percent of the electorate placed themselves at the right-of-center. It is noticeable that the left-of-center in the country is continuously shrinking in size in a period when the country was hit by two major economic crises one in 1994 and another in 2001.

In April 2004, another nationwide representative sample survey was conducted.[3] While the left-of-center electorate remains constant at about 16 percent, the right-of-center seems to have somewhat shrunken down to about 39 percent. As a result, the center seems to have grown to about

Figure 6.1 Distribution of the Electorate along the Left-Right Ideological Scale

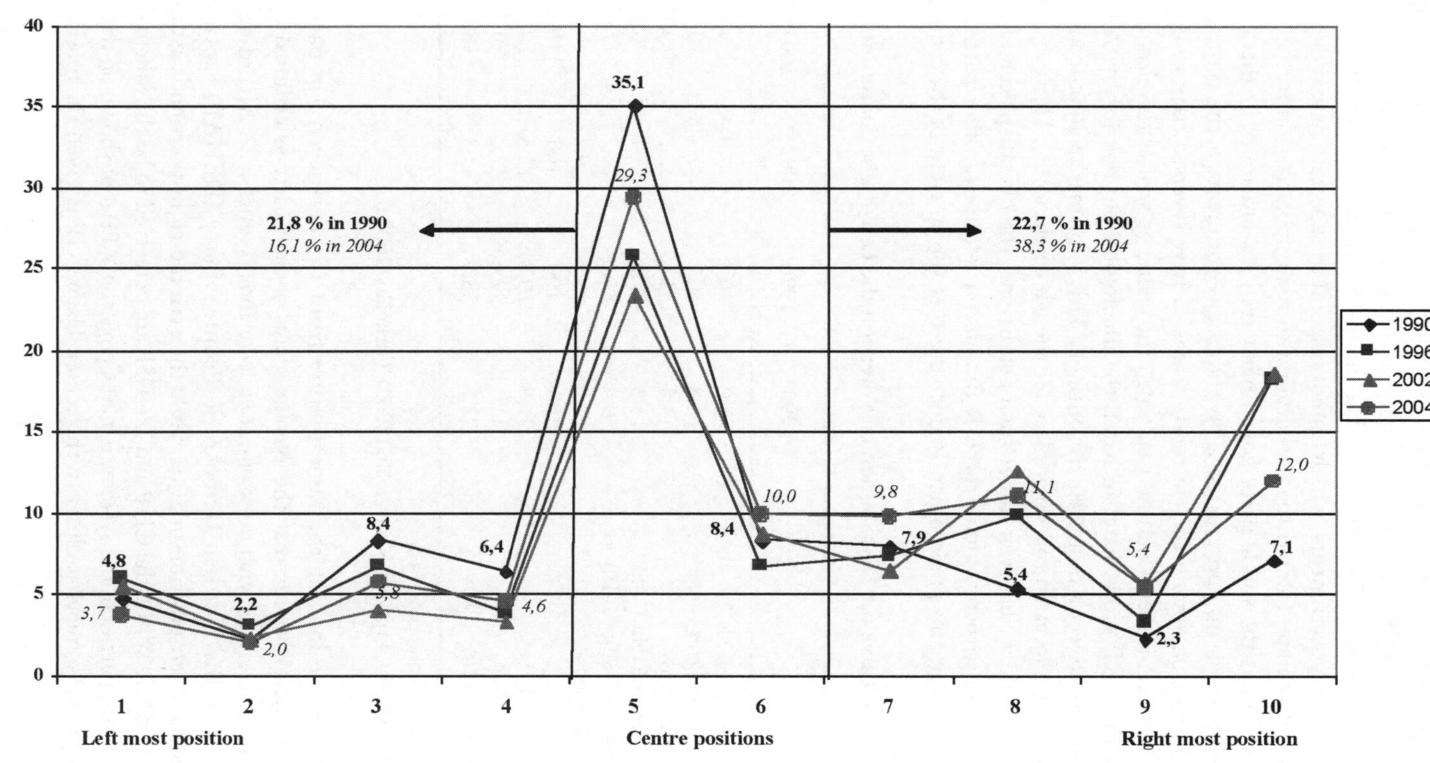

39 percent. It is interesting that, as the AKP's single party tenure completed its first year, the Turkish electorate seems to have become, once again more centrist. One could conjecture that increasing uneasiness with fractionalized coalition governments, which cannot respond to expectations and demands of the electorate, formed the background to rising polarization in the country. As soon as the single party government restored order and predictability in policy-making and created a favorable environment in the economy, the polarization among the electorate seems to have reversed back to centrism. Therefore, it seems natural that when the center as well as the electoral basis of the AKP grows hand in hand, the ideological outlook for the AKP will tend to project a more centrist outlook. This is primarily an outcome of the centrist relocation that took place for the whole electorate. However, we will show below that even under such conditions, the overall placement of the AKP constituency along the L-R dimension relative to other parties in the system remains predominantly unchanged at the far right of the center.

Table 6.1 Distribution of Voters on the Left-Right Continuum

	1990*	1996*	2002**	2004***
Extreme Left (1–2)	7,0	9,1	7,9	5,7
Moderate Left (3–4)	14,8	10,7	7,4	10,4
Centre (5–6)	43,5	32,6	32,2	39,3
Moderate Right (7–8)	13,3	17,3	19,1	20,9
Extreme Right (9–10)	9,4	21,6	24,2	17,4
No Response	12,0	8,7	9,2	6,2
	100	100	100	100
Left (1–4)	21,8	19,8	15,3	16,1
Centre (5–6)	43,5	32,6	32,2	39,3
Right (7–10)	22,7	38,9	43,3	38,3

*Kalaycıoğlu (1999, 58),
**Çarkoğlu, Ergüder, Kalaycıoğlu (2002), Çarkoğlu (2005a)

When we look at the same picture from the perspective of party constituencies, we see that the average scores of each party as assigned by their voters, overlaps with most of our expectations (Figure 6.2). According to the voters, the Kurdish Democratic People's Party (DEHAP) captures the extreme left position in 2002 while the extreme-right position is assigned to the MHP. While the CHP and the DSP are perceived to be the other two left-leaning parties of the system, Ismail Cem's the YTP (not shown on the figure) is placed somewhat closer to the center. Uzan's GP is given the most centrist position, reflecting a lack of ideological orientation in its populist stands. While the ANAP and the DYP are seen as leaning toward right-of-center, the other extreme-right wing group is placed on the distinct right-wing end of the spectrum. In other words, the constituencies of the major parties that competed in the 2002 general election place themselves on the left-right ideological spectrum almost in full agreement with our expectations about the Turkish party system.[4] The MHP and DYP voters place themselves on average at the very end of the ideological spectrum while those of the AKP and ANAP follow them. In the eyes of their voters then, ANAP and DYP were within the right-of-center of the ideological spectrum. The fact that AKP voters are very close to ANAP and DYP voters and considerably towards the center compared to MHP voters should be underlined here. Ideologically speaking, the difference between the MHP and AKP voters are much larger than those found between the AKP and ANAP, as well as DYP voters. One thing is clear then, while AKP voters see themselves similar to those of ANAP and DYP positions, these three parties are all, in the eyes of their own voters, quite away from the center of the ideological spectrum. The center (5 and 6 on our 1 to 10 scale) prior to 2002 general election was left empty by all party constituencies and only the GP and DSP voters see themselves closer to the center than either one of the extremes.

Figure 6.2 Party constituencies' positions on the left-right ideological spectrum

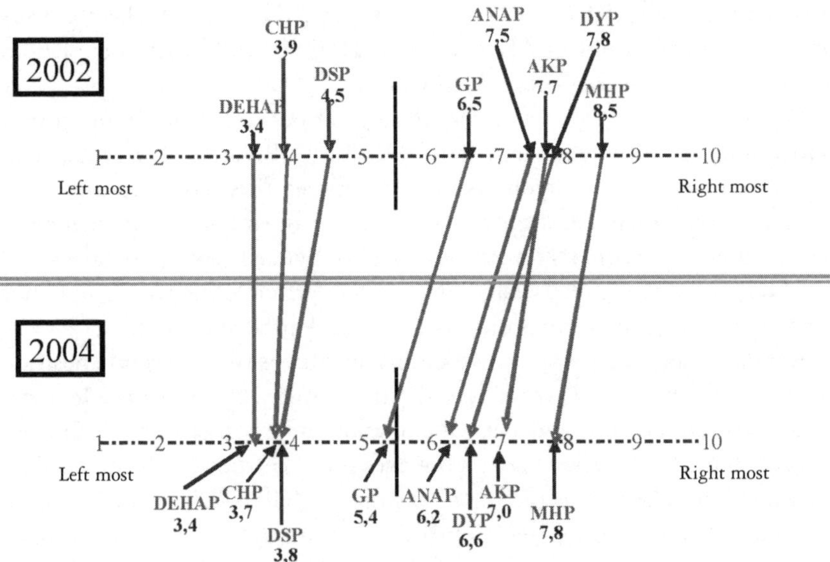

*Where do party constituencies see *themselves* on the left-right scale?

Figure 6.2 also shows a comparison of the party constituency placements in 2002 and 2004 surveys. After the municipal elections of March 2004 we see that the above-mentioned move to the center of ideological orientations becomes clearer by taking the party constituencies into account. We see that with the exception of DEHAP voters, for whom the average position remained the same at around 3.4 on a 1 to 10 scale, all other parties' voters have changed their average positions. The center-left party constituencies, those of the CHP and DSP, have moved to the left and thus becoming more leftist on average during the tenure of the AKP government. The fact that on average DEHAP and CHP voters place themselves very similarly along the left-right ideological spectrum is also noticeable and reflects perhaps the limits of CHP appeal to a larger audience by simply maintaining a similarity to an ethnic left-wing party constituency, which does not even vote for the CHP.

In contrast, centre-right and right-of-centre party constituencies have shifted towards the centre and thus mellowed their ideological stands during the course of the AKP's tenure. We also see that these shifts are not insignificant shifts. For the GP, on average, the positions are 1.1 points more leftist in orientation taking the GP voters from 6.5 points on average down to 5.4 points. Similarly, ANAP voters move from 7.5 to 6.2, DYP voters from 7.8 to 6.6 and AKP voters from 7.7 to 7. Even the right-most placement of the MHP moved from 8.5 on average down to 7.8, still occupying the right-most position. The only leap-frogging, to use a spatial voting jargon, occurred between DYP and AKP voters' average positions. While the DYP voters were on average to the right of AKP voters in 2002, in 2004 they occupied on average a position to the left of AKP voters.

Despite mellowing down of the ideological positions and more centrist positioning in 2004 compared to 2002, the AKP voters still occupy the second most-right position on average. In between these two measurements, the AKP constituency has grown considerably in size and thus includes a larger number of people. Nevertheless if an individual reports to have voted for AKP he or she is on average only to the left of MHP voters and thus occupies a clear right-wing position on the ideological spectrum.

Another important point to note in this juncture is that the centre position of the Turkish party system is still unoccupied by credible electoral organizations. The GP and ANAP command a very small group and GP leadership has been buried under a big package of corruption charges against its leader Cem Uzan. This picture shows that the GP constituency is still up for grabs. The constituencies mobilized by the populist rhetoric of Uzan remains to be lured by any one of the existing parties and thus form a potential threat to more responsible policy positioning in the system. However, this group is relatively small and obviously not growing. Given the successful showing of the DYP in the 2004 municipal elections it remains to be seen if the DYP leadership can continue its long route back to the centre of Turkish politics and start appealing to the centrist constituencies.[5]

As we underlined above in chapter two and four the Turkish party system is characterized by high volatility and fragmentation, deep regional cleavages and low nationalization of electoral forces. A number of additional micro individual level findings complement these macro characteristics. As demonstrated above, survey research shows a consistent shift of voters from centrist left-right ideological positions towards the extreme-right end of the spectrum. As a result, only a small minority seems to have remained left-of-centre. While the centrist positions have shrunk by half, the right-of-centre positions have grown continuously and nearly 20 percent of the voters seem to be placed on the far right position; (i.e. at point 10 on a 1 to 10 L-R ideological scale). Multidimensional analyses show two dimensions that command the ideological competition in the Turkish party system (see Kalaycıoğlu, 1998; Hale, 2002; Çarkoğlu and Hinich 2002, 2006). The first and relatively more dominant dimension is the secularist vs. pro-Islamist cleavage. It is noteworthy that this cleavage largely overlaps with the centre vs. periphery formations in Turkish politics and also with left-right orientations, thus being similar in many respects to western European traditions. The second dimension is the ethnic cleavage, setting the Turkish and Kurdish identities in opposition to one another and reflecting pieces of a larger reform debate in the country around the Copenhagen political criteria for EU membership.

In micro individual level analyses, a rising disenchantment of the electorate with the existing parties becomes evident. For a long time, commercial and academic surveys have revealed that not only is a large segment of the electorate undecided as to which party to vote for, but an equally large segment simply refuses to vote for any one of the available parties (Çarkoğlu, 1997).[6] Negative affection or simple anger is evident among this group of the electorate. The inability of governments to respond to emergency needs, even in the aftermath of the devastating 1999 earthquakes and the following economic crisis, obviously occupy an important place in the popular anger towards politicians and politics at large. Turkish voters seem simply unhappy with their lives and outraged with the politicians' inability to deliver satisfactory policies to counteract these tendencies.

Similarly, as underlined before, religiosity, more than any other variable, is found to determine Turkish voters' choice among competing parties. The impacts of retrospective or prospective economic evaluations are relatively weak on party choice.[7] When these effects are present, their magnitudes are small compared to the effect of religiosity. In the 1999 elections, when the ultra-nationalist MHP scored high gains, Çarkoğlu and Toprak (2000) indicate that both right-of-centre parties, namely the FP and MHP, as well as the centre-right DYP appealed to pro-Islamist constituencies.[8] In line with the shift in ideological orientations of the voters, determinants of vote choice seem to have been shaped by increasing tension between pro-Islamists and the secularists. While three of the five parties that obtained representation in the 1999 Parliament appealed to pro-Islamist sentiments, the rest of the bunch seem to cater to secularist constituencies thus keeping religious issues a top priority in their respective agendas.

Given the above diagnosis of the ideological characteristics of the Turkish electorate within the conventional L-R ideological dimension, we now turn to the attitudinal milieu that shaped voters' preferences in the November 2002 election.

Attitudinal Milieu of November 2002

As noted above, three interconnected factors were effective in moulding the attitudinal milieu of the electorate. One is religiosity of the voters. Another is the patriotic, nationalistic and xenophobic predispositions of the voters that seem to have been on the rise over the past decade. Last but not the least effective was voters' feelings of efficacy, or lack of it, in the political arena. Below, we address these multidimensional issues in greater detail with the help of data from our pre-election survey of October 2002.

A Multi-Dimensional Depiction of Religiosity of Turkish Voters[9]

As noted above, religion and religiosity has been frequently used by political scientists over the last nearly two decades to account for political change in Turkey. However, despite the fact that influence of religion is observed over many phenomena central to politics, a genuine understanding of the way religion works in the complex web of political interactions have not been offered for the case of Turkey. Following the line of the behavioral tradition religion is often treated as an integral part of our understanding of ideology. Hence religion in this approach is treated as yet another mental frame that helps individuals make sense of the political world around them. Religion is supposed to give individuals a particular orientation to their surrounding social and political environment, and shapes their political preferences and responses to salient political developments.[10]

We follow a similar approach in the ensuing sections by adopting the multi-dimensional treatment of piety based on earlier work by Stark and Glock (1965) and Hassan (2002). Hassan (2002) adapted the five dimensions of religiosity derived in Stark and Glock (1965) to Muslim piety.

Faith:

The ideological or faith dimension focuses on the set of fundamental beliefs with which the individuals are required to comply. A number of core doctrinal beliefs that shape individuals' approach to their religion can be identified for this dimension. Following earlier work by Çarkoğlu and Toprak (2000) and Hassan (2002) we presented the following beliefs to our respondents for evaluation: belief in God, in sin, in heaven and hell, in the existence of the spirit, in the afterlife and in the existence of the devil (Table 6.2).[11] Believers in God form the highest proportion, with about 98 percent. The existence of the devil, however, is believed by about 86 percent of the respondents.[12]

Table 6.2 Reflections of Religiosity: Belief

	Believes	Does not Believe	NR
God	98,0	1,6	0,4
Sin	96,6	2,7	0,7
Heaven/Hell	95,9	3,7	0,5
Existence of spirit	95,3	4,1	0,6
After-life	92,2	7,0	0,8
Devil	85,7	13,6	0,7

Religious Practice:

Rituals and worship practices are instrumental in showing devotion of believers to their religion. More importantly, such practices are expected to shape religious identities of individuals primarily through their socialization experiences. Such acts provide opportunities to form, strengthen and maintain communal links on religious grounds. Individuals tend to adopt certain key values and worldviews commonly shared by their fellow believers with whom they meet in their communal rituals and worship practices such as mosque attendance, fasting, religious donations and Haj in Islam. By way of such practices individuals become part of a community of believers.

The fact that worship practices are easily observable by other members of their community renders their impact upon individuals' place in their community much more effective. An individual may hold private beliefs of all different sorts, but as long as he or she conforms to the majority practices their access to community resources through their use of the majority religious identity will typically not be restricted. Their religious practices thus place them in different roles in society and give them a distinct social identity. Fellow community members can easily observe worship practices and thus impose restrictions and pressures on individuals, especially of minority religious denominations, to conform to their community's valued practices from the perspective of the majority.[13] A large number of rituals exist in Islam. We however, adopted only two in our questionnaire, both referring to prayer. The first asked how often the respondents pray (a private act) and again how often they go to the mosque (a public act). The reported frequencies are given in Table 6.3.[14]

Table 6.3 Reflections of Religiosity: Worship

	Pray	*Go to mosque*
More than once a week	49,1	18,2
Once a week	19,1	23,1
Once a month	3,7	2,5
In the month of Ramadan and religious festivals (kandils)	15,4	17,7
In bairam holidays, once or twice a year	3,1	3,9
Less than once a year	1,0	1,3
Nearly never, never	6,5	30,4
NR	2,2	2,9
	100	100

Religious Attitudes:

Attitudinal differences on issues related to religion have been addressed by providing the respondents with certain statements. They were then asked to evaluate these statements by providing their degree of agreement with them on a 1 to 10 scale. All such statements were worded so that those who agree with them could be grouped as individuals with religious attitudinal characteristics, as opposed to those who disagree, who were grouped as less religious.[15]

Table 6.4 reports the distributions of the answers.[16] As reported earlier by Çarkoğlu and Toprak (2000), head covering for girls at universities is a policy position supported by nearly three quarters of the respondents. As we will note below, the issue of turban wearing women in Turkish universities and public offices at large is quite a potent one among a large segment of the electorate. So much so that positions taken concerning the turban issue are effectively an important factor shaping the vote decision for especially the AKP. The apparent heavy support for lifting of the legal restrictions on turban over the last few years prior to the November 2002 election is indicative of the political potency for that issue over which the AKP seems to have developed a credible position.

Nearly 69 percent object to having their daughters marry a non-Muslim. Such high level of objection to the statement concerning inter-faith marriages is a clear indication of contrast between the tolerant and the conservative circles.

While nearly half of the sample agrees with having restaurants and coffeehouses remaining closed until the breaking of the Ramadan fast, the other half disagrees with this position. Similarly, nearly half of the sample agrees with sending their children to religious *Imam Hatip Schools* (Prayer Leader Schools) while the other half objects to such an idea. In fact, for both of these last two statements there are slightly more people disagreeing with the religious interpretation of the statement. For the next two statements, the disagreeing group is significantly larger than the other, suggesting that religious interpreters are a relatively smaller group. 54.9 percent disagree with the statement that "a religious person is more trustworthy in commercial life than non-religious individuals." When it comes to the statement suggesting that girls and boys should be separated in schools we observe an even larger group disagreeing while only about 35.2 percent of the respondents agreed with the statement approving separation.

Looking at the distribution of the answers across a one-to-ten level of agreement scale presented to our respondents, we observe that for all statements there is a bi-modal distribution. In other words, one group of people tends to agree and another sizeable group tend to disagree with the statement at hand. For the first two statements concerning turban and one's daughter marrying a non-Muslim we see that there is a dominant group who agrees with the provided statement while a much smaller group disagreeing with it. For the next three statements concerning Ramadan, Imam Hatip High schools and religious individuals in business life we observe that the group who disagrees with the statements is nearly double the size of the first two and comprise a sizeable group of about 25 percent. For the last statement the disagreeing group is nearly double the size of those who agree with the statement concerning girls and boys attending school in same classes. The shape of these distributions suggests that there exists two opposing groups on issues concerning religion in social life. On all issues addressed by our statements there exists a sizeable group which can be referred to as religious conservatives. These groups however are not always dominant over those who tend to disagree with the conservative perspective and thus face a significant group of people which can be, speculatively at this stage, considered as being open to socially liberal perspectives. Such apparent division is reflective of a pertinent divide between the socially more liberal secularists as opposed to conservative pro-Islamists in Turkish politics.

Approval of Shari'a (Şeriat) Rules

A prominent dimension in this apparent cleavage in Turkish politics around religion and religiosity has always been shaped around the issue of Shari'a rule. Shari'a, or *şeriat* in Turkish, is composed of a body of rules regulating the conduct of the pious Muslims in their rituals and foundations of their belief as well as their social lives within the framework of the customary law (Berkes, 1964, 9). An important point of contention between the centrist and secularist Republican elite and the reactionary peripheral forces has long been shaped around issues of religious significance and especially concerning the role of *Şeriat* in public and private spheres of the new regime.

From the early 1990's onward, questions about the popular bases of *şeriat* rule have been frequently used in public opinion surveys. The last question on Table 6.4 concerns the support for a *şeriat* -based religious state to be founded in Turkey. In the pre-election survey we observe that about 16.5 percent support founding of a *şeriat* state while 74 percent is opposed to it. Following the formation of the single-party government by the AKP, this post-election survey, conducted in early 2003, reveals a level of support for the founding of a *şeriat* state in Turkey that is significantly lower, at 14.7 percent, than that reported by Çarkoğlu on the basis of a survey in 1999 (see Çarkoğlu; 2004). To what extent this drop in support for *şeriat* can be attributed to the AKP's success in elections is obviously not clear. It may be that this question is simply a proxy variable for reflecting the level of unease among the religiously sensitive electorate. However, as Table 6.5 shows, the rise of support for *şeriat* seems to have been broken in 2002. No longer, do groups of about one fourth the size of the whole electorate support *şeriat* rule.

We should underline that the underlying meaning, social or political, attached to *şeriat* rule is not clear on face value. Çarkoğlu (2004) notes that those who seem to approve some kind of *şeriat* based state in Turkey are not clear in their minds as to what this new regime should entail. The same

	Totally Disagree	2	3	4	5	6	7	8	9	Totally Agree	NR
Girls at universities should be allowed to cover their heads if they want to.	11,4	1,3	1,3	1,0	6,0	1,9	2,7	4,7	5,2	63,2	1,4
I would object my daughter marrying a non-Muslim.	18,5	2,5	1,3	1,2	5,7	1,5	2,4	4,0	5,8	55,1	1,8
During Ramadan, restaurants and coffee houses should be closed until the breaking of the Ramadan fast.	28,5	5,2	2,9	2,1	9,4	3,1	3,0	4,7	4,2	35,0	1,7
I would consider sending my child to an Imam/Hatip High school.	26,8	3,7	3,9	1,6	15,3	3,8	4,9	5,8	4,4	27,2	2,4
A religious person is trustworthier in commercial life than non-religious individuals.	27,7	5,1	4,4	2,5	15,2	3,7	4,4	6,5	3,5	24,3	2,7
I do not approve of having boys and girls in the same class at high schools.	41,1	6,9	3,0	2,1	9,8	3,0	3,7	3,6	3,7	21,3	1,8

	Disagree	Agree
Girls at universities should be allowed to cover their heads if they want to.	20,9	77,7
I would object my daughter marrying a non-Muslim.	29,3	69,0
During Ramadan, restaurants and coffee houses should be closed until the breaking of the Ramadan fast.	48,2	50,1
I would consider sending my child to an Imam/Hatip High school.	51,4	46,2
A religious person is trustworthier in commercial life than non-religious individuals.	54,9	42,4
I do not approve of having boys and girls in the same class at high schools.	63,0	35,2

	Yes, would like to	No, would not like to	NR
Would you like to have a *şeriat*-based religious state founded in Turkey? (pre-election, October 2002)	16.5	74.0	9.4
Would you like to have a *şeriat*-based religious state founded in Turkey? (post-election, January-February 2003)	14.7	75.3	10.0

NR: No response

individuals who approve a *şeriat* based state in Turkey are found in an earlier study in 1999 to be overwhelmingly in support of the secular Civic Law which guarantees monogamy and equal treatment of women before the law for example. Such findings suggest that approval of Şeriat rule may simply be a proxy for reactions reflective of economic and political unease in the country rather than being a radical turn towards religion based legal and political order in the country.

Table 6.5 Would you or would you not favor establishment of a *şeriat* based religious state in Turkey?

	Yes	No	DK/NA
1995*	19,9%	61,8%	18,4%
1996*	26,7%	58,1%	15,2%
1998*	19,8%	59,9%	20,2%
1999**	21,0%	67,9%	11,1%
2002	16,4%	74,1%	9,5%

*TÜSES,
** Çarkoğlu (2004)

Another important dimension of the above attitudinal picture concerns the sectarian divide that it depicts. The attitudinal evaluations echo straightforward Sunni preferences as opposed to Turkish Alevism.[17] Those who place themselves on the religious conservative side on the statements given are likely to be of Sunni/Hanefi orientation while those who are on the opposing side are much more likely to be of Alevi orientation. With regard to turban wearing at the universities, for example, the Alevi community preferences are likely to oppose, in contrast to the approval by most of the survey respondents in the table. Women's liberal position in the Alevi community is an often-voiced view. Shankland (2003) also notes, together with many Turkish authors on Alevi movement, that, support for secularism is an integral part of the Alevi political stand in modern Turkey. So, Alevi preferences are more likely to reflect secularist tendencies rather than viewing turban as a liberalizing element for Muslim women. Any rise of Sunni Islamism that would make uncovered women's attendance of public spaces more difficult is thus expected to be opposed by Alevis. It is also very unlikely that Alevis would agree with the statement that boys and girls should be separated in school. This too runs against the Alevi tradition which treats women as more or less equals of men in public spaces.[18] Observance of the Ramadan fast and, in accordance, the closure of public places such as coffeehouses and restaurants is also likely to be opposed by Alevis who traditionally remained by and large unobservant of the formal rituals of Islam such as daily prayers and fasting.[19]

Objecting to one's daughter marrying a non-Muslim or thinking that a religious person is more trustworthy in commercial life than a non-religious person is difficult to interpret from a sectarian divide perspective. The first, that is, one's daughter marrying a non-Muslim is more a reflection of parochialism than religiosity. A Sunni respondent who is working in an international environment, which thus may be interpreted as being non-parochial in his/her attitudes, is not likely to differ in his or her preference concerning this issue compared to an Alevi of similar socio-economic background from the same environment. In other words, once controlled for parochialism sectarian divide is likely to disappear.

Evaluations of religious vs. non-religious tradesmen are again not likely to differ significantly between Alevis and Sunnis of similar backgrounds. Here a more subtle issue concerns whether or not or to what extent either the Sunnis or Alevis of similar backgrounds are acceptant of dealing with tradesman or shopkeepers from the other sectarian orientation. That is to what extent are Sunnis willing to deal with Alevis and to what extent are Alevis are ready to deal with Sunnis who for instance might be highly pious. We have however not asked this version of inter sectarian trust in this survey.

Given the Alevi tradition's historical experience, it is almost unimaginable that Alevis would support the establishment of a *şeriat* state in Turkey. Nevertheless we should always remember that reactions to this, as well as any of the other questions, may be subject to *taqiya* in certain environments and more so for some groups of respondents, especially among Alevis, than others. Despite the fact that all the survey's interviews were conducted in the privacy of respondents' households, it is conceivable that some respondents of both Sunni and Alevi orientations would shy away from revealing their true private preferences during the interviews. Keeping this difficulty of preference falsification in mind, it is nevertheless feasible that in as large a sample as the one used here, such deviations would not change the direction of causal links, but perhaps only have a minimal effect in altering their strength. In short, the overall picture from these evaluations is a likely dichotomy to arise between those who support the Sunni preferences on the one hand as opposed to those likely to be attractive to Alevis.

Besides the sectarian and *şeriat* demand dimensions and obviously directly correlated with them is yet another aspect of religiosity in Turkish politics that potentially can prove to be potent in shaping political preferences. It concerns the degree to which the obvious tension between the secularist forces and those of the pro-Islamists have given rise to a perception among the electorate that leads some to believe and feel that Muslims in Turkey are not fully free to practice their religion. We approached this issue with three questions in sequence (see Table 6.6). We first directly asked our respondents whether they believed that people in Turkey are free to practice worship requirements of Islam. Since the same question was asked earlier in another study by Ali Çarkoğlu and Binnaz Toprak, we can easily trace the changes in people's feelings concerning this issue. We, however, see that there is nearly no change in their answers to this question since 1999. About 63 percent of our respondents indicate that people are free to practice their religious commitments. However, a relatively larger group of about 34 percent report that there are restrictions on religious practices. The rise in these critical views is primarily due to a drop in the number of people who chose not to respond or who happen to have no view on this issue. In short, the number of people who feel that there are effective restrictions on religious practices have increased since February 1999 to October 2002.

Similar to the earlier 1999 study, we also asked all our respondents whether they believe that there is oppression of religious people in Turkey. Compared to 1999 those who report that there is oppression on pious people, have declined. Nevertheless, about 40 percent still claim that there is some repression. Next, we asked those who claim that there is oppression to give examples regarding these cases in an open-ended fashion where the respondent can actually give any example he or she desires without being directed to one specific example already prepared by the researchers. Looking at these answers, we observe that the prominence of turban and headscarf pressures have raised in their salience compared to 1999. In line with our earlier findings about encumbrances on religious practices, we see that hindrances on religious services or practices have nearly tripled compared to three years earlier.

In short, prior to the November 2002 election the attitudinal atmosphere clearly shows a religious conservative constituency that has been gaining ground over the last couple of years that preceded it. More importantly, although support for *şeriat* was in decline, feelings of the people at large that oppression upon pious people by the state was on the rise, is noticeable. In other words, since there seems to be no increase in the demand for *şeriat*, we can safely argue that religious sensitivities were on the rise for a party that is supported for resembling its constituency that is religiously conservative, and sensitive, but at the same time quite well mannered and docile in these reactions. All such tendencies suggest that such a rise in conservatism should have helped the secularist parties very little, while significantly helping the new generation pro-Islamists of the AKP.

Table 6.6 Are people in Turkey free to practice worship requirements of Islam?

	Yes	No	DK/NA
1999	63,8	30,9	5,3
2002	63,3	33,8	2,9

Is there oppression of religious people in Turkey?

	Yes	No	DK/NA
1999	42,4	50,2	7,4
2002	40,0	55,6	4,4

Examples of oppression given by those who believe that religious people are being oppressed in Turkey:

	1999	2002
Headscarf/turban pressures	53,7%	67,7%
Hindrances on the freedom of religious practices.	2,2%	7,3%
The status of *Imam-Hatip* High schools	5,0%	4,6%

We now have a total of 15 variables, shown in Tables 6.2 to 6.6, all tapping various aspects and different levels of an individual's religiosity. By including all of these variables into a factor analysis, (see Table 6.7), three dimensions emerge. The first clearly captures belief in core doctrinal aspects of Islam and accounts for about 24 percent of the total variation among the 15 variables. The second has high loadings for attitudinal evaluations. Since all of these variables are scaled so that increasing values indicate increasing religious attitudes, their interpretation in a factor analysis is straightforward. There is a noticeably high correlation between those who would want a *şeriat*-based religious state founded in Turkey and this dimension, which captures nearly 21 percent of the total variation. Lastly, the two worship indicators of prayer and mosque attendance appear together highly loaded on the third dimension, which captures about 10 percent of the total variation. Altogether, these three latent dimensions account for nearly 55 percent of the total variation in all 15 variables included in the factor analysis. Our expectation that faith, attitudes and worship practices constitute different dimensions of religiosity is supported by these findings.[20]

Factor analysis allows the derivation of scores for each of the three dimensions, reflecting a summary measure of individual orientations for all respondents according to the estimated factor loadings, as shown in Table 6.7. As such, we obtain for each individual respondent a score on each one of the three dimensions that has a standard normal distribution with a mean of zero and variance of unity.[21] We use these individual scores on our three dimensions as independent variables later on to explain the variation in party preferences.

Table 6.7 Religiosity

Rotated Component Matrix	Faith	Attitudes	Practice	Communalities
Belief in Heaven/Hell	**0,832**	0,133	0,040	0,712
Belief in sin	**0,792**	0,086	0,020	0,634
Belief in the existence of spirit	**0,758**	0,104	0,049	0,588
Belief in after-life	**0,719**	0,112	0,083	0,537
Belief in God	**0,711**	0,023	0,044	0,509
Belief in the existence of devil	**0,562**	0,067	–0,001	0,320
I would consider sending my child to a Imam Hatip High school.	0,094	**0,757**	0,115	0,595
A religious person is trust worthier in commercial life than non-religious individuals.	0,067	**0,753**	0,116	0,586
During Ramadan restaurants and coffeehouses should be closed until the breaking of the Ramadan fast.	0,069	**0,725**	0,017	0,530
I do not approve of having boys and girls in the same class at high schools.	–0,001	**0,674**	0,044	0,456
I would object my daughter marrying a non-Muslim.	0,166	**0,634**	0,123	0,445
Girls at universities should be allowed to cover their heads if they want to.	0,126	**0,559**	0,162	0,354
Dummy variable for those who go to mosques more than once a week.	0,018	0,126	**0,856**	0,750
Dummy for those who pray more than once a week.	0,110	0,259	**0,781**	0,690
% of Variance	*23,62*	*21,22*	*10,20*	*55,040*

Note: Extraction Method: Principal Component Analysis. Rotation Method: Varimax with Kaiser Normalization. Rotation converged in 5 iterations.

Patriotism/Nationalism, Xenophobia and Foreign Policy Preferences

In order to obtain individuals' relative positions with respect to one another concerning issues related to patriotism, nationalism and xenophobia we once again provided the respondents with certain statements as shown on Table 6.8. They were then asked to evaluate these statements on a 1 to 10 scale of their degree of agreement with them. All such statements were worded so that those who agree with them could be grouped as individuals with more patriotic/nationalistic or xenophobic attitudinal characteristics. Non-response rates to these evaluations were again quite low suggesting little problem in understanding the statements or making their evaluations about them. Table 6.8 reports the distributions of the answers.

Similar to above evaluations concerning religious attitudes, for most statements there exist a bi-modal distribution suggesting two groups of people at the opposing ends of evaluations. However, for the first statement concerning the Turkish flag for example, the numbers of people who disagree with it are quite small (7.9 percent). Despite economic difficulties, our given statement about buying more expansive Turkish goods still gets supported by nearly 70 percent of our sample.

A commonly used motto to refer to Turkish oddity and loneliness in the international arena is our statement concerning Turks not having any other friends than Turks themselves. Although nearly 79 percent agrees with this statement, a small but significant group of about 20 percent still disagrees with it. Similarly, a well-known slogan of the nationalist camp, that is: "one should either love or leave" Turkey, is given for evaluation. Surprisingly, a much higher percentage of our sample (31.3 percent) disagreed with this statement than either one of the previous two discussed.

The divisive nature of other statements concerning foreigners and tourists display a much sharper bi-modal distributions along the 1 to 10 scale of agreement. For example, although 56.4 percent agree with the statement that "foreigners settling in our country take our jobs", 41.2 percent disagree with it. Foreigners settling in our country are detrimental to our culture" gets only 48.2 percent agreeing with it; a smaller percentage than those who disagree with it. A slight majority of 50.5 percent disagrees with the detrimental impact of tourists on "our moral values". A much larger group of about 60 percent suggests that they would not mind having a foreigner as their neighbor. In other words, when we deal with statements that reflect some degree of xenophobia, groups that reflect attitudes of non-xenophobic nature become larger than those who can be grouped as non-nationalistic or non-patriotic. In short, patriotism or nationalism seems much more powerful among our respondents than it is the case for xenophobic attitudes.

Table 6.8 Patriotism, Nationalism and Xenophobia

	Does not agree at all 1	2	3	4	5	6	7	8	9	Fully agree 10	NR
Seeing the Turkish flag gets me excited.	2,2	0,7	0,7	0,5	3,8	1,6	3,7	5,3	5,4	74,7	1,3
I would prefer Turkish goods even if they are more expensive.	12,6	2,5	2,9	2,5	8,6	5,4	5,5	8,2	6,8	43,3	1,6
Turks don't have friends other than Turks.	9,5	1,4	2,0	1,2	5,8	2,7	3,1	6,0	6,3	60,8	1,2
One should either love Turkey or leave it.	16,4	2,1	1,8	1,8	9,2	3,7	4,8	7,9	4,9	45,2	2,3
Foreigners settling in our country are detrimental to our culture.	25,6	5,0	5,0	4,0	9,9	3,5	5,7	6,4	4,8	27,8	2,3
Foreigners settling in our country take our jobs.	18,6	5,4	4,3	3,7	9,2	4,7	5,5	8,1	6,4	31,6	2,4
I would not want a foreigner as a neighbor.	31,5	7,3	5,6	3,6	12,4	3,9	4,1	4,7	3,2	22,1	1,5
Tourists destroy our moral values.	26,9	5,7	3,9	3,6	10,4	3,6	5,1	6,5	3,9	28,7	1,7

	Does not agree	Agrees
Seeing the Turkish flag gets me excited.	7,9	90,8
Turks don't have friends other than Turks.	19,9	78,9
I would prefer Turkish goods even if they are more expensive.	29,1	69,3
One should either love Turkey or leave it.	31,3	66,5
Foreigners settling in our country take our jobs.	41,2	56,4
Foreigners settling in our country are detrimental to our culture.	49,5	48,2
Tourists destroy our moral values.	50,5	47,8
I would not want a foreigner as a neighbor.	60,5	38,1

Our statements about patriotism and nationalism only reflect a Turkish version and perhaps are alienating to other major ethnic groups. If this is so, then the degree of agreement with the patriotic and nationalist statements among the Turkish ethnicity might be even larger than meets the eye at first sight. A simple test for this is to separate those of the Kurdish ethnicity and see if their degree of agreement with these statements is significantly lower than those who are non-Kurds. The problem with this testing strategy is that we have only an indirect way of detecting who is a Kurd and who is not. We ask our respondents to tell us whether they can speak several different languages such as Arabic, major European languages and Kurdish. 12.8 percent of our respondents indicated they can speak Kurdish. Obviously, what exactly they speak is not clear from this question. Is it Zaza or Kırmanç? We simply do not know. To what degree are these people conversant with the Kurdish version they seem to indicate? We again do not know. Perhaps they are very fluent, perhaps they can only use a few words. In order to leave our respondents comfortable in being a part of our survey we did not go into the details of this question. It is noticeable nevertheless that the percentage of Kurdish speakers in our sample reflects a very comfortable estimate of the Kurdish ethnicity in the whole country.

When we look into the differences of responses between Kurdish and non-Kurdish speakers to the above statements on patriotism and nationalism, we do detect certain patterns. Those Kurdish speakers have an 8.1 as opposed to non-Kurdish speakers of 9.3 mean score of agreement out of 10 with the statement that "seeing the Turkish flag excites them". Clearly, among non-Kurds agreement rate is much higher. For all the rest of the four statements that reflect patriotic/nationalistic attitudes we see that Kurdish speakers have a mean score of agreement that is significantly lower than non-Kurdish speakers. When however, we look into statements about xenophobic attitudes we see just the opposite trend. Kurdish speakers seem to be less in agreement with the xenophobic statements than non-Kurdish speakers; perhaps due the fact that they are being seen as part of the "other" or "foreign" groups. However, this will have to remain as a speculative explanation before being subject to a deeper analysis which we do not go into here.

Foreign policy preferences are obviously directly related to patriotic/nationalistic and xenophobic attitudes. Given the complex nature of foreign policy we only delved into two policy areas. One concerns the relations with Europe within the EU membership debate. The other is on broad preferences concerning policy aimed at the Middle East. Table 6.9 reports the distribution of support for two broad policy stands for Turkey. Should Turkey develop closer relations with Muslim or Western countries? Posed with basically this broad religious divide in foreign policy, nearly 53 percent prefer Muslim as opposed to about 30 percent who prefer Western countries. More directly relating to the present situation in the Middle East, we asked our respondents to choose between Israel and "other Middle Eastern countries". We specifically refrained from naming the "other Middle Eastern countries" as being Muslim. Nevertheless, only about 7 percent prefers Israel over other Middle Eastern, not Muslim, countries. In other words, for the Turkish electorate support for Israel as opposed to other regional countries in the Middle East as a target for cooperative Turkish foreign policy is very low. West as opposed to Muslim countries does better, but still it remains in minority with sizeable back up. There obviously is an expected pattern of more religious people being more supportive of the Muslim and other Middle Eastern countries as opposed to Western countries and Israel. However, we leave an in depth analysis of these patterns out of our scope at this stage.

Table 6.9 Broad Foreign Policy Preferences

	Muslim countries	Western countries	Both	NR
Would you prefer Turkey to form closer relations with Muslim or Western countries?	53,3	30,1	1,4	15,2

	Israel	Other Middle Eastern countries	Both	NR
Should Turkey give priority in its foreign policy to Israel or other Middle Eastern countries?	6,8	61,6	0,4	31,3

One peculiar pattern that remains to be underlined however concerns the mass support for EU membership. Despite religious conservative as well as nationalist and somewhat xenophobic attitudinal traits of the Turkish electorate prior to November 2002 election there also existed a comfortable level of support for EU membership in the country. Figure 6.3 summarizes the historical development of EU membership support for the electorate since 1996.[22]

Figure 6.3 Support for EU Membership, 1996–2003

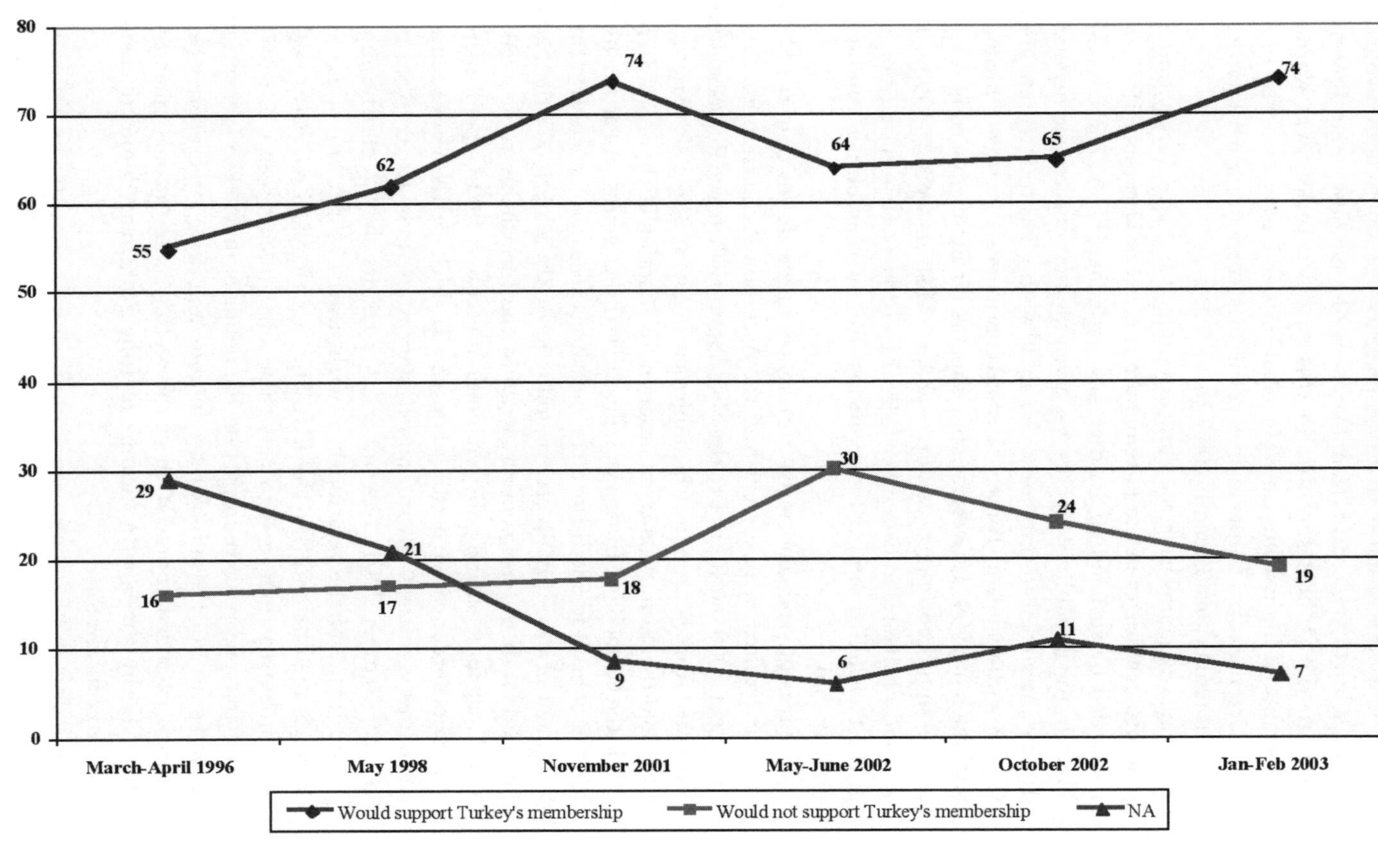

The first observation with a bare majority of supporters in favour of EU membership (55 percent) is from March-April 1996, just about three months prior to the Dublin summit. In this summit Turkey was warned for observance of highest human rights standards and was also urged to use its influence to seek a solution in Cyprus in accordance with UN Security Council resolutions (Erdemli 2003, 6).

About 18 months later, the European Council excluded Turkey from its list of formal candidates in the Luxembourg summit of December 1997. Turkey responded by suspending its dialogue with the EU. At the Luxembourg summit, the Republic of Cyprus was given the start of accession negotiations. Turkey threatened in response to go ahead with plans to integrate northern Cyprus with mainland Turkey. Tensions continuously increased during 1998 and much of 1999. However, public support for EU membership was found to have significantly increased up to about 62 percent by May 1998. About a year and a half later in December 1999, EU-Turkey relations were normalised at the Helsinki summit by recognising Turkey as an official candidate for membership.

The friendly and cooperative atmosphere in the aftermath of the Helsinki summit resulted in agreement over the Accession Partnership for Turkey in December 2000 – just prior to the Nice Summit where the European Council welcomed Turkey's progress in implementing its pre-accession strategy and requested the submission of its program for adoption of the *acquis*. In March 2001, the Council of Ministers adopted EU-Turkey accession Partnership that set the short and medium term measures necessary to ensure Turkey's fulfilment of membership criteria followed by the adoption of the National Program for the Adoption of the *Acquis* by the Turkish government. As such, a road map for legal and policy adaptations necessary for EU membership was set. In accordance with this plan, the Turkish parliament adopted 34 amendments to the Constitution necessary to meet the Copenhagen criteria in early October 2001. November 2001 results show a clearly improved public image of the relationship, with nearly 75 percent in support of Turkey's membership for the EU. The fact that a three party coalition government has managed to pass these amendments seems to have had a convincing a nd positive impact on the public opinion. The Laeken summit of December 2001 also took place in quite a positive atmosphere where the Council extended appreciation of the recent Constitutional amendments. However, by the Seville summit of June 2002, the domestic scene has changed considerably.

In February 2002 European Commission Representative Karen Fogg's personal e-mail account was hacked. Her private exchanges were published by the nationalist left as well as right wing media in a predominantly selective and manipulative manner. The messages were manipulated in such a way so as to create an image of Fogg and others who were in contact with her as traitors who were on EU pay, for working against Turkey's national interests.[23] At a time when the Turkish political elites and the Parliament were debating the necessity of and the strategy for handling the impending adjustments to the Copenhagen criteria, this hacking of e-mail messages and the ensuing discussion that developed around them created a nationalist upsurge.[24] This very period also curiously coincided with the start of bilateral talks on Cyprus, in Turkey. There was growing concern in the nationalist circles in the country about the need to resolve the conflict on the island. The issue was being extensively debated on the media and the public was being extensively exposed to views and information about the conflict that could potentially be detrimental to the preferences of these nationalist circles. Karen Fogg's e-mail messages were also used to discredit advocates of the idea of a solution in Cyprus and led to the accusation of Fogg for interfering in the TRNC's internal affairs (Çarkoğlu and Kirişci, 2003).[25]

As a result of this media campaign, public support for membership had significantly dropped to about its 1998 level of 65 percent. From the perspective of public support, all the gains in favour of EU membership since May 1998 were lost. Nevertheless, even at this point where anti-European forces were at their peak and the campaign against EU through personal attacks on Fogg had its full impact on the public at large, the nature of public support was such that it still commanded a clear majority in favour of EU membership for almost all smaller sub-national public opinion constituencies.[26]

The surprise passage of the EU adjustment package in early August 2002, and the election campaign that took full force in its aftermath, does not seem to have had much impact on the level of public support in favour of EU membership. Despite the revolutionary character of the legislation package that lifted the death penalty and allowed teaching and broadcasting of native languages other than Turkish which liberated the usage of Kurdish in public space, these issues were not much discussed in the campaign. Our October 2002 results show almost an unchanged level of support at around 65 percent. Our results from mid January to early February however, clearly show that the normalisation of the political environment in the aftermath of the election has increased the level of support back to its 2001 level of about 75 percent. It seems that the failure of the AKP government to receive a firm date for the start of negotiations in Copenhagen meetings of

December 2002 did not adversely affect public opinion. The AKP leadership's clear support for the EU cause has helped solidify the public opinion support for EU membership especially amongst the traditionally Euro-sceptic pro-Islamist constituencies.

An overall feature of the developments in the public opinion support for EU membership over the last seven years since spring 1996 is that the percentage of answers indicating no opinion to questions concerning EU membership is almost constantly dropping. This indicates the level of alertness of the mass public to the issue of EU membership. Not only do the people have clear support for EU at levels above 60 percent since 1998, but also they seem to be increasingly attentive on this issue and willing to express their preferences concerning EU membership at higher and higher levels over time.

Political (In)Efficacy

As the date of the election of November 2002 became clear, a distinct pattern of interaction between the politicians and the masses also became apparent. This dimension of mass-elite interaction was characterized with endemic alienation of the masses from the Turkish political system. The concepts of political alienation (or its antonym, political efficacy) have gained salience with the rise of mass citizenry. Two main questions seem to shape this literature: To what extent do the citizens have connections with the exercise of political power? How do the citizens feel connected with their governments? The roots of the concept can be traced back to Marx's treatment of Hegel's concept of *alienation* (entfremdung), later on resurfacing in Durkheim's (1933) concept of *anomie* and Simmel's (1950) analysis of uprooted individualism of the modern metropolis. While these early conceptions treated the condition of social estrangement as an objective condition, the modern empirical treatments have approached it as a micro individual level phenomenon. Political alienation and efficacy thus became a social psychological or subjective attitudinal characteristic of individuals rather than an objective property of the social system. Consequently, the measures developed aimed at the citizens' feelings of their abilities to effectively shape the performance of the political system that they are a part of.

The collapse of the centre in Turkish politics can be partially attributed to rising alienation from the political system. As noted above, the 1990s were full of instances where mass preferences were either not met, or simply manipulated for short term benefits. More importantly, a chronic deficiency started to emerge amongst the dynamic young population who increasingly became convinced that their expectations for the future are more likely to be left unrealized. The large ethnic minority of Kurds in the Southeastern Anatolian provinces took up a separatist movement that gained momentum in the early 1990s. Regional disparities and dismal living conditions together with a sense of cultural discrimination seem to have fuelled this movement which led to thousands of deaths in a prolonged ethnic warfare in the region until the capture of its leader in early 1999. Besides ethnic conflict, religious divisions between the Alevis and Sunnis, as well as pro-Islamists and secularists have become more pronounced over the last decade, prior to the 2002 election. As noted above, in 1994, the pro-Islamists did come to power but were unable to remain in control. Their coming to power disheartened the hard core secularist segments of Turkish society. However, their inability to resist secularist reactions and impositions from the Republican establishment, spearheaded by the military, also demoralized the pro-Islamist constituency of especially covered women.

Economic crises were also omnipresent during most of the decade that preceded the election. As noted above, the country was just emerging from its deepest economic crisis in history at the time when the 2002 election took place, which caused massive unemployment, especially amongst the white-collar urban constituencies. However, amongst the hardest hit segments were the informal sector workers of the lowest social strata dominated by Kurdish ethnicity as well as newly urbanized conservative Islamist segments of Turkish society. Finally came the earthquake disaster which was the last straw that broke the balance of trust amongst the mass electorate, between the state and civilian forces in favor of the latter. However, the Republican establishment or its co-opted political parties were not willing to open themselves up to mass scrutiny and intensified participation which would allow them to respond to the needs, demands and expectations of different segments of Turkish society. Such irresponsiveness continued despite ethnic and inter-sectarian conflicts or clashes between secular or religious segments of the society. Nor could the rising economic disparities or even the clumsy performance of the political establishment in response to a major natural disaster could push the establishment towards responsive democratic scrutiny by allowing participation mechanisms to "clean" the system. The major reason for pervasive feelings of inefficacy and alienation from politics is likely to be due to the closed patronage organization of the political parties, which have remained closed to any meaningful participation of the large masses. The legal arrangements during the military regime years of the early 1980's have banned parties to maintain branches to reach out to different constituencies like the youth, women, workers, farmers and so on. Students, government employees were not allowed to become members in political parties. Organizational facilities of the working classes were curbed by the effective growth of the informal sector, which was never been fought against effectively by the governments of the post-1980 period.[27]

In addition, the military as well as the civilian leadership of the post-1980 era, has made it clear that getting organized in search of group or class rights and seeking organized interests were to be approached with cynicism and suspicion. Given the harsh realities of the pre-1980 years, which witnessed mass demonstrations paralyzing the ineffectively organized Turkish society, deep divisions between ideological, ethnic, sectarian as well as simple parochial bases, led to bloody urban guerilla warfare. Restrictions imposed by the military regime of the 1980 were well-received by masses who welcomed the stability and sustained economic relief and growth during the early 1980s under the military junta. In short, legal and organizational bases for a prolonged lack of meaningful participation in politics and the consequent feeling of inefficacy were present for most of the post 1980s. At the intellectual level, a deep sense of apolitization also took root in Turkish society. Instead of seeking political solutions for mass community wide problems, Turks seem to have reverted back to their private domains wherein they were primarily engaged in economic activities as necessitated by the newly introduced market reforms of the early 1980's. At a deeper intellectual level, this reversion into the private domain had its reflections in the arts and social activities.

Reflections of political efficacy, or lack of it, are apparent in the three statement evaluations summarized below in Table 6.10. For all three items proposed, a 1 (complete disagreement) to 10 (full agreement) scale of evaluation were used. We see that for all three items given, nearly two thirds majority tended to agree with them.

All eleven items pertaining to xenophobia, nationalism and political efficacy were subjected to a principle components analysis which revealed a clear three dimensional attitudinal structure (Table 6.11). Nearly 57 percent of the variation in these 11 items was captured by three dimensions that reflected first a dominant xenophobia dimension, with negative evaluations of "foreigners". In the second dimension, evaluations apprais-ing Turkish ethnicity appeared highly effective (with high factor loadings). The third dimension clearly groups the evaluations concerning political efficacy as opposed to other items of xenophobic or nationalistic features.

Table 6.10 Political (In)Efficacy

	Does not agree at all 1	2	3	4	5	6	7	8	9	Fully agree 10	NR
Simple citizens cannot affect political decisions	11,9	3,0	2,2	2,2	11,8	4,3	5,5	7,1	5,0	42,1	4,8
A small but powerful group runs Turkey	12,1	3,6	2,7	1,8	11,8	6,0	5,4	8,1	5,0	37,7	5,8
Despite the fact that I work hard I still cannot get anywhere.	12,8	3,9	3,3	3,0	11,2	6,4	6,0	6,1	4,1	39,7	3,5

	Does not agree	Agrees
Simple citizens can not affect political decisions	31,1	64,1
A small but powerful group runs Turkey	32,0	62,2
Despite the fact that I work hard I still cannot get anywhere.	34,2	62,2

Table 6.11 Xenophobia-Nationalism and Political Efficacy

Rotated Component Matrix	Xenophobia	Nationalism	Political Efficacy	Communalities
Foreigners settling in our country are detrimental to our culture.	**0,825**	0,095	0,080	0,696
Foreigners settling in our country take our jobs.	**0,745**	0,167	0,097	0,593
Tourists destroy our moral values.	**0,692**	0,201	0,226	0,571
I would not want a foreigner as a neighbor.	**0,660**	0,225	0,124	0,502
Turks don't have friends other than Turks.	0,258	**0,775**	0,037	0,669
Seeing the Turkish flag gets me excited.	0,041	**0,729**	0,055	0,536
One should either love Turkey or leave it.	0,260	**0,691**	0,073	0,551
I would prefer Turkish goods even if they are more expensive.	0,152	**0,674**	0,158	0,503
Despite the fact that I work hard I still cannot get anywhere.	0,144	0,144	**0,723**	0,564
A small but powerful group runs Turkey	0,129	–0,064	**0,705**	0,517
Simple citizens can not affect political decisions	0,097	0,186	**0,692**	0,522
% of Variance	*33,55*	*12,42*	*10,61*	*56,57*

Extraction Method: Principal Component Analysis. Rotation Method: Varimax with Kaiser Normalization. Rotation converged in 5 iterations.

Economic Performance Evaluations

Before the general election of November 2002 perhaps the single most important issue in the minds of the voters was the condition of the Turkish economy at large and in particular their own family's economic condition. The economy has gone through the worst crisis in republican history and the Gross Domestic Product contracted by 7.5 percent in 2001 (Figure 6.4). However, this was by no means an exceptional experience for the Turkish electorate; for two years earlier in 1999, the economy contracted by a sizeable 4.7 percent and only about 7 years ago, by 5.5 percent.

The inflation rate peaked in the economic crisis of 1994 up to around 120 percent. Ever since, it has declined and reached about 33 percent in 2000, a year before the big economic crisis. In 2001 the inflation rate rose up to about 89 percent. By the end of 2002 it reached about 50 percent and a year later 14 percent. Compared to only 2 years ago, the inflation rate has come down to about one sixth of its former level.

In 1999, the unemployment rate was about 8.1 percent, and was even lower at 6.2 percent in 1996. Ever since 1997, the unemployment rate has remained between 6.5 to 7.4 percent. However, in 2001, the economic crisis caused the unemployment rate to rise up to 8.4 percent, which was unprecedented for the last decade or so. Despite recovery in growth and inflation indicators for the Turkish economy, the unemployment rate has remained consistently high at around 10 percent for the election year of 2002.

Looking at these three most commonly used performance indicators for incumbent governments, a few questions linger in one's mind about the dynamics shaping voting behavior of the Turkish electorate. Given the volatility of the Turkish economy, it makes more sense to think of rational voters who one way or another can come to predict the developments awaiting them in the future. Moreover, given the history of paralyzing economic contractions with high inflation and unemployment rates, punishment for the incumbent government in 2002 should perhaps not be exaggerated. After all, the economic crisis was comparable to an earlier one just 6–7 years ago. In addition, the attribution of responsibility was even more difficult, since in 2002, the coalition partners were greater in numbers than in 1994.

More importantly, at the time when the general election was being held, the economy was already recovering from its wounds. The responsibility of this apparent recovery cannot possibly be attributed to the newly founded, inexperienced AKP. Hence if there is no easy way of attributing blame to the incumbent DSP-MHP-ANAP coalition, and there is no easy way of rewarding the AKP for anything they had accomplished since seizing power, is it possible that economic voting was not effective in shaping the electoral choices of the voters in the November 2002 election? Our answer to this question is that unless one looks into factors that shape the affectionate feelings of the electorate that are based in non-economic factors, one is bound to get a distorted picture regarding the nature of the 2002 election.

Figure 6.4 Growth of GDP and Unemployment

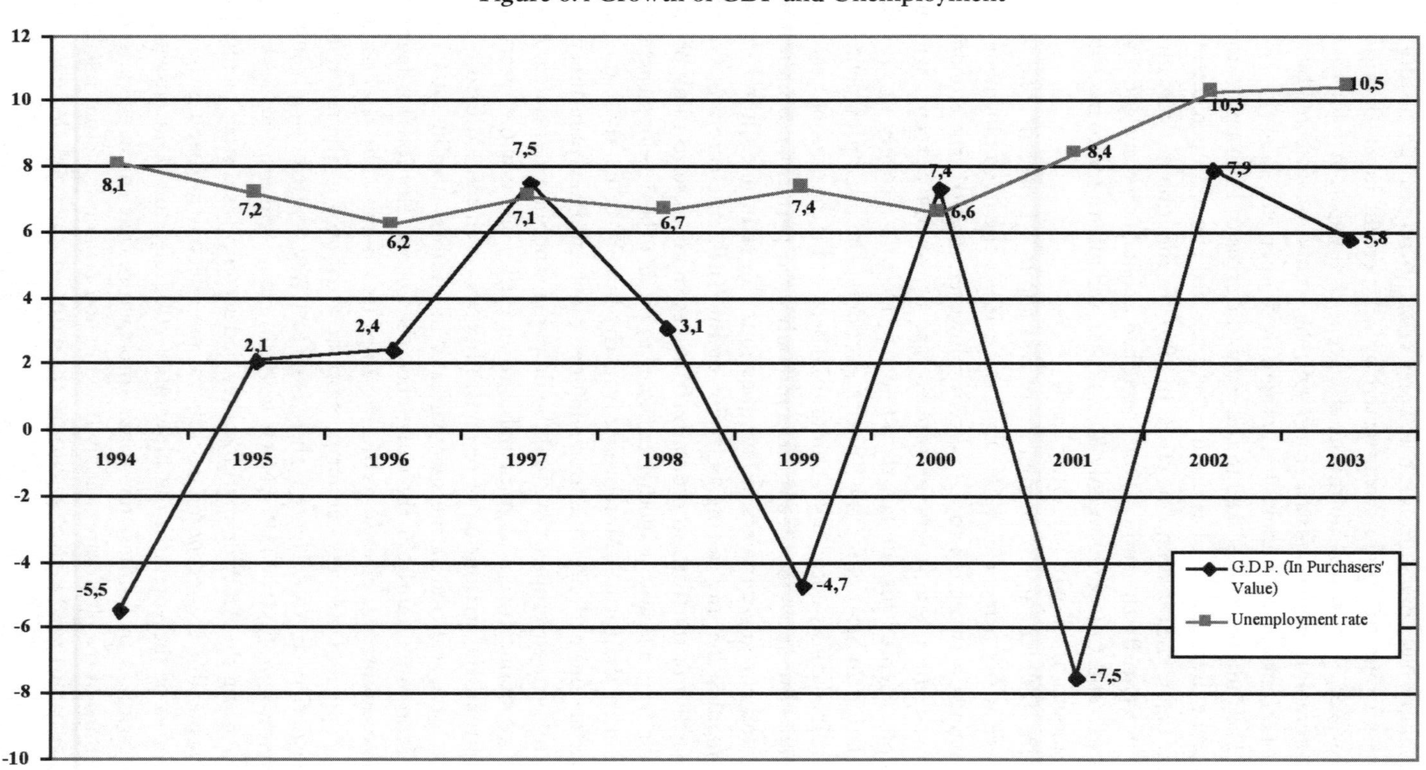

Figure 6.5 Inflation (Consumer Price Index)

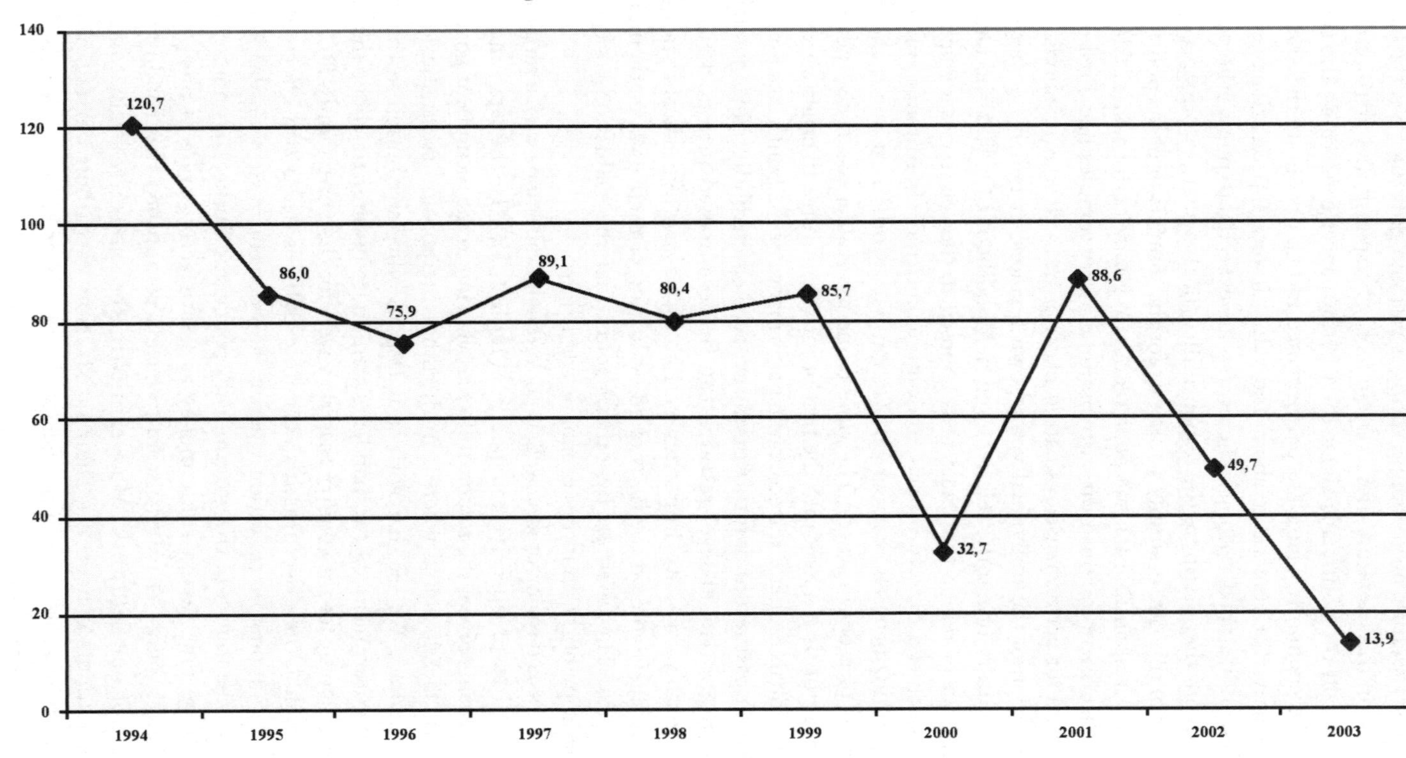

The literature on economic voting is vast and growing.[28] At the base of all work, in this literature, lies a certain sense of responsibility attribution by the voters on the politicians about their performances concerning the condition of the economy. There are performance indicators about the state of the economy that voters care about and value. If voters' perceptions concerning these indicators deteriorate, then voters are expected to punish the politicians to whom they attribute the responsibility for this poor performance. Punishment in this case is simply a vote cast for the competitor of the politician who is held responsible for the poor economic policy performance. Clearly, the mechanism of responsibility attribution is a very complex one. First of all, the criteria for performance evaluation may not be as clear as it sounds. Is it the condition of the individual voters' own finances, or is it his or her close-by community of family, relatives and neighborhood? Or is it the larger city, province or region that matters as opposed to the country as a whole? What do we mean exactly by the economic condition? Is it about inflation or unemployment? Is it about satisfaction with work? Is it about the buying power of money earned? The time frame for evaluations is also not clear at first sight. Is it a look into the past or into the future? In other words, do the individuals evaluate the economic performance of the politicians on the basis of their past record or future promises and their credibility? In a nutshell, the micro individual level research can be decomposed into pocketbook vs. sociotropic voting hypotheses. The *pocketbook* hypothesis states that individuals vote on the basis of an evaluation of their own, or their family's finances. The *sociotropic* hypothesis states that the evaluation concerns the condition of the country's economic conditions.

We asked sociotropic as well as pocketbook evaluations with a retrospective as well as prospective perspective (Table 6.12). In the first and second statements given, the responsibility attribution to the incumbent government is also clearly stated whereas in the others, responsibility attribution is left ambiguous. We see that with clear responsibility attribution to the incumbent government, our respondents were more pessimistic about the state of the economy for the country than they were for their own family. 86.7 percent state that the government's economic policies had a bad effect on their family's economic condition whereas 90.3 percent made a similar judgment about the impact of the government's policies on Turkey's economy.

If we take saving some money as a satisfactory state of one's personal finances, only 3.5 percent seem to have accomplished that condition at the time of our fieldwork. More explicitly, the subjective evaluations of our respondents concerning their satisfaction with their current economic conditions at the time of our fieldwork in October 2002, we see that only 7.1 percent were satisfied.

Looking at the prospective evaluations we see a brighter picture. Nearly one third of our respondents indicate on a pocketbook as well as sociotropic basis that the economic conditions will improve over the next year that is from November 2002 to November 2003 which obviously was a successful prediction, given the state of the economy depicted by Figures 6.4 and 6.5 above. However, it is also worthy to note that besides optimists, one third of our sample indicated that conditions will remain the same and that cannot be good given the miserable evaluations of the present state of the economy at the time of our fieldwork. Yet another one third of the sample indicated that on a pocketbook or sociotropic basis, the economic conditions will get even worse. Such variation in evaluations does not make much electoral sense unless we look into the partisan divide that differentiates respondents on each evaluation.

Table 6.12 Retrospective and Current Economic Condition Evaluations prior to the November 2002 Election

1. How did the government's policies affect your family's economic condition over the last year? (pocketbook)	
Had a good impact	1,8
Had a bad effect	86,7
Not much of an effect	10,9
NR	0,6
2. How did the government's policies affect Turkey's economic condition over the last year? (sociotropic)	
Had a good impact	2,4
Had a bad effect	90,3
Not much of an effect	6,8
NR	0,6
3. How is your family's economic condition over the last year? (pocketbook)	
Had to take a loan	36,0
Spent from past savings	11,1
Barely could make ends meet	49,2
Could save some money	3,5
NR	0,2
4. How satisfactory do you find your current economic condition? (pocketbook)	
Not at all satisfactory	40,9
Not satisfactory	31,6
Neither satisfactory nor dissatisfactory	20,1
Satisfactory	6,7
Very satisfactory	0,4
NR	0,4

Table 6.13 Prospective Economic Condition Evaluations prior to the November 2002 Election

How do you think your family's economic condition will evolve over the next year?	
Will be much worse	8,5
Will be somewhat worse	22,1
Will be the same	35,8
Will be somewhat better	28,1
Will be a lot better	1,3
NR	4,3
How do you think Turkey's economic condition will evolve over the next year?	
Will be much worse	10,0
Will be somewhat worse	22,0
Will be the same	30,1
Will be somewhat better	31,5
Will be a lot better	1,8
NR	4,6

To analyze the partisan differences concerning economic performance evaluations of individuals, we conducted a logit analysis wherein the dependent variable is the zero-one coding on the basis of the above presented retrospective/prospective pocketbook and sociotropic evaluations (Table 6.14). More specifically for the first evaluation, we coded all individuals who indicated that the government's policies had a bad effect on their family's economic condition over the last year as one, and all of those who indicated that it did not have much effect or had a good impact as zero. We see then that those respondents who intend to vote for the AKP were significantly more likely to be in the group who state that the government's policies had a bad effect on their family's economic condition over the last year. Compared to AKP voters, CHP voters were much less likely to be in the same group. MHP voters were the least likely to be in this group. The rest of the party constituencies cannot be differentiated in terms of their likelihood of being in or out of this group.

Table 6.14 Economic Evaluations and Partisan Choices

Dummy variable fort hose who say that government's policies had a bad effect on their family's economic condition over the last year	B	Sig.	Exp(B)
Dummy variable for those who intend to vote for ANAP	–0,33	0,44	0,72
Dummy variable for those who intend to vote for CHP	**–0,42**	**0,04**	**0,66**
Dummy variable for those who intend to vote for DEHAP	0,01	0,99	1,01
Dummy variable for those who intend to vote for DSP/YTP	–0,64	0,15	0,53
Dummy variable for those who intend to vote for DYP	0,24	0,51	1,27
Dummy variable for those who intend to vote for GP	–0,23	0,34	0,79

Dummy variable for those who intend to vote for MHP	**–0,77**	**0,01**	**0,46**
Dummy variable for those who intend to vote for SP	–0,11	0,84	0,90
Dummy variable for those who intend to vote for Other smaller parties	0,33	0,59	1,39
Constant (AKP)	**2,12**	**0,00**	**8,37**

Model Summary	–2 Log likelihood	Cox & Snell R Square	Nagelkerke R Square
	1142,78	0,01	0,02

Dummy variable for those who say that government's policies had a bad effect on Turkey's economic condition over the last year	B	Sig.	Exp(B)
Dummy variable for those who intend to vote for ANAP	–0,38	0,45	0,68
Dummy variable for those who intend to vote for CHP	**–0,50**	**0,04**	**0,61**
Dummy variable for those who intend to vote for DEHAP	–0,57	0,16	0,56
Dummy variable for those who intend to vote for DSP/YTP	**–1,66**	**0,00**	**0,19**
Dummy variable for those who intend to vote for DYP	–0,39	0,27	0,68
Dummy variable for those who intend to vote for GP	–0,02	0,95	0,98
Dummy variable for those who intend to vote for MHP	**–0,76**	**0,03**	**0,47**
Dummy variable for those who intend to vote for SP	–0,22	0,73	0,80
Dummy variable for those who intend to vote for Other smaller parties	1,06	0,30	2,88
Constant (AKP)	**2,55**	**0,00**	**12,86**

Model Summary	–2 Log likelihood	Cox & Snell R Square	Nagelkerke R Square
	931,44	0,02	0,03

Dummy variable for those who say that their present economic condition is unsatisfactory	B	Sig.	Exp(B)
Dummy variable for those who intend to vote for ANAP	–0,06	0,87	0,95
Dummy variable for those who intend to vote for CHP	**–0,33**	**0,04**	**0,72**
Dummy variable for those who intend to vote for DEHAP	0,65	0,07	1,91
Dummy variable for those who intend to vote for DSP/YTP	–0,42	0,24	0,66
Dummy variable for those who intend to vote for DYP	–0,09	0,72	0,92
Dummy variable for those who intend to vote for GP	**–0,38**	**0,03**	**0,68**
Dummy variable for those who intend to vote for MHP	**–0,49**	**0,05**	**0,61**
Dummy variable for those who intend to vote for SP	–0,05	0,89	0,95
Dummy variable for those who intend to vote for Other smaller parties	0,10	0,81	1,10
Constant (AKP)	**1,07**	**0,00**	**2,93**

Model Summary	–2 Log likelihood	Cox & Snell R Square	Nagelkerke R Square
	1803,04	0,01	0,02

For the second evaluation, a much clearer picture emerges. Once again AKP voters were the most likely ones to be within this group of respondents who made an adverse evaluation of Turkey's economic conditions due to the government's performance. For this sociotropic evaluation however, the major coalition partners that is the DSP and then YTP followed by the MHP voters appeared to be the least likely ones to be part of the adverse evaluation group.

When we move from clear responsibility attribution on the basis of retrospective evaluations to an evaluation of the present state of economic conditions, without a clear responsibility attribution in the last evaluation, we see a different picture (Table 6.14). This time GP voters came into the picture in a significant way. Once again AKP followed by CHP voters were the most likely ones to be in the group of respondents who made an adverse evaluation of their present economic conditions. The least likely ones to be in this group were once again the MHP voters followed this time by the GP voters. This is surprising but perhaps indicative of the reasons why the GP was never able to gather together a large enough momentum to get over the 10 percent nationwide threshold in 2002.

When we look into the prospective pocketbook and sociotropic evaluations we see a similar picture (Table 6.15). We see that the least likely party constituency to be part of the group of respondents who indicate that their family's economic condition over the next year will be worse is those who intended to vote for the DSP followed by those who intended to vote for the AKP. The most likely constituency to be part of this pessimistic group were those who intended to vote for DEHAP. For the case of sociotropic evaluations DSP/YTP voters dropped out of the picture and we see that DEHAP voters were the most likely to be part of the pessimistic group, while the AKP voters were the least likely ones to be part of the pessimistic group.

In a nutshell, the AKP seems to have gathered together a group of individuals who hold a very distinct negative performance evaluation of the incumbent government in October 2002, while at the same time maintaining a relatively more optimistic perspective for the future of the economy from both a sociotropic as well as pocketbook perspective. CHP voters are similar to the AKP constituency in their retrospective evaluations as well as the present state of their economic conditions. However, when it comes to prospective evaluations, they seem to be indistinguishable from the rest of the party constituencies. They are neither more nor less optimistic it seems about the future of the economy from a pocketbook or sociotropic perspective. This certainly stands as a barrier in front of the CHP's efforts to gather a significant group of voters to capture executive office.

Table 6.15 Economic Evaluations and Partisan Choices

Dummy variable for those who say that their family's economic condition over the next year will be worse	B	Sig.	Exp(B)
Dummy variable for those who intend to vote for ANAP	0,00	0,99	1,00
Dummy variable for those who intend to vote for CHP	–0,09	0,57	0,91
Dummy variable for those who intend to vote for DEHAP	**0,67**	**0,01**	**1,95**
Dummy variable for those who intend to vote for DSP/YTP	**–1,03**	**0,03**	**0,36**
Dummy variable for those who intend to vote for DYP	–0,01	0,97	0,99
Dummy variable for those who intend to vote for GP	0,03	0,87	1,03
Dummy variable for those who intend to vote for MHP	–0,28	0,31	0,76
Dummy variable for those who intend to vote for SP	0,52	0,15	1,68
Dummy variable for those who intend to vote for Other smaller parties	0,44	0,20	1,55
Constant (AKP)	**–0,82**	**0,00**	**0,44**
Model Summary	–2 Log likelihood	Cox & Snell R Square	Nagel-kerke R Square
	1798,10	0,01	0,02
Dummy variable for those who say that Turkey's economic condition over the next year will be worse	B	Sig.	Exp(B)
Dummy variable for those who intend to vote for ANAP	–0,17	0,60	0,84
Dummy variable for those who intend to vote for CHP	–0,27	0,09	0,76
Dummy variable for those who intend to vote for DEHAP	**0,56**	**0,03**	**1,76**
Dummy variable for those who intend to vote for DSP/YTP	–0,45	0,25	0,64
Dummy variable for those who intend to vote for DYP	–0,04	0,87	0,96
Dummy variable for those who intend to vote for GP	–0,33	0,08	0,72
Dummy variable for those who intend to vote for MHP	–0,22	0,40	0,80
Dummy variable for those who intend to vote for SP	0,38	0,29	1,46
Dummy variable for those who intend to vote for Other smaller parties	0,47	0,16	1,61
Constant (AKP)	**–0,69**	**0,00**	**0,50**
Model Summary	–2 Log likelihood	Cox & Snell R Square	Nagel-kerke R Square
	1826,83	0,01	0,02

Perceived Political Agenda of the Country

To what extent then were economic problems on the agenda at the time of the election? We asked an open ended question about what the most important problem of the country was at the time of our fieldwork. The results were given in chapter three above in Table 3.1. What is striking in these responses is that inflation, unemployment and economic instability comprise nearly three quarters (77 percent) of the responses given.

Besides the economy, political uncertainty and instability were mentioned by 13.7 percent of our respondents as an important problem comprising about 7 percent of the total responses given. However, before an uncertain election, such answers should perhaps be seen as normal. All in all then voters tended to see only the economy as problematic before the election. It is interesting to note that some very prominent issues do not appear on the top of the voters' agenda. For example, education is mentioned by only about 8 percent (about 4 percent of the responses), bribes and corruption by about 6 percent (about 3 percent of the responses). Foreign policy issues also do not appear in this top problem area list. The problems related to the EU, foreign policy, Iraq and war, all together comprise only about 1.8 percent of the responses mentioned by 3.3 percent of our respondents. More interestingly, turban, religion or religious practices were mentioned as a problem for the country by less than 1 percent of our respondents.

It is important to note here that these figures only represent problem perceptions of the people and only those problems seen as being within the top two most important problems facing the country. In other words, we are not asking whether or not turban, or human rights are or are not an important problem here. What we are given, are simple judgments as to what can be included within the top two most important problems. We should thus interpret the results carefully and conclude that very few non-economic problems appear in the top two most important problem list of our respondents. This however does not mean that these non-economic issues are not important in Turkish electoral politics.

Who Can Resolve the Problems?

We wanted to know if people first of all tended to vote for a party on the basis of a belief that it could resolve an important problem of the country. Is issue voting prevalent therefore amongst Turkish voters? When we specifically asked whether there is a party which the respondents vote for, believing that it could resolve an important problem for Turkey, we see that only about 56 percent indicate that they will vote for such a party (Table 6.16). Nearly 36 percent however indicate that there is no such party for which they intend to vote for the resolution of a problem. In other words, nearly two thirds of the voters seem to vote for a party thinking that it could resolve an important problem, while the remaining one third's vote is not shaped by such issue oriented concerns.

Table 6.16 Is there a party which you will vote for, believing that it would resolve an important problem?

Yes, there is such a party	56,1
No, there is no such a party	36,2
I don't plan to vote	2,8
NR	4,9

For those who indicated that they consider casting a vote for a party to specifically resolve a problem, we asked a second question as to what this particular problem was (Table 6.17). Once again the answers given for this question indicate that nearly 68 percent of the responses consist of economic issues, with nearly 78 percent of the respondents mentioning an economic problem. Turban and religion as a problem whose resolution derives voters decisions to vote for a party is minimal in this question (3 percent of the responses and 3.5 percent of the respondents). Once again we see that in shaping voters' decisions for a party, mostly economic issues come to their mind in an open-ended question format and not turban or anything related to religious practices.

More specifically we also asked whether our respondents believe that there existed a party in November 2002 which can resolve Turkey's problems (Table 6.18). Those who answered affirmatively indicated that the AKP with 26.1 percent support behind it, is seen as a party that can resolve the country's problems while the CHP got only about 11 percent. It is once again worthy of note that at the time of our fieldwork, nearly 29 percent indicated that there was no such party in the November 2002 election. The striking phenomenon worthy of note here, is the pervasive alienation that could be attached to these findings. About less than a month before the election the electorate was still not convinced that anyone of the competing parties could effectively tackle the country's problems.

Table 6.17 If there is a party which you will vote for, believing that it would resolve an important problem, what is that problem?

	Count	Percent of Responses	Percent of Cases
Inflation	55	4,8	5,6
Unemployment	266	23,4	27,1
Economic instability	444	39,1	45,3
Bribes, corruption	34	3	3,5
Health/Social security	28	2,5	2,9
Education	37	3,3	3,8
Political uncertainty/instability	59	5,2	6
EU/Foreign policy	11	1	1,1
War/terror	16	1,4	1,6
Parliamentary immunities	9	0,8	0,9
Agriculture	25	2,2	2,6
Infrastructure/environment	8	0,7	0,8
The future of Turkey	31	2,7	3,2
Democracy/Human rights/Freedoms	38	3,3	3,9
Turban problem/Religion/Religious practices	34	3	3,5
IMF	13	1,1	1,3
Other	28	2,5	2,9
Total responses	1136	100	115,9

1.004 missing cases; 980 valid cases

Table 6.18 Do you believe that in the November 2002 election there competes a party which can resolve Turkey's problems? If you believe that there is one, which one is that party?

	%
AKP	26,1
ANAP	1,9
CHP	10,8
DEHAP /HADEP	2,3
DSP/YTP	1,0
DYP	3,7
Genç Parti	7,4
MHP	2,8
SP	1,3
Others	1,2
No there is no such party	29,3
NR	12,2
	100,0

We next questioned, one by one, whether a given problem can be resolved by a specific party coming to power (Table 6.19). It is interesting to note that for every single problem area the number of respondents indicating that no one could resolve it, is larger than the group which offers a party name for its solution. Once again the respondents seem to clearly tell us that the country's problems were irresolvable by the existing parties. This again might be a convenient way of avoiding to provide an answer. However, we tend to believe that it also reflects a certain degree of lacking political efficacy, or a feeling of remoteness from the political system or a belief that the political system can address the issues on the agenda.

Continuing to look at the same picture from the perspective of problem areas, we see that for each problem area the front runner in electoral competition, that is, the AKP, is seen as the most able to overcome it. This is hardly surprising since once individuals have already made up their minds as to which party to vote for, they tend to see that party as the most able to tackle almost any issue. It is nevertheless interesting that the AKP is not seen as able to tackle all issues at the same level of effectiveness. For instance, while for EU membership only about 16 percent seem to think that the AKP would be effective in resolving problems, this group remains at around 18 percent for resolving the Cyprus issue or restricting parliamentarians' immunities. In other words, there is a great degree of variation in the level of conviction of the respondents about the ability of the AKP to deal with different problems. Such variation is also visible for all other parties around different levels of conviction for their ability to tackle problems.

When we look at the same question from the perspective of different parties we therefore see a much more striking feature. While the AKP is seen as the most effective in dealing with the issue of turban by nearly 30 percent of the electorate, the CHP is seen as most effective for dealing with restrictions on MP immunities. The GP is seen as most effective in dealing with unemployment, while the DSP is indicated to be most effective in resolving the Cyprus issue. For ANAP, EU is seen as the most credible issue area where it could be effective, and the DYP is seen as most effective for resolving the problems of the agricultural sector. In a sense, parties seem to have a relative credibility in the eyes of the voters about their ability to resolve certain problems. This is a relative credibility issue and not an absolute one. However, it signals that parties may be "owning relative advantages" in different issue areas. From this perspective we observe that no one party seems to have relative advantage in reducing taxes, or revitalizing the economy, or reducing inflation, or solving health and education problems, or reinforcing moral values in the country. These "un-owned issues" are mostly economic issues and perhaps this is an indication that they tend to be the most salient issues in the eyes of the voters wherein no specific party rises above others even in relative terms.

It is interesting that the highest percentage of people indicating that no one could resolve a given issue appears for the Cyprus issue with a group of about 39 percent behind such a position. In other words, in the eyes of the voters there is no hesitation about indicating who among the parties is more likely to be effective in dealing with different problem areas. This party was the AKP. However, reflective of the pervasive alienation, a larger group of respondents were always present in saying that no one could resolve these issues. Another interesting point to note is that different problem areas emerge as relative credibility areas for different parties. From this perspective, it is interesting that the AKP's most credible problem area appears to be the issue of turban about which it consistently tried to create some opening after it came to power, but has consistently failed in its attempts.

Voter Anger

As suggested above, a major outcome of the economic crises, lacking openness of political parties to mass participation and the inability of the centrist political establishment to respond to the needs, demands and expectations of the voters was a pervasive sense of powerlessness in and alienation from the political system at large. An immediate consequence of such a mind set was anger amongst the voters especially towards the political parties. We directly tackled this issue by first asking our respondents whether or not they have recently encountered a situation that made them angry (Table 6.20). Nearly 29 percent of our respondents responded affirmatively. To those who said they encountered a situation that made them angry we asked whether or not a number of people or institutions were responsible for their anger. What is striking is that while a fraction of less than 5 percent indicated to have been angry with their wives or husbands, their children, other family members, their employers, municipality, labor union, sports club or government employees, nearly 14 percent said that they were angry with political parties and 10 percent said that they were angry with the government.

To those who said that they were angry with political parties we asked which among them were responsible for this anger in an open-ended format. Nearly 34 percent mentioned the ANAP, 47 percent the DSP and 30 percent mentioned the MHP. Other parties which eventually were successful in gaining seats in the parliament, like the AKP (nearly 13 percent mentioned it) and the CHP (nearly 9 percent mentioned it) were also high on the list.

Table 6.19 Who can resolve these problems?

Problems\Parties	AKP	CHP	GP	DSP	MHP	ANAP	DYP	No one	Others	NR	
Restricting MP immunities	18,3	**13,4**	6,3	0,4	2,2	1,8	2,1	38,2	3,3	14,0	100
Reducing unemployment	24,0	9,2	**10,0**	0,4	1,7	1,7	3,1	35,1	4,0	10,6	100
Reducing taxes	21,0	8,8	9,8	0,3	1,6	1,9	3,1	37,3	3,7	12,6	100
EU membership	16,1	10,1	5,8	0,6	1,4	**8,3**	3,8	36,3	3,4	14,2	100
Fighting with corruption	25,0	10,1	6,3	0,9	**3,2**	1,8	2,6	34,0	4,7	11,3	100
Revitalizing the economy	26,2	11,2	7,6	0,4	1,9	1,9	4,1	32,2	3,7	10,9	100
Resolving the Cyprus problem	18,5	8,8	4,7	**2,9**	**3,2**	1,9	2,5	**38,5**	3,6	**15,4**	100
Reducing inflation	25,4	9,6	7,7	0,7	1,9	1,5	3,1	36,0	3,6	10,5	100
Solving health and education problems	23,2	10,5	7,5	0,5	2,4	1,7	3,2	34,7	4,2	12,2	100
Solving the turban problem	**30,3**	7,8	4,9	0,4	2,2	1,4	2,0	33,9	**5,3**	11,9	100
Solving the problems in agriculture	23,8	9,5	6,9	0,8	2,3	1,9	**4,6**	34,3	3,9	12,1	100
Reinforcing moral values in the country	28,2	8,5	5,2	0,4	2,5	1,7	2,2	33,6	5,1	12,7	100

Note: Table values are percentages.

Table 6.20 Voter Anger

	Yes	No
Have you recently encountered a situation that made you angry?	28,5	71,5
Who among the following made you angry?		
You wife/husband	2,9	97,1
Your children	3,3	96,7
Other family members	4,4	95,6
Your employer	3,7	96,3
Municipality	1,6	98,4
Labor union	0,4	99,6
Sports club	1,1	98,9
Government employees	1,4	98,6
Political parties	13,9	86,1
Which one among the political parties made you angry?	**% of responses**	**% of cases**
AKP	7	12,7
ANAP	18,7	33,8
BBP	0,9	1,7
CHP	5,2	9,3
DEHAP /HADEP	4	7,2
DSP	26	46,8
DYP	6,1	11
GP	6,3	11,4
MHP	16,6	30
SP	2,6	4,6
YTP	1,2	2,1
All of them	5,4	9,7
Total responses	100	180,2
The government in Ankara	10,0	90,0
Which one among the coalition parties made you angry?	**% of responses**	**% of cases**
AKP	0,6	1,6
ANAP	30,5	72,9
CHP	0,6	1,6
DEHAP /HADEP	0,3	0,8
DSP	38	90,7
DYP	1	2,3
GP	0,3	0,8
MHP	28,2	67,4
YTP	0,3	0,8
Total responses	100	238,8

However, the most striking thing was that among the three coalition partners the blame was not equally shared. In both questions where we ask about the political parties at large and coalition parties in specific, it looks like the DSP was remembered more frequently as making people angry than any of the other two coalition members. Among the other partners ANAP came second in attracting, anger followed by the MHP. This ranking according to anger instigated by the coalition partners directly reflects their ability to attract support in November 2002. The MHP with about 8.3 percent of the popular vote was the most successful among the coalition parties followed by ANAP (5.1 percent) and the DSP (1.2 percent).

Conclusion

Several features of the Turkish electoral scene emerge from our mostly descriptive account of the November 2002 election. Foremost among those is the long-term corroborated finding of increasing domination of the right-wing ideological predispositions among the voters. Time after time, all survey research evidence suggests that voters are leaving their once centrist positions for right-of-center stands. Although there is evidence to suggest that ideological positions in Turkey exhibit a multi-dimensional picture, we find no evidence that progressive ideological orientations are becoming attractive to the Turkish electorate. Instead, more and more voters seem to be attracted to conservative orientations with a certain unmistakable nationalist flavor.

Religiosity is also an integral part of these rising right-of-center orientations. Although support for *Şeriat* is declining, voters predominantly express evaluations that there exists in Turkey a certain degree of oppression of the religious people by the state. Foremost among the examples given for such oppression is the turban ban in universities and restrictions upon covered women. However, taken together with our previous findings concerning the decreasing impact of religiosity upon unconventional participation in the form of protest behavior we see mostly a docile nature of religious conservatism in the country. Since there seems to be no increase in the demand for *Şeriat*, we can safely argue that religious sensitivities were on the rise for a party that is supported for being closer to its supporting constituency. It is quite telling that while nearly one third of our respondents report no party to resolve Turkey's problems, among all the parties in the party system, the AKP tops the list for being the party to resolve the country's problems. Equally telling is that the AKP is seen as a solution primarily for the turban and headscarf problem. However, in all other major issues the AKP still commands a domineering position as a party of solution for problems. Given the unassuming decline in the demand for *Şeriat* in the country and the controlled non-threatening rise of its electoral support, the AKP projects an image that is religiously conservative, and sensitive. However, at the same time quite well-mannered, especially compared to its predecessors, and docile in its reactions to secularist circles. All such tendencies suggest that such a rise in conservatism should have helped the secularist parties very little, while helping the new generation pro-Islamists of the AKP to a great extent.

There was a great deal of resentment among the electorate for the then still in effect economic crisis at the time of the November 2002 election. All economic evaluations show a miserable state of affairs from a pure familial perspective as well as a more general sociotropic one. However, we also diagnose that at the time of the election in November 2002, people were aware of the expected recovery in the economy. Their future expectations in comparison to their evaluations of the past were much better. While those who intended to vote for AKP were significantly more likely to have a negative evaluation of the state of the economy and past economic performances, they were less likely to have an adverse evaluation for the future. In other words, from a single-variable perspective the AKP seems to have benefited from the economic crisis and was able to attract those who were optimistic about the future at the time of the election.

Given the dismal performance in the economy and the overall homogenously negative evaluations concerning this performance, an affectionate evaluation on the basis of anger might have been at play in the country. Our analyses suggest that anger was relevant for only a small segment of the electorate. The incumbent DSP-MHP-ANAP coalition was seen as responsible for the poor performance and most likely punished due to anger. However, was this factor helping the AKP gather support is not clear.

The issue around the EU membership debates seems to be mostly ineffective in mobilizing masses for or against certain parties. While the AKP constituency seems reluctant to be supportive of the EU cause, the party leadership seems to have been very successful in guiding these conservative constituencies especially after they came to power and thus raising their support for the EU membership. However, from the perspective of factors shaping party choice it remains to be seen if the EU membership issue would survive in multifaceted analyses and remain to be a significant factor that differentiates voters of one party from another. We now turn to an in-depth multivariate analysis of the determinants of party choice in November 2002.

7

EXPLAINING THE VOTE CHOICE IN NOVEMBER 2002

Explanation and prediction of voting behavior in Turkey, or elsewhere, is very difficult. There are many facets to this confession. One is certainly a practical one that is rooted in the lack of interest and investment in data collection about voters' preferences in most democratic countries. When there is no data, there is very little that has any credible convincing power to talk about. While the details of national economies of comparable significance are followed by well-endowed national official data collection programs, typically, electoral choices have time-wise a much more infrequent following and many democracies like Turkey have no national election program that follows electoral choices in any systematic way. This in turn leads to a deficient understanding of electoral dynamics in particular and leaves multi-faceted problems in especially the developing democracies unresolved.

Having acknowledged the difficulty of making electoral explanations and predictions, we should note nevertheless that some individuals' choices are highly predictable while others remain largely idiosyncratic. Given the same level of sophisticated information about individual preferences however, such unpredictability in the political arena is hardly more acute compared to other social phenomena. Our belief nevertheless is that controlling for the sophisticated data collection efforts about the political phenomena perhaps the only shortcoming in making a successful explanation comparable to consumer behavior or other areas of individual choice, as well as predictions, concerning electoral choices, remains to be at the level of conceptual clarification. As noted above, despite the fact that even descriptive data about electoral preferences are lacking in the Turkish electoral scene, we are inclined to see this factor to be the main issue in Turkish electoral studies' lack of success in providing its readers with satisfactory predictions as well as explanations about the choices voters have been making in the electoral market.

What then is the stage of the conceptual frameworks concerning voters' motivations in choosing a party? From a functional perspective voting is in many respects similar to behavior in other choice settings. Voters are choosers who act on the basis of benefit maximizing principle. These benefits may be in the form of identity pronouncements or material benefit or a combination of the two. However, in all cases, there exists a set of criteria that a candidate or party is expected to fulfill. As Evans (2004, 3) succinctly argues "the different theories either try to find *criteria* which best characterize as broad a number of voters as possible, or they try to find *characteristics* of voters which indicate that they are likely to share similar desires and consequently similar voting choices (*italics* ours)." A criterion based conceptualization of voting behavior best characterizes the spatial voting theory of Downs (1957) and Black (1961) and directional spatial voting approaches of Rabinowitz and Macdonald (1989), wherein utility maximizing voters implicitly calculate the return in terms of their personal gratification in the conceptual form of utility from amongst the alternative candidates or parties for whom to cast their votes. The party or candidate that brings the highest return receives the vote.

Alternatively, the search for characteristics that voters of the same party or candidate tend to share yields a large list of distinct traits defined by demographics such as age, gender, socio-economic group, ethnic and religious groups as well as ideological groups (see Evans, 2004, 6). Amongst these, ideological groups are best defined in terms of issue motivations of individuals. For instance, in the case of Turkey issue positions concerning the ban on headscarves in universities, membership in the EU, closer ties with the West as opposed to the Muslim countries or issues as underlined by the xenophobic or nationalistic preferences outlined in the previous chapter all define an ideological stance more than anything else. Such an extensive search for voters' characteristics has long been adopted in a systematic way by the followers of Campbell, Converse, Miller and Stokes' *The American Voter* (1960) or the so-called Michigan modelers.

Both of these broadly defined approaches are only able to account for a portion of the decisions by voters. A large segment remains characterized by individual idiosyncrasies. Nevertheless, unless an attempt is made to account for individual-to-individual variation in vote choice, the true character of the party and then the electoral system is bound to remain blurred. The aggregate election outcomes on the basis of polling stations at the lowest level of aggregation, up to the national election outcomes are restricted in their ability to account for individual level calculations. As such, aggregate level geographic election data can be used, on the one hand, to reveal the volatility and fragmentation in successive elections or constituencies. On the other hand, by combining the election outcomes with socio-economic indicators collected from the same geographic constituencies they can be linked to the election outcomes in a causal manner.

In such efforts, explanatory frameworks that relate the prevailing economic conditions to incumbent party support have long been researched. Similarly, in a more descriptive manner, socio-economic development indicators are linked to different party constituencies across different geographies. In all these kind of analyses however, the argument is of the following form: "when a given geographic constituency's level of economic prosperity changes so does the level of support for a given party or party family." The problem with such an argument is not that it does not offer an explanatory framework or an answer to the question of why support for a given party changes. The explanatory framework may be crude and unsatisfactory, but it nevertheless does exist. Voters value economic prosperity and social development. So, changes in these lead to changes in the level of support for parties. Different types of parties are affected more by such developments than others. However, a causal relationship does exist between election results and economic prosperity and development indicators.

The real problem with such explanations is that they do not offer satisfactory information as to how individuals behave when they choose a party or a candidate. One is inclined to generalize from aggregate vote analyses into the individual level of behavioral patterns. However, ever since Robinson's (1950) famous article such attempts are used as classic examples of the ecological fallacy.[1] Patterns from aggregate data cannot be used to deduce any micro-individual level behavioral patterns. If our questions concern the factors that underlie the individual decision to cast a vote for a party or candidate then we need to study individuals. Obviously, the environmental factors may play a significant role in the way individual decisions are made. However, all of these will have to be observed directly from the perspective, or evaluations, of the individual.

A typical example of the necessity to appropriately measure factors that shape the individual vote can be found in the long tradition of linking the economy to the elections and voting decisions. As early as mid-1970s a sizeable literature had taken shape around the issue of the extent to which economic conditions affect the incumbent party vote. The underlying argument was that voters keep ruling politicians responsible for the prevailing economic conditions. If the prevailing economic conditions are favorable then the incumbent is expected to benefit, while unfavorable economic conditions deteriorated their electoral basis. Voters in other words, tend to support the incumbent party during the tenure in which they prospered in greater proportions. The incumbent is expected to be symmetrically rewarded, or punished, in the sense that if good times occur then a reward with high electoral support follows, but if bad times occur then punishment follows with the support shifting to the opposition.

At the aggregate level of analysis, years of relative economic prosperity are diagnosed to lead to an increased level of support for the incumbent party or coalition. For a long time a comparable, strong support for this hypothesis was lacking at the individual level of analysis. Individuals were asked in survey settings as to what degree their individual or family finances have developed over the tenure of the incumbent. However, no matter how the respondents' reported economic prosperity or suffering changed, the expected reflection of these changes onto the individual level of voting decision for the incumbent or the challengers was not found. Individuals in other words, seemed to pick a party or candidate without much respect for their changing individual or family finances.

Only in late 1970s Kinder and Kiewiet's (1979, 1981) analyses re-established the expected link between the economy and the polity at the individual level. Their argument was that individuals do not necessarily act on the basis of their judgment of their own individual or family finances. One important reason for this is that, in the American setting at least, individuals do not keep the governments responsible for their own personal suffering or prosperity. However, individuals' judgment as to the degree to which the whole collectivity or nation has prospered or suffered during the tenure of the incumbents is more important. These sociotropic evaluations need not always be in line with judgments about individual finances. When individuals subjective evaluations of the way the whole country's economy has evolved during the incumbent's tenure are obtained, then the expected link between economy and voting, no matter how weak, is also obtained.

The literature on economic voting and its sociotropic versions is still evolving.[2] However, for our purposes it is important to note that the nature of the questions that can be answered by different levels of empirical observations drastically differ. Our position here is that for only a limited number of questions are the aggregate-level analyses appropriate. In order to grasp the factors that account for individual-to-individual variation in vote choice we need to go deep into the individual level data analysis.

Below we briefly review the voting models and their empirical variants. Then we present the nature of our dependent variable. Lastly, we present an explanatory empirical framework to account for party choice in Turkey for November 2002.

Models of Vote Choice

Explanatory frameworks of vote choice can be grouped under two branches of modeling exercises. As suggested by Evans (2004, 3) a criterion-based conceptualization fits the approach depicted in the spatial voting models, which dates back to Hotelling's (1929) model of firm competition. Downs (1957) adopted the same approach where firms are replaced by parties who compete for votes of individuals along the conventional one-dimensional issue space. Black (1958) contemporaneously developed the same framework for voting in committee settings. The idea however, in both, is the same. Individuals have a most preferred position in an issue space. This issue space could easily be conceptualized as multi-dimensional, to reflect a more realistic depiction of political competition. Parties take positions on the same issue space and voters calculate which one's declared position brings a higher pay-off. Since moving away from the most preferred position brings lower levels of payoff, voters simply calculate the distance between their ideal position and the parties' positions. Whichever party is closest to their most preferred position gets the vote. Since parties also compete for most votes this model actually offers an explanatory framework for both party competition as well as vote choice. Parties in this setting place themselves in accordance with their perceptions as to where the majority of voters' most-preferred positions in the issue space are to be found. Every election setting offers a new configuration of voters' positions, as well as the party or candidate positions on the relevant issue space. All voters and parties take their positions and make up their minds as to what to do in this particular electoral context according to a simple criterion. That is, to maximize their payoffs/utilities or electoral support. Once this criterion of decision-making is set, the rest is determined by the context that shapes the relevant players' positions in the issue space.

Radically different sets of dynamics are presumed to underlie the voting decision within the framework of the search for characteristics that voters of the same party or candidate tend to share. Voting decisions are assumed to be an outcome of a long-term process of political socialization and psychological conditioning. Campbel et al. (1960) argue that group membership and family influence in early childhood and youth form, what they call, a *party identity* (PID) establishes a causal link in the choice of the individuals' party preference (within the so-called *funnel of causality*). As time passes, all attitudinal characteristics concerning policies, group related benefits and all relevant issues, as well as attractions towards, or away from certain parties and candidates are all shaped after a continual evaluation under the light of the partisan identity. The most recent influences on these evaluations during the election campaigns are all again scrutinized through the glasses of the PID. In consequence, individual vote decision tends to be consistently in favor of one party for which the individual is positively pre-disposed and against the others. Only those who have a low level of PID tend to change their party of choice; i.e. the intensity of PID is highly and positively correlated with the likelihood of vote for a given party. Equally importantly, vote choice is for the most part predetermined by earlier socialization experiences. Given the earlier socialization of individuals that mold the intensity of PID, there is very little, if any real choice depending on the context of the election shaped by the issue content and the positions taken by the parties. In short, while the spatial model places individual maximization drives at the core of the vote decision, the socio-psychological Michigan model builds a more deterministic argument.

The empirical reflection of the spatial model has for long been missing. The spatial modelers offered eloquent analytic depictions of the election contexts and derived behavioral hypotheses which by and large remained untested in light of empirical evidence. Only relatively recently the empirical extension of the spatial model was developed by Hinich and Pollard (1981) and then extended by Enelow and Hinich (1984) and Hinich and Munger (1994).[3] Besides offering tests of the basic expectations concerning vote criteria and median voter results, these empirical extensions of the spatial voting models offer an interesting approach to the description of the ideological space in different polities. The main finding about the nature of these ideological spaces is that they are low dimensional; e.g. usually they are two-dimensional. Another interesting extension of these models is the linkage they offer with the prevailing issue preferences of the voters. As such, the estimated ideological space becomes the issue space defined on the basis of voter evaluations of the major issues on the agenda.

Unlike the spatial model, the Michigan model has been built upon empirical rather than analytical foundations. Ever since the early voting studies that form the foundation to the Michigan model undertaken by Lazerfeld and Berelson (1948) and followed up by Berelson et al (1954), all pointed out that instead of election specific influences more stable attachments to parties were found to dominate the voting decisions. All of these findings were rooted in the panel surveys carried out in a few localities. These panel designs allowed the researchers to trace local influences, so much so that local newspaper coverage of the campaigns, neighborhood meetings and the like were all controlled by repeated interviews carried out with the same individuals over a period of time. However, after controlling for the impacts of all these locality and campaign specific effects, people's longer-term attractions or repulsions to a party seemed to determine the vote choice. Only with a nation-wide representative sample used in the *American Voter*, these results were solidly generalized for the whole American electorate. Besides vote choice, people's PID's were measured along with other issue specific measurements of ideological sophistication, group membership, demographic characteristics and the like.

For the Turkish case the spatial framework has only very recently been adopted by Çarkoğlu and Hinich (2006, forthcoming) who offer a spatial interpretation of the issue space in Turkey as of 2001 about a year and a half prior to the November 2002 election. Their claim is that the Turkish ideological space is primarily two-dimensional. The first dimension is a left-right dimension *a la Turca*. The left or secularist positions are opposed by right-wing pro-Islamist positions around the issues of religious rights, turban ban and overall religiosity. The second, relatively less salient dimension reflects issues in transition that reflect positions on social and economic reforms in the country. Positions that posit individuals of pro-EU orientations who support the Copenhagen political criteria reforms against those who are Euro-skeptics and Turkish nationalists are found to be reflective of this second dimension. Party positions are clearly differentiated along the first dimension that conforms to well-known left-right or secularist vs pro-Islamist ideological cleavage. Equally striking differentiation is also observed along the second dimension of pro-reform vs anti-reform cleavage in the country.

The remaining literature is closer to the Michigan Model in conceptual orientation and is composed of a limited number of articles based on studies that target issues mostly other than voting determinants.[4] Several exceptions to this pattern exist. We focus here on Ergüder (1980–81) from the pre-1980 period and on Esmer (2002) in comparison to Çarkoğlu and Toprak (2000) and the series of surveys by TUSES (*Türkiye Sosyal Ekonomik Siyasal Araştırmalar Vakfı*-Turkish Social Economic and Political Studies Foundation).

Üstün Ergüder and Selçuk Özgediz co-directed the 1977 pre-election study funded by the Turkish daily *Hürriyet*. Ergüder (1980–91) provides the only report of the findings of this study. Ergüder reports that a three item ideological scale (left of center, center and right of center) does help one to differentiate major party constituencies. However, it is worth noting that about 21 percent of the respondents back in 1977 could not place themselves along this simple scale. Later evidence suggests that much lower percentages fail to place themselves along the conventional left-right scale in the 1990s and more recent years.

The RPP is reported to be more attractive to housewives than the JP while a larger group of RPP voters exists among workers and civil servants than farmers compared to those who intended to vote for the JP. The RPP was more popular among higher levels of education than the JP. In contrast, the JP was more attractive to older generations than the RPP which was more popular among the younger generations of voters. More significantly perhaps, was the finding that is to be corroborated later on in studies of 1990s as well as in our most recent study, which concerns the impact of religiosity on party choice. The RPP was found to be nearly twice as popular among those who do not practice religion by praying than among those who reported to be praying daily. Among those who do not report to practice prayer on a daily basis, the RPP comprise a group of 79 percent while the JP voters appear to have a group of only about 14 percent.

Ergüder (1980–81) also reports that party choice differs on the basis of ethnicity. Among those whose mother tongue is other than Turkish, the CHP voters comprise a group of 55 percent while the JP voters are merely 25 percent. From another angle, the same result is also found. Among those who could speak Kurdish or other Middle Eastern languages (mostly Arabic), the RPP voters comprised about 63 percent while the JP had a share of only 23 percent. In short, Ergüder's univariate analyses revealed clues that were to be further corroborated for the elections of post-1980 era. Left-right ideology, religiosity and ethnicity were all significantly related to differentiating the two major party constituencies while age and gender were also significant in the same vein.

Esmer (2002) is based on a post-election fieldwork funded by another Turkish daily, *Milliyet*, a week after the April 1999 election. Unlike the TÜSES studies this survey reflects genuine efforts to adopt a coherent and internationally comparable conceptual framework for the study of the Turkish electorate. Unfortunately, the only two publications that came out of this study is Esmer's (1999b) report in early May 1999 in *Milliyet* and later in his rather short essay in an edited volume (2002). Esmer (2002) uses a wide array of variables in this study. Besides basic demographic variables, variables measuring geographic location of the respondents, their economic status, subjective well-being, religious and political values were all covered.[5] Similar to Çarkoğlu and Toprak (2000) who actually report a pre-election study carried out a few weeks before April 1999 election, Esmer uses a series of binary logistic regressions to delineate differences in party constituencies. Although no comparisons exist in the literature, our observation is that Çarkoğlu and Toprak (2000) and Esmer (2002) corroborate many of one another's findings concerning the April 1999 election.

The major finding in both Esmer (2002) as well as Çarkoğlu and Toprak (2000) is that for all party constituencies the self-reported left-right ideological position turns out to be significant.[6] Çarkoğlu (1998) have noted earlier on the basis of party manifesto data that Turkish ideological space appears two-dimensional and that at least one of the two dimensions reflects the features of a western style left and right. However, these are the first of its kind of result that suggest that the conventional left-right is still meaningful in determining party choice in the Turkish electoral context.

Another important finding in both of these studies is that different factors are significant in determining choice for different parties. A single unqualified homogenous statement about the impact of a variable upon party choice cannot be made for any variable besides left-right ideology placements.

Both studies report that religiosity is significant in differentiating the pro-Islamist party constituencies from the others. Age is found by both studies to be significant in delineating the MHP from the rest of the parties. The ANAP is found to be more attractive to women than men. Both studies also report either no impact of economic condition evaluations (Esmer, 2002) or simply a secondary small impact (Çarkoğlu and Toprak, 2000) upon party choice. Kurdish identity was not at all measured in any ways by Esmer (2002) but found to be of significance for differentiating the MHP constituency by Çarkoğlu and Toprak (2000).[7]

The other notable exception is a series of fieldworks and publications undertaken by TÜSES which were designed to analyze voting behavior. TÜSES studies, as far as published ones are concerned, date back to fieldworks carried out in late 1993 and early 1994 (TÜSES, 1995, 1996, 1999, 2002). Our primary objective here is not to offer a comprehensive critique of these studies. However, very briefly, a few notable issues can be underlined. First of all, quota sampling is used in all these studies. As noted in our appendix on methodology, probability sampling is difficult in the Turkish context. However, we find the interview dynamics created by incentives to fill up the quotas is far too damaging during the interview phase of the fieldworks.

Second, these studies are carried out without much concern for conceptual clarity and with reference to other comparable studies elsewhere. Measurement concerns around issues like religiosity, ethnic and other identities, ideological positions, attitudinal tendencies shaped around issues of nationalism, social democracy are either addressed in a very simplistic way or ignored all together. A typical example is question 25 in TÜSES (2002, 151) concerning political positions a respondent might take: "If someone were to ask you 'What are your political inclinations?' which of the following would you pick as an answer?" Then answers, as many as the respondents might choose to pick from the card shown to them are recorded. The options given are as follows: rightist, leftist, nationalist, patriot, a supporter of Sharia rule,

Turkist, social democrat, socialist, communist, liberal, conservatist, revolutionary and other. All of these options require an in depth analysis as to what they might mean to the Turkish electorate. The choices reported are most likely to mean completely different things to different respondents who may happen to have picked the same descriptors for themselves. Similar ambiguous and difficult to comprehend list of options are offered to respondents concerning a question (#27) about their racial, national, and religious identities (TÜSES, 2002, 152).[8] On the basis of this question alone respondents' identity, that is, whether or not they were Kurds or Alevis, is determined.

Third, the impact of question sequencing is also not adequately addressed. In all of these studies party choice in a hypothetical election at the time of the fieldwork is asked before the question concerning the party that the respondent feels closest to for example. For most individuals the only logical answer to this question is the party of choice in the hypothetical election and as such, it fails to form a basis for evaluating one's PID. In none of these studies the degree of attachment to any one of the parties is asked as a reflection of PID measurements.

Fourth, there is not a single question in these studies that conforms in its wording with the questions used in other comparative election studies. Although ideology seems to occupy an important concern in these studies, self-placements along the left-right index is not asked for example. Lastly, most of the questions other than those concerning the demographics are aimed at addressing the daily political atmosphere at the time of the fieldwork. As such, very little long-term conceptually meaningful information is embedded in them.

Clearly these studies cannot be considered to follow along the Michigan nor the spatial model. They are a mixed bag of various simplistic measurements. Two of the most sophisticated statistical analyses of the most recent November 2002 election, using multinomial-logistic regression, are based on data from this series of research.

We have to first classify the work by Başlevent et al (2004, 2005) not as studies of the November 2002 election since the fieldwork that provides the data for both was conducted in April 2002 when the decision to go for an early election was not even on the agenda. As a consequence, a critical party such as the GP was not even on the electoral market.[9] It is not surprising that voters at the time were not choosing their party preferences with an eye towards actually voting for them. The meaning of the no vote or the no response group also is not the same as the pre-election undecided group that we will be dealing with in the ensuing sections. Since the actual setting for the election of November 2002 was radically different from the one that could be grasped by a fieldwork of April 2002, we tend to see these results as mere tendencies not really reflective of the vote decision of November 2002.

In some respects our results below are quite similar to those obtained in Table 1 of both articles.[10] Our results concerning the impact of religiosity, age, gender are similar for almost all parties. However, we disagree on the significance of economic voting. Such a disagreement is most likely due to the timing of both fieldworks as well as possible differences in our measurements. We for example tend to think that the issue variables included in this study has eventually lost their significance as the election campaign progressed (see our discussion chapter 6 above). Similarly, as noted above, the measurement of Kurdish and Alevi identities are severely problematic and thus most likely blur the impacts of the variables in the model.

We now move on to discuss our dependent variable of party choice and next the findings of our analysis.

The Dependent Variable: What does it really measure?

Before we actually analyze the determinants of vote choice in November 2002 elections we first want to underline the characteristics of our dependent variable; that is, the reported vote intention in the pre-election fieldwork. Typically in election studies two types of fieldworks are conducted. One is a pre-election study that takes place a few weeks prior to the election and the other is a post-election study that takes place a few days a weeks after the election. In the pre-election studies the question of interest is one about the intention of the respondent to cast his or her vote in the up-coming election. Our question was worded in the following way: "Which party do you intend to vote for in the up-coming general elections on 3 November 2002?" Party names are not read to the respondent who was expected to come up with a party name on his or her own. If the respondent stated that he or she is undecided then and only then, a second question was asked: "If you are undecided which party do you feel closer to voting for?" Table 7.1 reports the results of the vote shares within our pre-election survey in the first column leaving the undecided group unprocessed in any way. Typically, in election result prediction exercises a number of different techniques are used to distribute these undecided voters amongst the party constituencies so as to create an election prediction.[11] We refrain from such exercises and instead focus on the post-election survey to diagnose some of its characteristics.

In the post-election studies typically respondents are asked to report their party of choice from a couple of days or weeks back. In our case, we first asked if the respondent actually had the opportunity to cast a vote in the general election. If the answer was affirmative then the individual was asked which party he or she voted for. Our post-election survey included 971 individuals who took part in the pre-election study, which included a total of 1984 respondents. We reached nearly half of our respondents (49 percent), about 4 months after the first fieldwork and interviewed them for a second time. The same sampling frame was used to derive a control sample (N=1068) with which we conducted only the post-election questionnaire. In short, when joined together the post-election sample consisted of 2039 interviews.

Two important points to keep in mind when evaluating pre as opposed to post-election surveys is that in the pre-election surveys we only have reported intentions within a great deal of uncertainty about the election's outcome and in the post-election only the reported votes after having observed the election results. In the pre-election outcome the degree of uncertainty is not the same for all voters. Voters of low education and interest in politics are expected to make up their minds under much greater degree of uncertainty than others who are more able to process information and who have access to such information. For the November 2002 election, the real uncertainty was not about who was going to be the largest party and who was going to be its main opposition or the second runner up. Weeks before the election it became clear amongst the opinion leaders and the elite that the AKP was going to be the largest vote gainer and that the CHP would be the second largest party. Their vote shares were obviously uncertain but for the constituencies of these parties there was no uncertainty as to whether their votes could be wasted by remaining below the 10 percent electoral threshold. However, for all the other parties this was a major concern. Faced with the difficult task of deciding for a party, which might not be able to actually represent one's preferences, voters are likely to resort to last minute changes in their votes. Such switches are likely to originate within the ranks of the smaller parties towards larger parties who are more likely to get into the Parliament.

Another difficulty with the pre-election declarations is that they are more likely to group behind politically mainstream or acceptable parties. Ideological margins are less likely to show up for two main reasons. One is the difficulty, in the context of a survey setting, of portraying a political image for one's self as the supporter of a marginal, ideologically extremist party. The other is the difficulty of admitting to support a "looser", or a party that is very likely to remain out of parliament. Even if one is going to vote for one such party that is small and ideologically marginal, when asked before the election, that individual may be misrepresenting his or her preference by declaring a more acceptable party and avoid projecting a difficult image. Obviously some types of voters are more likely to resort to such misrepresentations than others. However, there is no concrete information that would tell us who is in one way or another "lying" to us and who is sincere in the declared party choice.

Looking at the post-election studies we have similar difficulties to keep in mind. In these studies, the outcome of the election is known. Although individuals differ in their level of information about politics it is difficult to conceive of an adult voter who would not know in rough terms how his or her party of choice has performed in the election; that is whether or not it won seats in the parliament or what share it roughly got in the election. Similarly, the "winner" of the election, however ambiguous this term might be in a multi-party setting where coalitions of different sorts are quite common, is also very likely to be known to almost all individuals interviewed. In January or February 2003 no such ambiguity about the "winner" existed since the AKP was quick in forming a single party government after the election. Given this information, we observe that individuals tend to project an image of a voter for the "winning" party rather than admitting to have supported a "loser", at least in their own minds. We see reflections of such a tendency in Table 7.1 as well.

Several patterns are worthy of note in Table 7.1. When we look at the pre-election results we notice that compared to the observed election results, our sample included a large GP constituency. The GP obtained about 7 percent of the valid votes in November 2002. However, at the time of our fieldwork, the GP supporters were about 10 percent of the sample. The undecided group is about 12 percent of our sample. Our analyses below will have a more in depth depiction of who these undecided individuals were. However, we want to underline here that this group is likely to include not only the real undecided voters who simply are unable to decide who to vote for but also those individuals who simply do not want to share their decisions with our interviewers. Such strategic motives are more likely to play a role amongst women of low socio-economic status who are expected to shy away from declaring their party of choice. Similarly, small marginal party constituencies and parties of controversial platforms at the margins of the ideological spectrum are more likely to be included in this group. About 4 percent of the valid votes went to the smaller parties included under our "other parties" category. DEHAP obtained nearly 5 percent of the vote while our sample had about 3 percent. So, more likely than not these undecided voters could be voters of the smaller parties and DEHAP. The fact that the GP shows up quite high in our pre-election sample makes more sense when we consider the post-election results. There the GP only gets a share of about 5 percent.

We also observe that the AKP vote share is 8 to 10 percentage points higher in all three post-election samples. The highest AKP vote share is observed amongst our panel sample respondents. Those individuals with whom we talked for a second time tended to declare to have voted for the AKP in much larger shares compared to, for example, our control group whom we only visited once after the November 2002 election. While the AKP supporters' share increases in the post-election samples, GP voters' shares persistently decline to about half their size in the pre-election. Interestingly, while we observe about 8 percent of respondents in the pre-election sample who declare that they will not vote in the post election samples, this group increases to a share of 11 to 16 percent. Amongst the control group respondents those who declare to have not voted nearly doubles and reaches 16 percent. Other party constituencies and the non-respondents remain more or less the same across our post-election samples.

Table 7.1 Reported Vote Intentions in the Panel Study (%)

	Pre-election		Post-election	
		Panel (1)	Control (2)	Total (1+2)
AKP	30	42	38	40
ANAP	2	3	4	4
BBP	1	0	0	0
CHP	14	14	13	13
DEHAP /HADEP	3	2	3	3
DSP	1	1	1	1
DYP	5	4	4	4
GP	10	5	3	4
MHP	4	5	5	5
SP 2	1	2	2	
YTP	1	1	1	1
Will not vote*	8	11	16	14
Undecided	12			
Other smaller parties	1	2	2	2
NA	7	9	8	9
	100	100	100	100
N	1984	971	1068	2039

*For pre-election study "will not vote" includes "none of the present parties". For all post election study columns "will not vote" includes those who did not vote and those who cast an invalid or empty vote.

Our panel design allows for a test of stability in the party choices declared to us in our pre-election interviews. Table 7.2 shows the correspondence between pre-election intentions for party choices and the post-election declarations of actual votes cast for the parties. Since some party constituencies are too small for a meaningful analysis we can only concentrate on a few parties in this analysis. In our panel sample of 971 interviews, 99 declared in the post-election interviews that they did not vote in November 2002 and were left out of this analysis. Similarly BBP, DSP, YTP, SP and voters of the smaller parties are too few in this panel sample to make meaningful judgments. However, we nevertheless see that, for instance, the AKP voters in our pre-election interviews have predominantly voted for AKP (85 percent) according to their post-election declarations. About 15 percent declared to have voted for a wide range of parties along the left-right ideological spectrum. Some declared to have voted for ANAP, CHP, DYP and MHP (2 percent of the total AKP voters in the pre-election interviews) while others declared to have even voted for the DSP, GP and SP (1 percent of the total AKP voters in the pre-election interviews) despite the fact that besides the CHP, all have remained below 10 percent and thus were out of the parliament.

The interesting observation is that those voters who reported to us that they intended to vote for the GP before the election predominantly report to have voted for other parties. Only 44 percent of the pre-election GP voters reported to have actually cast their vote for the GP after the election. About 46 percent of those who reported to us that they intended to vote for GP before the election actually reported after the election that they voted for either the AKP or CHP. Most of these seem to have switched to the AKP (38 percent of the total GP voters in the pre-election interviews) but some have also gone to the CHP (8 percent of the total GP voters in the pre-election interviews). Most likely, after having considered the impossibility of GP passing the 10 percent threshold, these individuals chose the parties that are most likely to get in the parliament.

The undecided and the pre-election individuals who gave no answer for their party choice, reported to have predominantly voted for the AKP (43 percent and 45 percent respectively) and CHP (12 percent and 6 percent respectively). Among the undecided some went to the DYP (4 percent) and MHP (5 percent) and even to the GP (6 percent) but most significantly only 3 percent of those undecided individuals report after the election that they did not vote at all. So, the undecided individuals do eventually make up their minds and cast a vote most likely for the sure "winners" in the election. Another case in point is the declarations of the individuals who reported to us before the election that they do not intend to cast a vote in November 2002 after the election. Only 12 percent after the election reported to have not voted. 41 percent reported to have voted for the AKP and 19 percent for the CHP.

Table 7.2 Vote change from Pre to Post-Election

Post-election		Pre-Election Choice of Parties Declared															
		AKP	ANAP	BBP	CHP	DEHAP	DSP	DYP	GP	MHP	SP	YTP	Will not vote	Other	Un-decided	NA	Total
	AKP	**85**	20	29	17	25	25	26	38	21	33	13	41	18	43	45	47
	ANAP	2	**64**	14	2	0	0	0	3	3	0	13	2	0	3	3	4
	BBP	0	0	**29**	0	0	0	0	0	0	0	0	2	0	0	0	0
	CHP	2	4	0	**66**	3	13	9	8	3	0	13	19	18	12	6	15
	DEHAP	0	0	0	0	**63**	0	0	0	0	0	0	0	0	0	0	2
	DSP	1	0	0	1	0	**38**	0	0	0	0	0	0	0	1	0	1
	DYP	2	0	0	1	0	0	**51**	1	0	0	0	3	0	4	6	5
	GP	1	0	0	0	0	0	2	**44**	0	0	13	2	0	6	3	5
	MHP	2	4	0	1	3	0	2	3	**67**	0	0	3	0	5	2	5
	SP	1	0	0	1	0	0	0	0	0	**67**	0	0	0	1	0	1
	YTP	0	0	0	1	0	0	0	0	0	0	**38**	0	0	1	0	1
	Other	0	0	29	2	0	13	0	0	3	0	0	2	**64**	1	0	2
	Did not vote	0	0	0	0	0	0	0	0	0	0	0	12	0	3	2	1
	NA	3	8	0	9	6	13	9	3	5	0	13	14	0	21	**32**	10
Total		100	100	100	100	100	100	100	100	100	100	100	100	100	100	100	100
	N	261	25	7	130	32	8	43	71	39	12	8	58	11	105	62	872

*Total number of interviews does not include the 99 respondents in the second interview who declared that they did not vote in November 2002.

These panel interviews are in many respects disheartening for election forecasters. On face value they show how volatile reported party choices could be especially when one focuses on the smaller parties that are likely to remain out of the parliament. The strategic calculations around the parties who are likely to waste individuals' votes by remaining out of the parliament are significant. However, we also believe that there is also a certain tendency to "make up" convenient answers before, as well as, after the election results are known. It is understandable that for example 38 percent of the GP intenders before the election reported to have switched to the largest party of the election, the AKP. However, nearly 17 percent of those who intended to vote for the CHP also, declare after the election that they voted for the AKP. These two parties are not only the farthest apart on the ideological left-right scale, but they were known to be able to win seats in the parliament and thus not waste one's votes. We see very little reason in these observations, if any other, than the attempt by the respondents to portray a politically more acceptable image after the elections.

Given these observations, forecasting exercises remain highly questionable in Turkey. Our impression from this panel evidence is that pre-election vote intention reports do provide a rough tendency on the part of the voters. However, precise dependable predictions are impossible on the basis of such reports. Voters especially of the smaller and ideologically less coherent parties tend to change their votes in the last moment mostly in favor of the larger parties. The post-election actual vote declarations are also equally less dependable to provide an accurate picture of the past election since many party constituencies tend to misrepresent their true votes simply to look like supporters of the winning party. Both pre as well as post-election methodologies have their shortcomings. We choose to use our pre-election data for analyzing the party constituencies simply because we find the intentions reported before the elections when results of the election are still uncertain to be more reliable and sincere reflection of individuals' true electoral identities.

A Voting Choice Model for November 2002

Empirical testing of hypotheses about Turkish voting behavior is scarce and has so far neglected the multi-party basis of voters' choices. Besides primarily tabular analysis of Ergüder (1980–81) and Esmer (1995), analyses by Kalaycıoğlu (1994a, b and 1999) used discriminant analysis and the recent work by Esmer (2002) and Çarkoğlu and Toprak (2000) used logit analysis. The methods used thus far all have their shortcomings. The discriminant analysis imposes some implausible normality assumptions on variable distributions and does not differentiate between different parties' electorates. While logit analysis resolves the restrictions of the discriminant analysis, it fails to account for the multi-party choice and its implications for modeling the voter behavior. As Alvaraez, Nagler and Bowler (2000, 135) note: "any model of voter choice in a multi-party setting should allow voters to consider simultaneously all viable parties . . . it should permit the effects of each independent variable to have a differential influence on the odds that a voter will pick each party, recognizing that the parties use different strategies to gain voter support. Also, and this is especially important in multiparty races, it should not impose the independence of irrelevant alternatives (IIA) property on the voters." The IIA property assumes that the ratio of the probabilities that a given voter chooses party A or party B when the available alternatives in the party system are parties A, B and C remains unchanged when the available alternative parties change.

In the Turkish party system this assumption is clearly violated since the expectations about which parties could obtain representation by passing the nation-wide 10 percent electoral threshold changes from one election to another, from one voter to another as well as for one voter within the campaign period. While HADEP and MHP were the major parties that failed to pass the 10 percent threshold in 1995, CHP and HADEP remained outside of the parliament in the 1999 elections. In 2002, despite expectations to the contrary, all major parties of the pre-election parliament formed after 1999 failed to capture any seats for remaining below 10 percent nationwide support. Assuming that voters cast their votes to obtain some representation in the parliament, this means that for at least 46.3 percent of the electorate which did not vote for either the AKP or CHP, the viable alternatives could not have been the same as those who voted for the parties that gained representation in the parliament. Since the IIA assumption is very strong and most probably untrue for the Turkish case, we adopt a multinomial logistic specification that does not impose the IIA assumption.

Before going into the results obtained in our analysis we first underline the descriptive properties of the dependent variable used in these analyses.

In addition to the shortcomings and salient characteristics of our pre-election vote intention question, which forms the basis of the ensuing analyses, there is yet another shortcoming that we should underline. That shortcoming is due to the missing data that reduces the number of observations in the final analysis and the distribution of party vote within the final dataset.

The distribution of the party support according to our vote intention question was given above in Table 7.1. The below given Table 7.3 however, has considerably smaller number of observations and a substantially different vote distribution for the parties. The underlying reason for this is that when for any one of the variables used in the ensuing multi-nomial logit analysis a given observation is missing due to no-response for that given question, then that individual's observation for all other variables is dropped out of the analysis (a list-wide elimination method is adopted in other words).

Our ensuing analysis includes a total of 38 variables including all of the independent as well as the dependent variable. 882 observations included in the final analysis comprise 44.5 percent of the total sample of observations. However, for that portion of the sample we have data on all 38 variables in the analysis, i.e. those 882 respondents have an observation for all of these 38 variables.

Table 7.3 Multinomial Logit Estimation Results of the Vote Intention Function Case Processing Summary

	N	Marginal Percentage
AKP	362	41
CHP	180	20
DEHAP	35	4
DYP	64	7
GP	104	12
MHP	65	7
Undecided	72	8
		100
Valid	882	44,5
Missing	1102	55,5
Total	1984	100

Pseudo R-Square

Cox and Snell	0,71	Nagelkerke	0,74	McFadden	0,38

Model Fitting Information

Model	-2 Log Likelihood	Chi-Square	Sig.
Intercept Only	2923,02		
Final	1825,75	1097,27	1,1E-113

We should also note that not all relevant parties are included in our analyses of vote determinants. This is primarily due to insufficient observations, as noted earlier in this chapter, for these parties in our sample. Besides the minor parties of the 2002 election we had to eliminate DSP, YTP, ANAP, and SP from our analysis due to small number of respondents indicating their intentions to vote for them in our sample. We should note that given the number of variables in the ensuing analyses we have barely enough degrees of freedom for the analysis of DEHAP's vote. Table 7.3 also shows that in our sub-sample for the multi-nomial analysis includes more AKP (6.8 percent point more), GP (4.5 percent points more) and CHP (1 percent points more) voters compared to the election results. DEHAP (2.3 percent points less), DYP (2.3 percent points less), and MHP (1 percent points less) voters are under represented in our sub-sample of analysis. The fact that we do not have all party constituencies in our analysis restricts the full use of possible comparisons that were possible at the time of pre-election calculations carried out by the voters trying to make up their minds about who to vote for in November 2002. However, since at the time our survey was carried out, the intentions of the voters for these parties comprised only a small fraction of the whole sample, such exclusion was a practical necessity we simply could not avoid.

Statistics on the fit of the model to our data show that we have quite a successful estimation at hand. However, given the encouraging estimation results the interpretation and significance of our findings are still quite difficult. The primary reason for this difficulty is the large number of parameters to take into account. In addition to the large number of independent variables, the multi-nomial logit also produces a large number of binary comparisons. Indeed, multi-nomial logit is a simultaneous estimation of binary logits for all possible comparisons among the outcome categories (Long, 1997, 149). In our case where we have 7 categories in our dependent variable, there are 21 relevant comparisons each one having 38 coefficients in total, creating 798 coefficients shown in the appendix to this chapter. Table 7.4 below simply gives a summary of the findings.

In order to facilitate this complex picture, we first will concentrate on just one comparison and give full interpretation of the results. Then we will move into groups of variables across all comparisons to make sense of the results.

We take the AKP vs CHP comparison as our starting point and reproduce these results in more detail in Table 7.5. We highlighted the significant coefficients at 90 percent as well as 95 percent level of confidence. The exp(B) term provides a convenient basis for interpreting the impact of a given independent variable. We provide here an odds-ratio interpretation as opposed to one based on predicted probabilities. Odds ratio interpretation is based on the ratio of the probabilities that the dependent variable takes on a value of one category of the dependent variable as opposed to the reference category. With a dependent variable taking on 7 different values we can cover all necessary comparisons by using six of the seven categories. The choice of the reference category is of no particular technical importance; since, once the model is estimated by using one of the categories as the reference category; all the rest of the comparisons necessitating the use of other reference categories could be easily calculated from the already estimated values. In order to facilitate the exposition of all comparisons, we already produced all comparisons with the use of all relevant reference categories and reported the results in the appendix to this chapter and summarized them in Table 7.4.

For a unit change in the independent variable in question, the odds (that is the ratio of the probability that a respondent votes for the CHP in this case over the probability that he/she votes for AKP) are expected to change by a factor of exp (B) holding all other variables constant. In other words, if the estimated coefficient for a given independent variable is positive (negative) then the exp (B) for that variable will have a value greater than equal to 1 (will have a value between 0 and 1). A positive coefficient implies that the probability of the reference category is smaller than the category with which it is being compared to. In a similar vein, a negative coefficient means that the probability of the reference category is larger than the category with which it is being compared. From a different perspective, we can claim that with a positive (negative) coefficient the respondent is more (less) likely to appear under the comparison category than under the reference category.

For example, the respondent's age is found to be significant with an exp (B) equal to 1.06, which indicates that for every additional year in the age of our respondent we see that the odds ratio for being a CHP voter as opposed to one who intends to vote for AKP increases by 6 percent. Taking into account the fact that our respondents are 18 years and older, a voter who is 28 as opposed to 18 is nearly 60 percent more likely to be a CHP, as opposed to an AKP voter. Following the same line of argument, we find that a 38 year old is 2.2 times more likely to be a CHP voter than an AKP voter of course keeping all other variables constant. In other words, younger voters are more inclined to choose the AKP rather than the CHP.

Left-right self placement on our 1 to 10 scale is also significant with a negative coefficient indicating that as respondents move one notch from left to right in their self-placement scores (that is a unit increase on our scale) they tend to be less likely to be a CHP voter as opposed to an AKP voter. So much so that a unit increase on the left-right scale, that is a unit move towards the right-most

Table 7.4 Multi-nomial Logit estimates of the Vote Intention Function-Summary Results

The Reference Category is . . .	AKP						CHP					MHP				DYP			GP		U
	DEHAP	CHP	GP	U	DYP	MHP	DEHAP	GP	U.	DYP	MHP	DEHAP	GP	U	DYP	DEHAP	GP	U	DEHAP	U	DEHAP
Intercept																					
DV for men		-	--	--	--				--					--							+++
Respondent's age		+		+	+			-			-						-			+	
DV for no-schooling								+++				+++	+++		+++					---	
DV for primary education				--					--											---	
DV for high school				--					---											---	
DV for rural areas																	--	--			
DV for those who report less than or equal to 350 million TL household income per month										+							1,00				
DV for those who can speak Kurdish	+++	+++						--	---		---	+++				+++			+++		+++
DV for those who indicated that over the last year the economic policies followed by the incumbent government have adversely affected their family's finances		--								+++					+++						
DV for those who indicated that over the last year the economic policies followed by the incumbent government have adversely affected Turkey's economy																					
DV for those who indicated that over the next year their family's economic situation will get worse			++					++									+++			--	
DV for those who indicated that over the next year Turkey's economic situation will get worse			--	++					++	++			--				---			+++	
L-R self placement	-	--	-	-		+		+	+	++	++	--	-	-	-	--	-	-	-		-
Religiosity-Faith	-	-			-				+												
Religiosity-Attitudes	-	--	--	--	-			+		++	++		-	-				-			
Religiosity-Practice		-	-	-	-						+		-	-	-						
Belief in destiny																					
Self-evaluated religiosity				-														-			
Xenophobia				+	+				+					+	+					+	
Nationalism																			-		
Political Inefficacy				+	+				+					+	+						

The Reference Category is . . .	AKP						CHP					MHP				DYP			GP		U
	DEHAP	CHP	GP	U	DYP	MHP	DEHAP	GP	U.	DYP	MHP	DEHAP	GP	U	DYP	DEHAP	GP	U	DEHAP	U	DEHAP
DV for those who support Turkey's membership in EU		+++		++	+++			--			---			+++	+++		---			++	
DV for those who prefer Turkey building closer relations with the Muslim rather than the Western countries	--	--	--		--				++		++		--							++	
DV for being angry to coalition partners DSP/MHP/ANAP	+++						+++					+++							+++		+++
Interest in politics		-	-		+		+		+	++	+		-				--		+	+	
Interest in the election campaign		+	+						--	-	-									-	
Strategic voters						-	--				--			++	++	--			--		--
DV for those who indicate that people in Turkey can practice their religious practices freely		++		++	++		--	--			--					--	--			++	--
DV for those people who give turban and headscarf ban as examples for pressures upon religious people		--					+++	+++	+++	++	++										
Region 2 Western Anatolia	+++	+++						--					-								
Region 3 Eastern Marmara		+++	++						--		---		+++								
Region 4–5 Aegean and Western Marmara		+++	+++	+++	+++	++															
Region 6 Mediterranean		+++		+++							---			+++							
Region 7 Western Black Sea	+++	+++	+++									+++			+++	+++					+++
Region 8 Centre Anatolia																					
Region 9 Eastern Black Sea				+++										+++							
Region 10 Southeastern Anatolia	+++																				
Region 11–12 Centre-east and North east A.																					

+ Increases 1 < Exp(B) < = 2; + + Increases 2 < Exp(B) < = 3; + + + Increases 3 < Exp(B);
- Decreases 0.5 < = Exp(B) < 1; -- Decreases 0.25 < = Exp(B) < 0.5; --- Decreases 0 < Exp(B) < 0.25
(dark shading) p < 0.05 (light shading) p < 0.1 U:Undecided

extreme, decreases the odds by a factor of 0.49. The same kind of a negative impact on the odds ratio of being a CHP voter as opposed to an AKP voter is observed for religiosity measures. While self-evaluated religiosity does not work significantly to differentiate between a CHP as opposed to an AKP voter, our faith, attitudinal and practice dimensions of religiosity are all significant with negative coefficients. It is interesting that the largest impact on the odds ratio is observed for the attitude dimension. That is, as individuals are one standard deviation more religious in the attitude dimension (more intense approvers of religious positions in our evaluation statements), their likelihood for being a CHP voter compared to an AKP voter is reduced by a factor of 0.28. This makes an AKP voter 3.6 times more likely than a CHP voter after controlling for the impacts of all other variables.

We also see that positions over foreign policy issues help significantly to distinguish the CHP from AKP voters. Those who support Turkey's membership in the EU are 3 times more likely to be CHP as opposed to the AKP voter (exp(B)=3). However, those individuals who support the view that Turkey should develop closer ties with the Muslim rather than Western countries are significantly more likely to be an AKP voter rather than a CHP voter. The strength of these two variables are comparable but in the opposite direction. Supporting closer relations with Muslim rather than Western countries renders the likelihood of being an AKP supporter (1/0.41=2.44) more than twice as likely, while supporting EU membership makes the likelihood of a CHP voter nearly 3 times more likely than being an AKP supporter.

Similarly, as the interest in the election campaign increases, so does the likelihood of that individual to be a CHP voter as opposed to an AKP voter, keeping all other variables constant. More interestingly perhaps is the observation that views of the respondents on the state of religious freedoms in the country help differentiate the party choice of these individuals. If an individual indicates that people in Turkey are free to practice their religious duties then the odds of that individual being a CHP as opposed to an AKP voter increases by a factor of 2.82 or makes that individual nearly three times more likely to be a CHP voter compared to one for the AKP. In terms of the magnitude of the impact for being a CHP as opposed to an AKP voter, this is very similar to being in support of EU membership. However, if the individual thinks that there is pressure upon religious people and gives turban/headscarf ban in the universities as an example to such pressures, then that individual is more than three times likely (1/0.27=3.7) to be an AKP voter as opposed to a CHP voter.

We also observe that, being a Kurdish speaker makes an individual nearly two and a half times more likely to be a CHP voter in contrast to an AKP voter. However, at a lower level of significance, women are more likely to support the CHP than the AKP. A counterintuitive finding is that those individuals who indicated that over the last year the economic policies followed by the incumbent government have adversely affected their family's finances are less likely to be a CHP voter compared to being an AKP voter. In other words, those individuals who make a negative evaluation of the incumbent government's economic policy performance at the time of our survey were more likely to prefer the AKP as opposed to the CHP. However, this impact is significant only at a lower level.

Interestingly, other demographic indicators such as education, urban-rural divide and income are not important in distinguishing the CHP voters from those for the AKP. Equally significantly, indicators of xenophobia and nationalism as well as political inefficacy turned out to be insignificant in explaining the likelihood of switching from the AKP to the CHP, or for that matter from the CHP to the AKP.

In short, the distinction between the CHP and the AKP voters is primarily built upon differences of opinion about religiosity and other religiously significant foreign policy issues. Ethnic and generational differences and preferential differences between men and women are also significant but of secondary importance. Figure 7.1 shows the exp(B) values of all the significant variables ranked according to their order of impact upon the odds ratio of being a CHP as opposed to AKP voter. We see that primarily structural or geographic factors increase the likelihood of being a CHP as opposed to an AKP voter. When an individual is from Western Black Sea region for example, then, after controlling for all other variable impacts, he or she is more than 6.5 times more likely to be inclined to vote for the CHP as opposed to the AKP. Similarly, just being a Kurdish speaker, increases the odds ratio in favor of CHP as opposed to the AKP by more than a factor of 4.1. From a political issue perspective, the top two most important impacts is made on the likelihood of being a CHP voter by the variables dealing with EU support and evaluation as to whether or not individuals freely practice their religious duties in Turkey. When looking into the factors that increase the likelihood of being an AKP voter as opposed to one for the CHP, we see that religious attitudes and statement that turban/headscarf ban constitute an example of pressures upon religious people comes at the top. When voters become more religious they tend towards the AKP. While the CHP has an advantage among women compared to men, the AKP has an advantage among the younger population. It is interesting that CHP is more attractive compared to the AKP among those who are interested in the election campaign but the AKP has an advantage among those who are interested in politics in general rather than remaining focused on the election campaign.

Table 7.5. The Vote Choice Function for CHP Voters in Comparison with the AKP Voters as the Reference Category

The reference category is: AKP.	B	CHP Sig.	Exp(B)
Intercept	0,30	0,81	
DV for men	–0,60	0,06	0,55
Respondent's age	0,06	0,00	1,06
DV for no-schooling	–1,23	0,16	0,29
DV for primary education	0,18	0,77	1,19
DV for high school	0,53	0,36	1,70
DV for rural areas	0,13	0,72	1,14
DV for those who report less than or equal to 350 million TL household income per month	0,00	0,30	1,00
DV for those who can speak Kurdish	1,42	0,02	4,12
DV for those who indicated that over the last year the economic policies followed by the incumbent government have adversely affected their family's finances	–0,83	0,10	0,44
DV for those who indicated that over the last year the economic policies followed by the incumbent government have adversely affected Turkey's economy	–0,20	0,71	0,82
DV for those who indicated that over the next year their family's economic situation will get worse	0,23	0,62	1,26
DV for those who indicated that over the next year Turkey's economic situation will get worse	–0,26	0,58	0,77
L-R self placement	–0,71	0,00	0,49
Religiosity-Faith	–0,43	0,03	0,65
Religiosity-Attitudes	–1,27	0,00	0,28
Religiosity-Practice	–0,62	0,00	0,54
Belief in destiny	0,00	0,93	1,00
Self-evaluated religiosity	–0,11	0,21	0,90
Xenophobia	0,20	0,29	1,22
Nationalism	0,20	0,22	1,22
Political Inefficacy	0,07	0,66	1,07
DV for those who support Turkey's membership in EU	1,10	0,01	3,00
DV for those who prefer that Turkey builds closer relations with the Muslim rather than the Western countries	–0,88	0,01	0,41
DV for being angry to coalition partners DSP/MHP/ANAP	0,38	0,47	1,46
Interest in politics	–0,38	0,07	0,68
Interest in the election campaign	0,51	0,01	1,67
Strategic voters	0,15	0,63	1,16
DV for those who indicate that people in Turkey can practice their religious practices freely	1,04	0,01	2,82
DV for those people who give turban and headscarf ban as examples for pressures upon religious people	–1,31	0,00	0,27

The reference category is: AKP.		CHP	
	B	Sig.	Exp(B)
Region 2 Western Anatolia	1,33	0,02	3,79
Region 3 Eastern Marmara	1,26	0,01	3,54
Region 4–5 Aegean and Western Marmara	1,24	0,02	3,46
Region 6 Mediterranean	1,52	0,04	4,57
Region 7 Western Black Sea	1,87	0,08	6,50
Region 8 Centre Anatolia	0,35	0,59	1,42
Region 9 Eastern Black Sea	1,40	0,14	4,05
Region 10 Southeastern Anatolia	0,17	0,85	1,18
Region 11–12 Centre-east and North east Anatolia	–0,08	0,95	0,93
DV: Dummy variable	p<0.05	p<0.1	

Table 7.4 shows the full spectrum of comparisons between different party constituencies. The significant variables for the analysis of the AKP vs. CHP constituencies are not all expected to be significant in another comparison between say for example, the AKP vs. MHP, simply because the constituencies of these parties are not expected to be significantly different in all respects that the constituencies of the CHP and AKP were. When we look at this particular comparison between the AKP and MHP voters, we see that although left-right self-placement is still significant in distinguishing AKP voters from those of the MHP, the religiosity indicators are not. In other words, being more or less religious in our three different dimensions or self-evaluation of religiosity really does not matter in changing the odds ratio of being an MHP as opposed to an AKP voter. Instead, we see that AKP and MHP voters are distinguished significantly on the basis of their tactical vote considerations and on the basis of geography. In terms of basic demographics such as age, sex, education, income and ethnic background there seems no significant differentiation exists between the AKP and the MHP voters. Geography however, does matter though at a low level of significance. Voters from regions four or five, that is from the Aegean and the Western Marmara regions are nearly three times more likely to be MHP voters (exp(B)=2.96) than the AKP voters.

Tactical Voting

More importantly, we see that tactical considerations also help differentiate the MHP voters from the AKP voters. We specifically asked whether our respondents would vote for a party who can be successful in the election while

Figure 7.1 Odds Ratio Plot for all significant coefficients (CHP vs AKP)

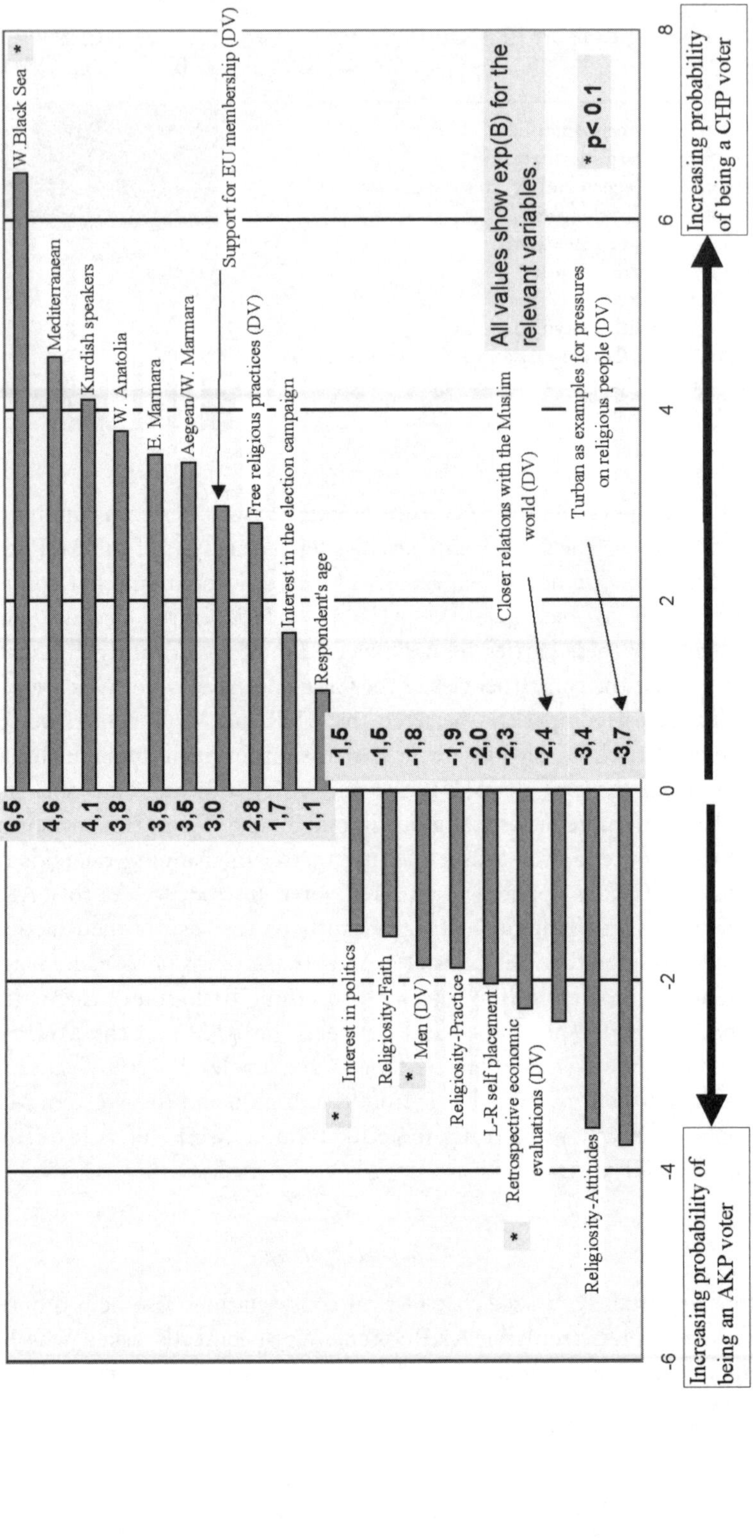

Variable	exp(B)
W.Black Sea *	6,5
Mediterranean	4,6
Kurdish speakers	4,1
W. Anatolia	3,8
E. Marmara	3,5
Aegean/W. Marmara	3,5
Support for EU membership (DV)	3,0
Free religious practices (DV)	2,8
Interest in the election campaign	1,7
Respondent's age	1,1
Interest in politics *	-1,5
Religiosity-Faith	-1,5
Men (DV) *	-1,8
Religiosity-Practice	-1,9
L-R self placement	-2,0
Retrospective economic evaluations (DV) *	-2,3
Closer relations with the Muslim world (DV)	-2,4
Religiosity-Attitudes	-3,4
Turban as examples for pressures on religious people (DV)	-3,7

All values show exp(B) for the relevant variables.

* p< 0.1

-6 -4 -2 0 2 4 6 8

Increasing probability of being an AKP voter ← → Increasing probability of being a CHP voter their most preferred party stands a chance of losing.[12] This scenario obviously was very applicable to the case of the MHP at the time, which in all likelihood was set to remain below the nationwide 10 percent electoral support barrier and thus fail to obtain any seats in parliament. However, we see that those respondents who reject such tactical change of party of choice in the election intend to vote for the MHP. In other words, even though these individuals know their party is likely to remain out of parliament, they still tend to vote for the MHP. Besides the MHP, there is no other party constituency where this variable turns out to be significant in comparison to the AKP as the reference party. However, comparing the MHP with the DYP and the undecided voters, we see that those respondents, who declare that they would change their vote if they think that their first party of choice is likely to be on the loosing side of the election, tend to vote for parties other than MHP. If the respondent is determined to change his or her vote for strategic reasons then that respondent is more likely to be a non-MHP voter. This can be taken as a reflection of a strong partisan basis among the MHP constituency, while for parties like the DYP and the undecided voters, tactical considerations seem to push these voters away from these parties. Similar results are observed for DEHAP and MHP voters in comparison to CHP voters, and DEHAP voters in comparison to DYP, GP and the undecided voters. In other words, tactical considerations do not seem to attract voters away from DEHAP and MHP while the undecided and the DYP voters do seem to make such tactical calculations in comparison to voting for MHP.

Left-Right Ideology

The most persistently significant variable in these analyses turns out to be the left-right self-placement scores. For all comparisons other than the ones between the undecided group and the GP, the AKP and DYP, and DEHAP and CHP, left-right ideology estimates on the basis of self-placements turns out to be significant. The left-right self-placement does not differentiate between GP and the undecided group. This is not surprising given the opportunistic non-ideological orientation of the GP and the undecided group. Similarly, the AKP and DYP voters as well as the CHP and DEHAP voters are indistinguishable on the conventional left-right scheme. Figure 7.2 shows the impact of movement along the left-right scale upon odds ratios for all comparisons. We see that the largest impact on the odds ratio is observed for the comparisons of two of the most extreme ends of the left-right spectrum, that is comparisons of DEHAP and CHP with the MHP. Then come comparisons of DEHAP and CHP with the DYP. An interesting point to notice is the situation of the AKP in comparison to other parties. After taking into account the impacts of all our independent variables, we see that movement towards the right end of the left-right spectrum increases the likelihood of being an MHP voter; that is AKP voters remain to the left of those for the MHP. With a similar logic, we see that the AKP remains to the right of DEHAP, CHP, GP and the undecided group, but it is not statistically significantly distinguishable from DYP voters. This once again confirms our previous claim that as of October 2002, AKP voters were not centrist but rather were situated to the right of the center. Only for the MHP there seems to be a decreasing likelihood of being an AKP voter as one moves from the left to the right of the ideological spectrum.

It seems that the left-right ideological self-placements are still significant in differentiating voter constituencies for many parties whereas other ideological indicators such as religiosity, nationalism and xenophobia are not as effective in shaping the distinction between party constituencies.

Religiosity

Religiosity is significant in differentiating the AKP and CHP from the rest of the party system while for other parties this impact is not as widespread. In other words, religiosity differences help us distinguish inclinations of voters primarily between the AKP and CHP and the other parties. However, when comparing other parties among themselves, indicators of religiosity appear insignificant. This is in line with an earlier remark by Çarkoğlu and Toprak (2000) that the levels of religiosity among the right-wing parties are not very significantly different and that their constituencies appear to be more or less of similar levels of religiosity. Our multinomial estimation allows us to detect this special role that religiosity plays in Turkish politics. Unless specific party-to-party comparisons are taken into account, religiosity appears significant in most single party logit vote intention estimates. However, these analyses are all comparing one party voters with the rest of the party system and ignore specific party-to-party comparisons. As such, they only show us that compared to all of the remaining party voters (coded as zero in the binary logit specification) the chosen party constituency (coded as one in the binary logit specification) religiosity appears significant. When we compare one party with all other parties on a one-to-one basis however, this impact of religiosity disappears for the right-wing party comparisons and only surfaces as significant for the two extreme ends of the Turkish ideological spectrum; that is, for the AKP and the CHP. Given increasing homogeneity of the voters of the right-wing in terms of their religiosity, such a result is not surprising

Figure 7.2 Odds Ratio Plot for the Left-Right self-placement scores across all comparisons

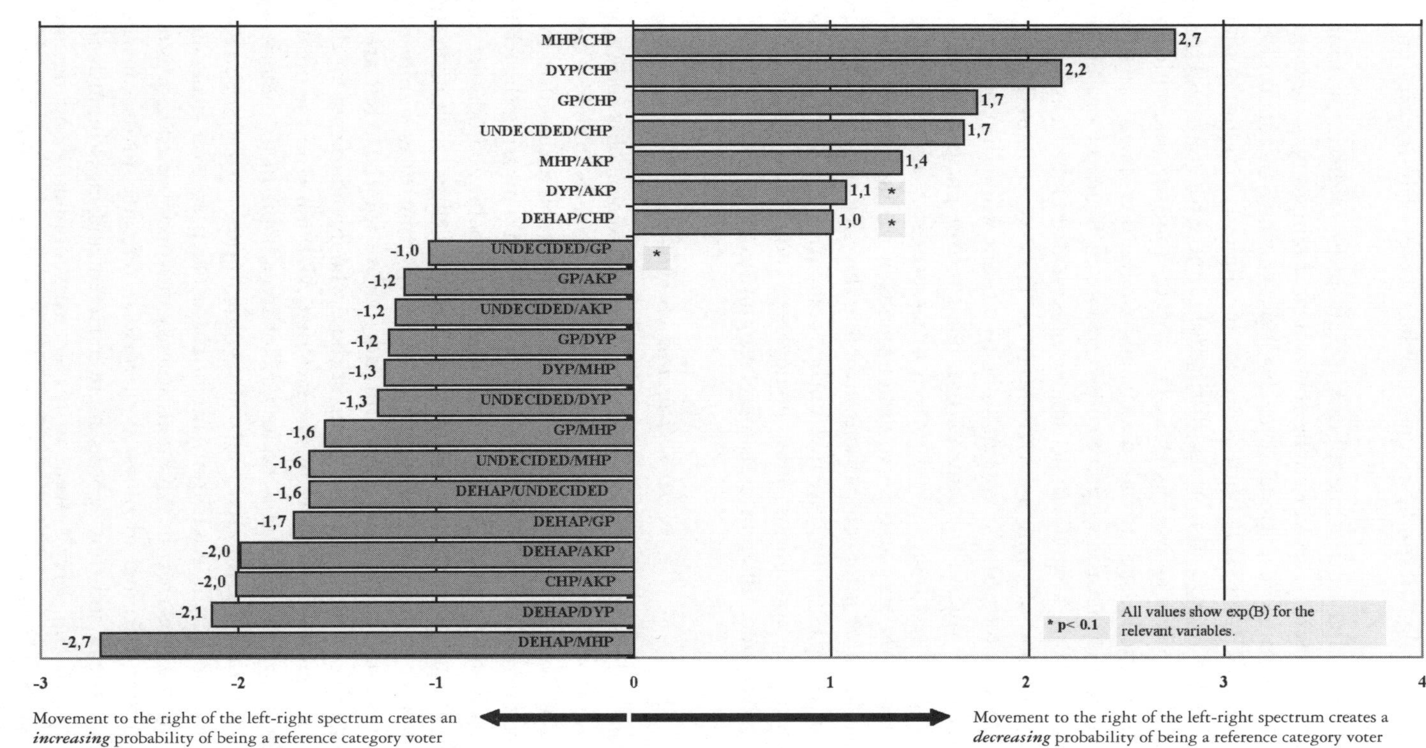

but highly significant in diagnosing the impact of religiosity on voting behavior.

While belief in destiny appears insignificant in distinguishing party constituencies for all comparisons, self-evaluated religiosity is only significant at a lower than conventional levels for distinguishing the undecided voters from the AKP and DYP. Faith dimension of religiosity is significant for 4 out of 21 comparisons and in those distinguishes the AKP from DEHAP, CHP and DYP voters as well as the CHP voters from the undecided voters. However practice and attitude dimensions of religiosity appear as a significant factor for distinguishing party constituencies in 8 and 11 out of 21 comparisons. For the attitudes dimension we observe that higher religiosity makes the likelihood of being an AKP, MHP or DYP voter more likely in the comparisons for which it appears to be significant while the opposite is true for the CHP voters. The same pattern holds for the practice dimension but this appears less frequently. In short, differences in religiosity shape party preferences for only at the two extreme ends of the underlying ideological dimension, that is for comparisons involving the AKP and the CHP with the rest of the parties in system. In other comparisons between parties the constituencies appear more or less homogenous and thus no significant impact is observed from different measures of religiosity.

Nationalism and xenophobia

When we look at the impact of nationalism and xenophobia indicators, we observe that they help distinguish party constituencies in only a few comparisons. Xenophobia appears significant in only 6 and nationalism in only 1 out of 21 comparisons. One such case appears when comparing the AKP with the DYP and the undecided groups. When xenophobic attitudes increase for an individual then the probability of that individual to be an undecided or DYP voter as opposed to a supporter of the AKP increases significantly. In other words, individuals who intend to vote for the AKP are not as xenophobic as the undecided group or those who intend to vote for the DYP. This is significant considering the fact that AKP relies on the pro-Islamist tradition, which had had a serious dose of xenophobia in its rhetoric. Given the fact that nationalism also does not appear to be significant in distinguishing the AKP from any of the other party constituencies, this finding suggests that the AKP constituency in November 2002 does not have much of a marginal ideological rhetoric as reflected in its constituency characteristics and thus appears more moderate and indistinguishable from the rest of the party system in respect to xenophobia and nationalism indicators. The fact that neither nationalism nor xenophobia indicators help distinguish the AKP voters from the CHP, GP, MHP and even DEHAP is quite telling of the lack of ideological color for the mixed-bag nature of the AKP constituency. In a sense, it helps the AKP to maintain a steady course in foreign policy as well as all policy areas that relate to the Copenhagen political criteria. In short, the AKP appears unconstrained from the right-wing ideological commitments for nationalist causes or by xenophobic knee-jerk reactions that crippled the MHP when they were in power as part of the DSP-MHP-ANAP coalition.

Another case is observed in the comparisons of the CHP with the undecided group. As the level of xenophobic attitudes increase, the probability of being an undecided as opposed to a CHP voter increases significantly. A similar positive coefficient is obtained for xenophobic attitudes when we compare the DYP and undecided voters with MHP voters. For both groups rising xenophobic attitudes increases the likelihood of not being an MHP voter in comparison to the parties in question. That is the MHP constituency seems to have less attraction on the basis of xenophobia compared to the DYP or the undecided group. Perhaps most surprisingly, the nationalist and xenophobic inclinations expected of the MHP constituency do not appear in any one of the other comparisons. In other words, neither xenophobic nor nationalist attitudes are significant in distinguishing the MHP voters from the other parties in one-to-one comparisons and in such one-to-one comparisons; the MHP constituency is less xenophobic compared to the DYP voters and the undecided group.

Political inefficacy

Our political inefficacy scale distinguishes the DYP and the undecided groups from the AKP, and MHP; as well as the undecided group from the CHP. In the remaining 16 comparisons it remains insignificant. The MHP voters also appear to be more politically efficacious compared to DYP voters and the undecided group. When political inefficacy indicator increases, the probability of an individual to be undecided or a DYP supporter increases significantly. A similar impact is also observed in comparison to AKP voters with the DYP voters and the undecided group.

Demographic Variables

Looking at the impact of respondents' sex as a distinguishing factor in party-to-party comparisons of vote intentions, we observe that men are less inclined to vote for the CHP, GP, DYP and being an undecided respondent, in comparison to being an AKP voter. In comparison to the CHP voters, the undecided group is more likely to include women (a negative coefficient for the Dummy variable for men is observed). DEHAP voters are more likely to be men as opposed to women in comparison to the undecided group.

These differential inclinations of women and men can be interpreted in at least two ways. One is that Turkish women appear to have an independent party choice within the largely patriarchal Turkish society. Their husbands', fathers' or big brothers' party preferences are not necessarily followed by women who tend towards some parties more than others. Another interpretation is based on a skeptic's view of the interview process in our fieldwork. Such differential tendencies for some parties may be a reflection of the fact that women do not feel equally comfortable as men do in expressing their preferences for certain parties. For instance, the observation that men dominate DEHAP may simply be a reflection of intimidation of women to admit that they are indeed going to vote for DEHAP. Whereas for the cases of the CHP who traditionally projected a secular perspective in gender issues, the DYP, which had a women leader in the past and the GP who had a purely reactionist colorless populist standing on most issues, women may have found it easier to report their inclinations for them rather than others, who may project a more problematic image in an interview setting. We tend to view the over representation of the GP in our sample partially at least as a result of such convenient reporting by women who simply could not deliver at the voting booth for the GP and followed their more patriarchal elders' preferences. It is interesting however that the MHP constituency does not appear to have a significant gender bias in favor of men in any comparisons except the one with the undecided group.

Age appears to be a significant distinguishing factor in comparisons of the AKP with CHP, DYP and the undecided group. Younger individuals in these comparisons tend to be AKP supporters. For the case of the CHP, we see that younger voters tend to be undecided or an MHP supporter when compared to the CHP. Younger voters tend to be inclined towards the GP in comparison to the undecided group. Similarly younger voters are inclined towards the GP compared to the DYP. However the MHP voters only appear to be younger in comparison to the CHP constituency.

It is telling that compared to the 1999 election where younger generations were more inclined to vote for the MHP, in 2002, the MHP seems to have lost that advantage to the AKP. The fact that the CHP could obtain the second largest vote share without much following among the young is also telling of the electoral strength of the CHP in the future. It is virtually impossible to strike a winning strategy in any Turkish election without somehow appealing significantly to the youth.

Levels of education appear to be significant in comparisons involving the undecided group as opposed to the AKP, GP and CHP voters, and the MHP constituency in comparison to DEHAP, DYP and GP constituencies. When comparing the AKP, GP and CHP with the undecided group, we observe that those individuals of primary education level and high school graduates are less likely to be part of the undecided group. In other words, if someone has neither very high level of education nor have no education at all then he or she is inclined to be decided in favor of either the AKP, CHP or GP rather than remaining as undecided. Some education pushes the voters towards these three parties rather than remaining undecided. However, when we look at the group with no formal education we see that they are more inclined to be a GP supporter as opposed to a CHP supporter. Similarly, voters with no education prefer DEHAP, GP or DYP to MHP or GP to being undecided. While the level of education does not affect being a supporter of the MHP in comparison to the AKP and CHP, such an observation is worthy of note since, on face value, low education level is usually attributed to the extreme right wing of the Turkish electoral space. We see that such an expectation is not supported for both the MHP as well as the AKP constituencies.

Level of income, as represented by the Dummy variable coded as one for the lowest income group, appears insignificant for all comparisons except for those of the GP vs. DYP and DYP vs. CHP. However, this impact is of low level of significance and of small magnitude.

Kurdish speakers appear significant in comparisons involving the DEHAP constituency and show that they are significantly inclined to vote for the DEHAP as opposed to any other party after controlling for all other socio-economic, attitudinal and ideological factors. Interestingly, comparisons involving the AKP constituency and CHP also show that Kurdish speakers are more inclined towards the CHP rather than the AKP. Similarly, in comparing the CHP with the GP, MHP and the undecided group we again see that Kurdish speakers tend toward CHP. In other words, Kurdish speakers tend toward DEHAP in comparison to all parties other than the CHP. However, Kurdish speakers are inclined to support the CHP in comparison to all other parties except the DEHAP. When CHP is compared with DEHAP then Kurdish speakers appear insignificantly inclined towards either one. Given the ideological closeness of the DEHAP and CHP along the left-right scale this is hardly surprising. Moreover, this may be an indication of a tactical preference by the Kurdish speakers to vote for the CHP knowing that their perhaps true first preference for DEHAP is not going to bring any seats in the parliament.

We also observe significant differences of party constituencies across the geographic regions we described above in chapter four. After controlling for the effects of other variables the dummy variable differentiating voters from different regions are most influential for the comparisons dealing with the AKP, and to a lesser extent with the CHP and MHP. We see from these comparisons that the CHP and AKP are clearly differentiable across our regions.

Economic Evaluations

The sociotropic retrospective evaluations, i.e. the dummy variable separating those who evaluate that over the past year, the government's economic policies have adversely affected Turkey as a whole, appears insignificant in explaining party choice in all comparisons. However, prospective evaluations of sociotropic or family's pocketbook type appear significant in 7 and 4 out of 21 comparisons respectively. Not surprisingly none of these significant cases (except the one with GP in comparison to MHP) involve a comparison with the MHP. Rather predominantly they involve a comparison with the GP and also the undecided group. For example, comparing the AKP with the GP, we see that while those who think that their family's economic situation will get worse tend toward the GP as opposed to the AKP; those who expect the economic fortunes for the whole country will get worse tend towards the AKP as opposed to the GP. Similarly, negative sociotropic prospective evaluations seem to push voters towards the DYP, as opposed to the GP, and towards the DYP as opposed to the CHP. Again for the case of comparisons with the DYP and the CHP, the GP and the MHP, and lastly the AKP and the undecided group, we see a low level of significance for the prospective evaluations. However, it is clear that for neither one of the two large parties of the November 2002 election, that is, the AKP and the CHP, do we observe a significant and large impact of economic evaluations, be it retrospective or prospective. In other words, despite expectations to the contrary, our micro-individual level evidence suggests that economic evaluations did not play a significant role in shaping the party choices of individuals especially for the two largest parties in the election in comparison with the other minor players in the last election. However, negative retrospective evaluations significantly push voter away from CHP and towards the AKP in their comparisons. Similarly the CHP and MHP have an advantage over the DYP from the retrospective pocketbook perspective. However, it seems clear that while economic evaluations are providing an advantage amongst parties of the opposition, no one seems to score any significant points against the incumbent parties' representative here; that is the MHP.

In hindsight, it is not surprising that retrospective evaluations are not effective in shaping party choice. As our descriptive discussion in the previous chapters shows, there was nearly a unanimous agreement as to the degree of impoverishing impact of the 2001 economic crisis during the tenure of the incumbent coalition of the DSP-MHP and ANAP. All incumbents' credibility was so badly tarnished that no punishment could be sensed for the incumbent parties in comparison to the others. One possible reason for prospective evaluations being significant for only a limited number of comparisons is again likely to be due to the devastating collapse of the credibility of the incumbent parties months before the election campaign.

It seems that neither the AKP, nor the CHP, were able to gather an advantage over the others in terms of their economic promises. In other words, our findings suggest that people did not really vote for either the AKP or the CHP on the basis of their expectations of a better economic future. However, the AKP seem to have an advantage over the CHP from a retrospective pocketbook perspective. In other words, in their mutual comparisons voters who had a negative evaluation of the past economic performance of the incumbents, and there were many of them as we discussed above in chapter 6, they tended to prefer the AKP over the CHP.

Economic matters could not get any worse than what the Turkish people have already experienced during the tenure of the DSP-MHP-ANAP coalition. Things could only get better irrespective of who may run the economy. In fact, it was perhaps clear to the people, in their simplistic gut feelings, that the management of the economy would not drastically change anyway, who ever may come to power. Economic evaluations seem to only matter in minor comparisons that involve the GP. There seems no significant economic evaluation basis for the success of the two largest gainers in the November 2002 election but only for the AKP in comparison to only the CHP.

Impact of Foreign Policy Issues

We included only two very boldly stated foreign policy issues in our estimations. Both have turned out to be of significance in many comparisons. Those who supported Turkey's membership in the EU, are more inclined to support the CHP, the DYP and to be undecided as opposed to a supporter of the AKP. In other words, despite its strong pro-EU position during its tenure, the AKP constituency does not appear to have a strong and clear tendency to support EU membership. In comparison, the CHP appears to be appealing to EU supporters in comparison not only to the AKP, but also to the GP and MHP. In no comparison does the MHP constituency appear to gather the EU supporters behind it. Supporters of EU membership appear to be behind the DYP in comparison to GP, but the undecided group is more inclined to be supportive of the EU cause compared to the GP. In other words, similar to the MHP, the GP as well seem to cater the Euro-skeptics.

Figure 7.3 shows the full spectrum of impact upon the odds ratios for all party comparisons. We observe that supporting Turkey's membership in the EU helps distinguish voters of parties not only from the opposing ends of the left-right ideological spectrum but also from within the right wing of the spectrum. For instance three of the largest impacts are observed in comparing the DYP with the MHP and the AKP, and in comparing the GP with the DYP. In other words, supporters of Turkey's membership in the EU are nearly six times more likely to be a DYP voter than an MHP voter. Similarly supporters of Turkey's membership in the EU are 4.1 times more likely to be a DYP voter than a GP voter and 3.6 times more likely to be a DYP voter than an AKP voter. Similarly the DYP attracts EU supporters compared to the DEHAP. In conclusion, the DYP seems to attract EU supporters much more than any other party of the right wing.

On the left wing, the CHP is attracting EU supporters in comparisons with the GP and MHP along with the AKP. In other words while the DYP and CHP seem to attract EU supporters, all other parties seem to have a predominantly euro skeptic constituency.

While the EU project does not seem appealing to the AKP constituency, closer ties with the Muslim world as opposed to the Western countries seem to be attractive to the AKP voters in most comparisons. When the AKP constituency is compared to the DEHAP, CHP, GP and the DYP, those who support closer ties with the Muslim world are more inclined towards the AKP. For the CHP's comparisons, only for the case of the MHP and the undecided group do the supporters of closer ties with the Muslim world appear to be inclined away from the CHP. For all other comparisons this issue appears insignificant in distinguishing the CHP from other parties. Similarly, comparisons with the MHP reveal that the MHP constituency, very much in line with that of the AKP, attracts those who prefer Muslim countries as opposed to Western countries. The same group also tends towards the undecided group as opposed to the GP.

Figure 7.4 shows the impact of support for Turkey, building closer ties with the Muslim world as opposed to Western countries, upon the odds ratio

Figure 7.3 Odds Ratio Plot for the supporters of Turkey's EU membership across all comparisons

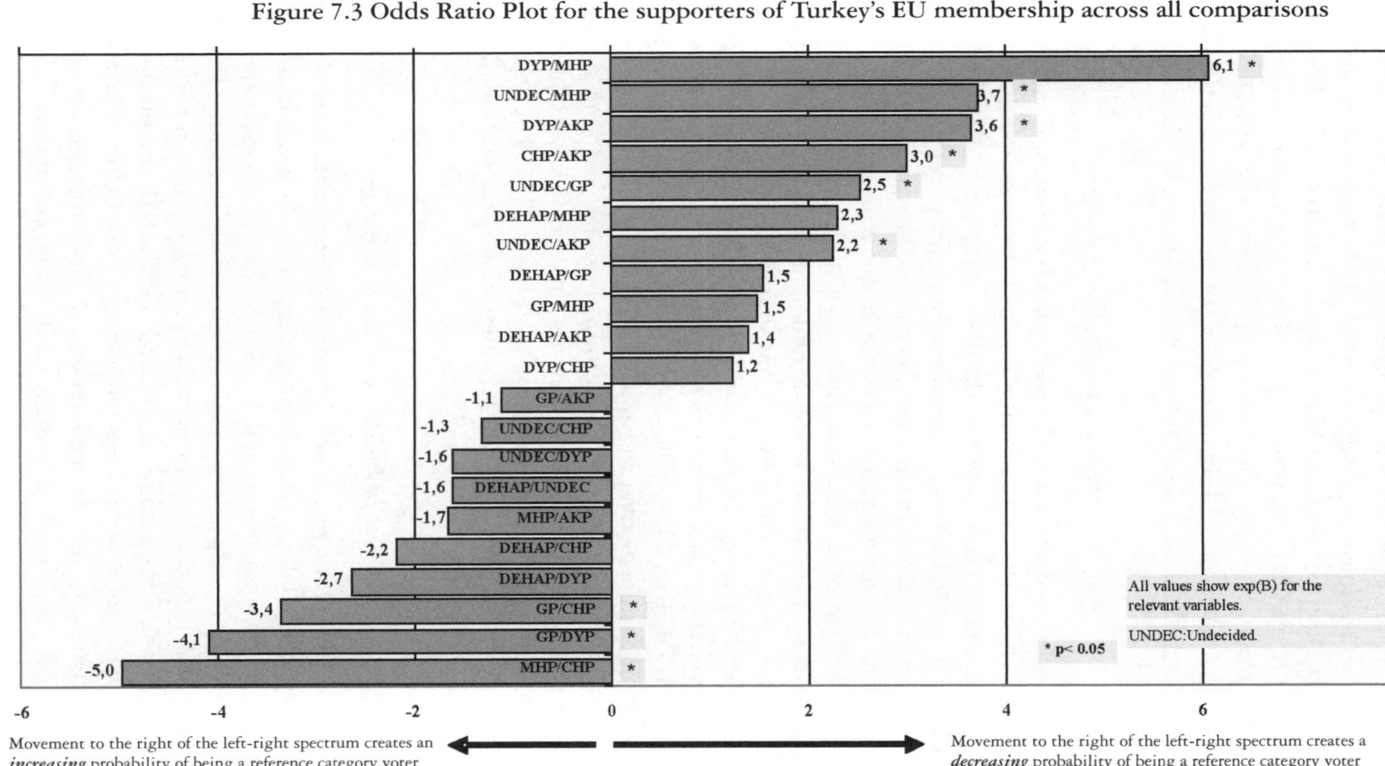

in all party comparisons. We see that statistically significant differentiation appears in comparisons involving mostly the MHP, AKP and the GP. Those who support closer ties with the Muslim world are attracted to the MHP in comparison to the CHP (2.3 times more), GP (2.7 times more) and the DYP (2.1 times more). Similarly, those who support closer ties with the Muslim world are 2.9 times more likely to be AKP voters compared to the GP and 2.2 times more likely to be AKP voters compared to the DYP.

Anger towards the Incumbent Coalition

We have underlined the level of anger towards the incumbent coalition parties during the election campaign due to their miserable performance facing the economic crisis as well as the devastating earthquakes that shook the country in 1999. However, anger towards the incumbents does not seem to be very determining in shaping party choices in different comparisons. We believe this is once again very similar to the lack of significant impact for the economic evaluations. Almost a unanimous anger seems to have been prevalent amongst the voters and thus finding a group that had a distinct party preference amongst angry voters was simply not possible.

What is striking is the observation that in only five comparisons out of 21 where a significant impact of anger factor is observed, the comparison involves the Kurdish DEHAP. Those who indicated that they were angry with the incumbent government tend to support DEHAP as opposed to the AKP, CHP, MHP, GP and the undecided group. In other words, if anger was effective in the November 2002 elections it seems to have vented through the mediation of the ethnic Kurdish issue used by DEHAP. For other party constituencies we observe no significant differentiating impact from the anger variable on party choice.

Interest in Politics and the Campaign

The general level of interest in politics and in particular the level of interest in the November 2002 election campaign appears to be a significant factor in 11 out of 21 comparisons and as such is the second most frequently observed impact upon party comparisons. Especially in distinguishing the CHP and AKP supporters from the other parties, interest in politics seem quite influential. Compared to the DEHAP, DYP, MHP and the undecided group, the CHP voters appear less interested in politics but more attentive to the election campaign. As the level of interest in the election campaign increases, the likelihood of being a CHP voter as opposed to one for

Figure 7.4 Odds Ratio Plot for the supporters of Turkey building closer ties with the Muslim world as opposed to the Western countries

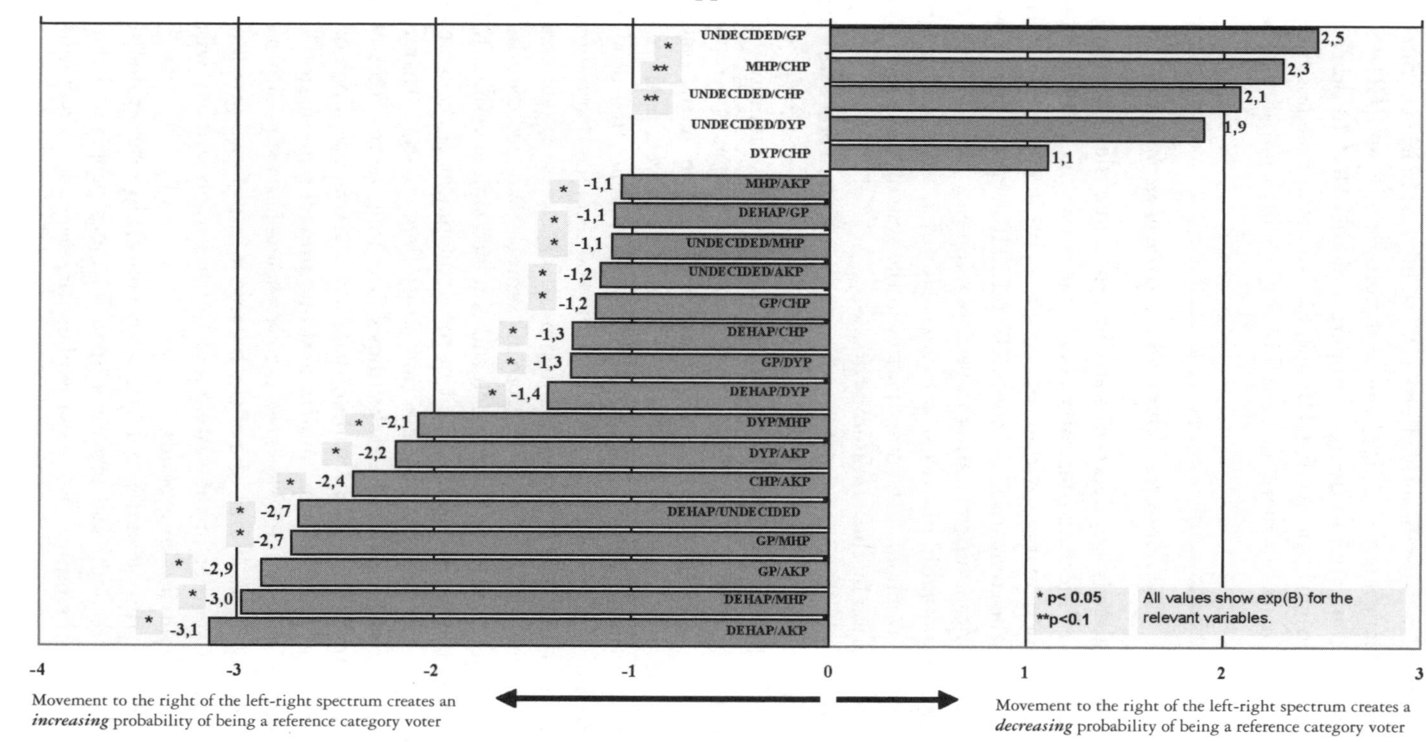

DEHAP is not significantly affected. With increasing level of interest in the election campaign the likelihood of being a GP and CHP supporter increases compared to being a supporter of the AKP. In other words, in comparison with the AKP, CHP and GP voters appear less interested in general politics but more interested in the specific campaign of November 2002.

Religious freedoms and the issue of turban ban

We have already pointed out that different dimensions of religiosity are effective in differentiating party constituencies at the extreme ends of the ideological orientations within the framework of the conventional left-right. Primarily, the comparisons of the AKP and CHP with the rest of the parties show significant differentiating impacts of religiosity measurements from the perspective of faith, practice or attitudes. However, more homogenous levels of religiosity amongst the other parties in the system lead to less significant differentiation by these measurements.

As part of the attitudinal predispositions of the voters we included a statement concerning the level of agreement with a statement that asserts support for the ongoing ban on turban in university campuses. This was a question first asked in the study of religiosity by Çarkoğlu and Toprak (2000). The same study included a series of questions concerning the evaluations of the state of religious freedoms in the country. Answers to these questions revealed that a significant portion of the respondents first of all saw that people in Turkey can not properly worship and secondly that religious people are under pressure. When asked to provide examples of such pressures, the turban and headscarf ban were given as examples. We used the same wording and sequence of the same question and obtained similar results. Kalaycıoğlu (2005) gives an in-depth account of the development of the issue of turban and uses our pre and post election study data to argue that religiosity primarily accounts for the evaluations concerning the freedoms of religious people. Interestingly, the turban issue never shows up as one of the most important issues of the country and our previous discussion above also reiterates this finding. However, it nevertheless has a special place amongst the salient issues of Turkish politics because it helps locate people and parties from one another in the system and touches upon a policy wise relevant activism on religious grounds.

We use this second set of questions concerning the evaluations about religious freedoms and pressures upon religious people and the examples given for these pressures as an explanatory variable in our multi-nomial analysis. The results are quite telling of the role this issue played in coming to power of the AKP after November 2002. First of all, it is very noticeable that these evaluations show up as significant only in comparing the AKP and CHP. For comparisons of other parties amongst themselves they are not significant. This is once again very much in line with our previous finding about the impact of religiosity on vote choice.

Secondly, the dummy variable separating those who indicate that people in Turkey can freely practice religion from those who disagree with this assertion shows up as significant with a positive coefficient for the comparisons of the AKP as the reference category and with a negative coefficient for the comparisons of the CHP as the reference category for a number of party constituencies. The implication of this pattern is that those respondents who agree with the assertion that people can freely practice their religion in Turkey tend to be supporters of the CHP, the DYP or remain undecided compared to being a supporter of the AKP. Similarly the same type of respondents who see freedoms for religious practice to be in place in Turkey tend to be supporters of the CHP as opposed to the DEHAP, GP or MHP. In short, compared to the AKP, GP, DEHAP and MHP, CHP voters tend to see freedoms of religious practice largely in place. Compared to the AKP, the DYP and the undecided group seem to agree with such a position. In other words, on the one side we have the CHP, DYP and the undecided group who tend to see practice of religious freedoms as non-problematic. On the other side we have the AKP, as opposed to primarily the CHP who see practice of religious freedoms as problematic.

When we look at the people who assert that religious people are under pressure and at the same time provide turban and headscarf ban as an example for such pressure we see that they are predominantly inclined towards the AKP, DEHAP, GP, DYP, MHP and the undecided group as opposed to the CHP. In other words, CHP voters seem to be alone in the party system in thinking that religious people are not pressured on the basis of the turban and headscarf issue.

Conclusion

Considering the totality of our results several important patterns become noticeable. First among these is that the multinomial framework that allows for an analysis of party to party comparisons in voter preferences yield significantly different results compared to previous methods. We, for instance, see that previously much stressed impact of religiosity on Turkish party choices may not be as important as we have once thought. Our analyses reveal that only at the two extreme ends of our ideological spectrum do we see important impact from religiosity. However, party choices between similar parties in between the two extreme ends are not greatly influenced by religiosity.

Nevertheless, as a category, the ideological predispositions tend to have a much more important impact upon party choice compared to demographic variables, economic evaluations, anger towards the incumbents and foreign policy issues. It seems that, the almost total collapse of the credibility of the incumbent parties in November 2002, led to a situation where economic evaluations and anger towards the incumbents are quite homogeneous and thus not helpful in distinguishing voter constituencies.

The impact of conventional left-right is by far the most important in distinguishing party constituencies. Next comes religiosity with its three different dimensions. However, our measures of nationalism and xenophobia are not at all of comparable importance in distinguishing parties. Religiosity as reflected in the attitudes and most importantly as reflected in the evaluation of the religious freedoms and the situation created around the turban ban appear to be most effective in separating the AKP from the CHP.

Similar to previous election experiences the predominant electoral victory of the AKP has its roots in the appeal of the party to the younger generations. The advantage of the MHP from the 1999 election in this respect now seems to have passed on to the AKP. The CHP's electoral picture reveals that not only is it not appealing to the young but also the CHP does not appear to have any significant advantage from the perspective of negative economic performance evaluations. The CHP seem to have distinct geographical advantages, a clear pro-EU stance and a distinct secular stand together with an appeal to the Kurdish ethnicity. However, the AKP seem to be appealing to the young, economically distressed, angry and the Euro skeptic masses at the time of the November 2002 election. Such a profile may be in quite a stark contrast to the present state of AKP supporters after the economy recuperated and after the AKP leadership has taken big domestic policy risks by portraying a clear and enthusiastic supporter of the EU cause. However, our analyses suggest that the new cleavage in Turkish politics around the issues related to the EU membership and the reforms that evolve within this project continue to shape the Turkish electoral scene.

It is also interesting to note that the issue of support for EU membership, and views on religious freedoms and whether or not religious people in Turkey are being oppressed act as litmus tests for differentiating the two extreme ends of the left-right ideological spectrum as well as distinguishing the AKP from the DYP which perhaps is potentially the most serious challenger to its electoral dominance in Turkish political scene. While the DYP and CHP maintain a clear pro-EU stance amongst its constituency the AKP at the time of the election seems to have appealed to Euro-skeptics more than Europhiles. The AKP also seems to have attracted voters who not only view religious freedoms as being curtailed but also assert that religious people are being oppressed in the country. The DYP, together with the CHP appear attractive to voters who disagree with those positions. For the CHP constituency this is not at all surprising. However, for the DYP constituency such an optimistic evaluation concerning religious freedoms is a signal of a major differentiation from the traditional peripheral constituency stands. In a sense the DYP portrays here a stance that is closer to the status quo on religious freedoms and the turban issue than the AKP constituency. As such, the DYP stands to play a critical role in the future debates concerning the resolution or normalization of the turban issue by being the only party with a clear status quo stance amongst the peripheral centre- right parties.

Appendix Chapter 7

Table 7A.1 Multi-nomial Logit Estimates of the Vote Intention Function

The Reference Category is AKP

	DEHAP			CHP			GP			Undecided			DYP			MHP		
	B	Sig.	Exp(B)	B	Sig.	Exp(B)	B	Sig.	Exp(B)	B	Sig.	Exp(B)	B	Sig.	Exp(B)	B	Sig.	Exp(B)
Intercept	1,23	0,60		0,30	0,81		0,77	0,53		–0,17	0,90		–6,84	0,00		–2,69	0,06	
Dummy variable for men	0,13	0,86	1,13	–0,60	0,06	0,55	–0,76	0,01	0,47	–1,35	0,00	0,26	–0,81	0,03	0,45	–0,52	0,16	0,59
Respondent's age	0,02	0,49	1,02	0,06	0,00	1,06	–0,01	0,40	0,99	0,04	0,00	1,04	0,04	0,00	1,04	0,02	0,16	1,02
Dummy variable for no-schooling	0,14	0,92	1,15	–1,23	0,16	0,29	1,15	0,15	3,15	–0,40	0,59	0,67	–0,73	0,49	0,48	–16,98	.	0,00
Dummy variable for primary education	–0,32	0,76	0,73	0,18	0,77	1,19	0,78	0,24	2,18	–1,07	0,08	0,34	0,16	0,84	1,17	–0,95	0,17	0,39
Dummy variable for highschool	–0,59	0,60	0,56	0,53	0,36	1,70	0,39	0,56	1,47	–1,31	0,04	0,27	0,10	0,90	1,10	0,54	0,41	1,72
Dummy variable for rural areas	–0,01	0,99	0,99	0,13	0,72	1,14	–0,16	0,60	0,85	–0,18	0,62	0,84	0,55	0,12	1,74	0,06	0,87	1,06
Dummy for those who report less than or equal to 350 million TL household income per month	0,00	0,40	1,00	0,00	0,30	1,00	0,00	0,16	1,00	0,00	0,56	1,00	0,00	0,26	1,00	0,00	0,85	1,00
Dummy variable for those who can speak Kurdish	2,64	0,00	14,06	1,42	0,02	4,12	0,20	0,69	1,22	–0,82	0,28	0,44	0,16	0,81	1,17	–0,15	0,85	0,86
Dummy variable for those who indicated that over the last year the economic policies followed by the incumbent government have adversely affected their family's finances	–0,02	0,99	0,98	–0,83	0,10	0,44	–0,46	0,30	0,63	–0,50	0,34	0,60	0,68	0,29	1,98	–0,54	0,27	0,58
Dummy variable for those who indicated that over the last year the economic policies followed by the incumbent government have adversely affected Turkey's economy	–1,09	0,34	0,34	–0,20	0,71	0,82	0,36	0,51	1,44	0,06	0,92	1,06	–0,71	0,24	0,49	–0,32	0,59	0,73
Dummy variable for those who indicated that over the next year their family's economic situation will get worse	0,73	0,36	2,08	0,23	0,62	1,26	1,04	0,01	2,82	0,10	0,84	1,10	–0,14	0,81	0,87	–0,23	0,69	0,80
Dummy variable for those who indicated that over the next year Turkey's economic situation will get worse	0,04	0,96	1,04	–0,26	0,58	0,77	–0,96	0,03	0,38	0,83	0,08	2,30	0,80	0,14	2,23	0,22	0,68	1,24

L-R self placement	–0,69	0,00	0,50	–0,71	0,00	0,49	–0,15	0,02	0,86	–0,19	0,01	0,82	0,07	0,41	1,07	0,30	0,00	1,35
Religiosity-Faith	–0,42	0,10	0,66	–0,43	0,03	0,65	–0,30	0,15	0,74	–0,01	0,97	0,99	–0,45	0,03	0,64	–0,23	0,36	0,79
Religiosity-Attitudes	–0,68	0,10	0,51	–1,27	0,00	0,28	–0,81	0,00	0,44	–0,93	0,00	0,40	–0,40	0,09	0,67	–0,26	0,24	0,77
Religiosity-Practice	–0,17	0,56	0,84	–0,62	0,00	0,54	–0,44	0,00	0,64	–0,31	0,07	0,73	–0,53	0,00	0,59	0,04	0,78	1,04
Belief in destiny	–0,02	0,61	0,98	0,00	0,93	1,00	–0,03	0,29	0,97	–0,01	0,84	0,99	–0,01	0,64	0,99	0,02	0,34	1,02
Self-evaluated religiosity	–0,12	0,36	0,88	–0,11	0,21	0,90	0,00	0,98	1,00	–0,16	0,07	0,85	0,04	0,70	1,04	–0,07	0,44	0,94
Xenophobia	0,21	0,48	1,24	0,20	0,29	1,22	0,22	0,18	1,24	0,60	0,00	1,81	0,42	0,03	1,51	0,01	0,98	1,01
Nationalism	–0,20	0,43	0,82	0,20	0,22	1,22	0,24	0,11	1,28	0,10	0,58	1,11	0,15	0,49	1,16	0,29	0,17	1,34
Political Inefficacy	0,21	0,53	1,23	0,07	0,66	1,07	0,13	0,35	1,14	0,42	0,01	1,52	0,40	0,02	1,49	–0,05	0,77	0,95
Dummy variable for those who support Turkey's membership in EU	0,32	0,64	1,37	1,10	0,01	3,00	–0,12	0,68	0,89	0,81	0,03	2,24	1,29	0,01	3,65	–0,51	0,12	0,60
Dummy variable for those who prefer that Turkey builds closer relations with the Muslim rather than the Western countries	–1,15	0,09	0,32	–0,88	0,01	0,41	–1,06	0,00	0,35	–0,15	0,68	0,86	–0,79	0,03	0,45	–0,06	0,88	0,95
Dummy variable for being angry to coalition partners DSP/MHP/ANAP	1,80	0,03	6,04	0,38	0,47	1,46	–0,25	0,61	0,78	–0,21	0,74	0,81	0,42	0,48	1,53	0,10	0,88	1,10
Interest in politics	0,23	0,53	1,25	–0,38	0,07	0,68	–0,42	0,02	0,66	0,14	0,51	1,15	0,44	0,03	1,55	0,20	0,34	1,22
Interest in the election campaign	–0,04	0,91	0,96	0,51	0,01	1,67	0,32	0,06	1,38	–0,26	0,18	0,77	–0,13	0,48	0,87	–0,08	0,71	0,93
Tactical voters	–0,94	0,12	0,39	0,15	0,63	1,16	0,14	0,59	1,15	0,14	0,64	1,16	0,29	0,37	1,34	–0,67	0,05	0,51
Dummy variable for those who indicate that people in Turkey can practice their religious practices freely	–0,34	0,56	0,71	1,04	0,01	2,82	0,02	0,94	1,02	0,83	0,02	2,28	0,85	0,02	2,34	0,22	0,52	1,24
Dummy variable for those people who give turban and headscarf ban as examples for pressures upon religious people	0,24	0,71	1,27	–1,31	0,00	0,27	0,05	0,86	1,05	0,24	0,50	1,27	–0,43	0,27	0,65	–0,31	0,41	0,74
Region 2 Western Anatolia	1,61	0,10	5,02	1,33	0,02	3,79	0,15	0,76	1,17	0,68	0,24	1,97	0,33	0,65	1,40	0,36	0,52	1,44
Region 3 Eastern Marmara	–14,79	.	0,00	1,26	0,01	3,54	0,87	0,04	2,39	–0,08	0,89	0,92	0,92	0,18	2,50	–0,41	0,50	0,67
Region 4–5 Aegean and Western Marmara	0,34	0,80	1,40	1,24	0,02	3,46	1,22	0,01	3,38	1,71	0,00	5,53	2,01	0,00	7,43	1,08	0,06	2,96
Region 6 Mediterranean	0,07	0,97	1,07	1,52	0,04	4,57	0,57	0,43	1,77	1,58	0,03	4,85	–0,37	0,78	0,69	–0,36	0,71	0,70
Region 7 Western Black Sea	3,60	0,02	36,53	1,87	0,08	6,50	2,43	0,00	11,41	–14,21	.	0,00	0,28	0,84	1,32	–14,03	.	0,00
Region 8 Centre Anatolia	–0,57	0,69	0,56	0,35	0,59	1,42	–0,06	0,90	0,94	0,07	0,92	1,07	0,30	0,68	1,35	–1,04	0,13	0,35
Region 9 Eastern Black Sea	–12,25	.	0,00	1,40	0,14	4,05	0,43	0,57	1,54	1,83	0,01	6,21	–0,32	0,80	0,73	0,07	0,93	1,08
Region 10 Southeastern Anatolia	1,85	0,10	6,33	0,17	0,85	1,18	0,11	0,86	1,12	–0,35	0,71	0,70	0,70	0,45	2,02	0,95	0,20	2,58
Region 11–12 Centre-east and North east Anatolia	–0,56	0,70	0,57	–0,08	0,95	0,93	–1,27	0,29	0,28	0,63	0,52	1,88	–0,73	0,60	0,48	–0,35	0,78	0,71

Table 7A.2 Multi-nomial Logit Estimates of the Vote Intention Function

	The Reference Category is CHP														
	DEHAP			GP			Undecided			DYP			MHP		
	B	Sig.	Exp(B)	B	Sig.	Exp(B)	B	Sig.	Exp(B)	B	Sig.	Exp(B)	B	Sig.	Exp(B)
Intercept	0,93	0,69		0,47	0,74		–0,47	0,76		–7,14	0,00		–2,99	0,09	
Dummy variable for men	0,73	0,30	2,07	–0,16	0,66	0,86	–0,75	0,05	0,47	–0,21	0,64	0,81	0,08	0,86	1,09
Respondent's age	–0,04	0,13	0,96	–0,07	0,00	0,93	–0,02	0,15	0,98	–0,02	0,30	0,98	–0,04	0,02	0,96
Dummy variable for no-schooling	1,37	0,33	3,93	2,38	0,02	10,81	0,83	0,37	2,30	0,51	0,68	1,66	–15,75	.	0,00
Dummy variable for primary education	–0,50	0,61	0,61	0,60	0,40	1,83	–1,25	0,05	0,29	–0,02	0,98	0,98	–1,13	0,17	0,32
Dummy variable for high school	–1,12	0,29	0,33	–0,14	0,84	0,87	–1,84	0,01	0,16	–0,43	0,61	0,65	0,01	0,99	1,01
Dummy variable for rural areas	–0,14	0,84	0,87	–0,29	0,48	0,75	–0,31	0,49	0,74	0,42	0,35	1,53	–0,08	0,88	0,93
Dummy for those who report less than or equal to 350 million TL household income per month	0,00	0,72	1,00	0,00	0,63	1,00	0,00	0,81	1,00	0,00	0,10	1,00	0,00	0,45	1,00
Dummy variable for those who can speak Kurdish	1,23	0,12	3,41	–1,21	0,06	0,30	–2,23	0,01	0,11	–1,26	0,13	0,29	–1,56	0,09	0,21
Dummy variable for those who indicated that over the last year the economic policies followed by the incumbent government have adversely affected their family's finances	0,81	0,48	2,25	0,37	0,50	1,44	0,32	0,60	1,38	1,51	0,04	4,53	0,29	0,64	1,34
Dummy variable for those who indicated that over the last year the economic policies followed by the incumbent government have adversely affected Turkey's economy	–0,89	0,44	0,41	0,57	0,37	1,76	0,27	0,69	1,30	–0,51	0,46	0,60	–0,11	0,88	0,89
Dummy variable for those who indicated that over the next year their family's economic situation will get worse	0,51	0,54	1,66	0,81	0,09	2,24	–0,13	0,81	0,88	–0,36	0,56	0,69	–0,46	0,50	0,63
Dummy variable for those who indicated that over the next year Turkey's economic situation will get worse	0,30	0,72	1,35	–0,70	0,17	0,50	1,09	0,04	2,97	1,06	0,09	2,88	0,47	0,47	1,61

L-R self placement	0,01	0,93	1,01	0,56	0,00	1,74	0,51	0,00	1,67	0,78	0,00	2,17	1,01	0,00	2,74
Religiosity-Faith	0,00	0,98	1,00	0,13	0,47	1,14	0,42	0,09	1,52	–0,02	0,90	0,98	0,19	0,48	1,21
Religiosity-Attitudes	0,58	0,17	1,79	0,45	0,07	1,57	0,34	0,21	1,40	0,87	0,00	2,38	1,00	0,00	2,72
Religiosity-Practice	0,45	0,16	1,57	0,18	0,38	1,20	0,31	0,15	1,37	0,09	0,67	1,10	0,66	0,00	1,94
Belief in destiny	–0,02	0,64	0,98	–0,03	0,36	0,97	0,00	0,90	1,00	–0,01	0,73	0,99	0,02	0,43	1,02
Self-evaluated religiosity	–0,02	0,89	0,98	0,10	0,26	1,11	–0,05	0,60	0,95	0,14	0,20	1,15	0,04	0,73	1,04
Xenophobia	0,02	0,96	1,02	0,02	0,92	1,02	0,40	0,08	1,49	0,22	0,36	1,25	–0,19	0,43	0,83
Nationalism	–0,40	0,11	0,67	0,04	0,82	1,04	–0,10	0,62	0,91	–0,05	0,83	0,95	0,09	0,71	1,10
Political Inefficacy	0,14	0,67	1,15	0,06	0,74	1,06	0,35	0,08	1,42	0,33	0,12	1,39	–0,12	0,58	0,89
Dummy variable for those who support Turkey's membership in EU	–0,78	0,27	0,46	–1,21	0,00	0,30	–0,29	0,55	0,75	0,20	0,74	1,22	–1,61	0,00	0,20
Dummy variable for those who prefer that Turkey builds closer relations with the Muslim rather than the Western countries	–0,26	0,70	0,77	–0,17	0,67	0,84	0,73	0,10	2,07	0,09	0,84	1,10	0,83	0,08	2,29
Dummy variable for being angry to coalition partners DSP/MHP/ANAP	1,42	0,08	4,14	–0,63	0,28	0,53	–0,59	0,39	0,55	0,04	0,95	1,04	–0,28	0,72	0,76
Interest in politics	0,61	0,09	1,84	–0,04	0,88	0,96	0,52	0,04	1,69	0,82	0,00	2,27	0,59	0,04	1,80
Interest in the election campaign	–0,55	0,12	0,58	–0,19	0,37	0,83	–0,78	0,00	0,46	–0,65	0,01	0,52	–0,59	0,03	0,56
Tactical voters	–1,09	0,07	0,34	–0,01	0,99	0,99	0,00	1,00	1,00	0,14	0,71	1,15	–0,81	0,06	0,44
Dummy variable for those who indicate that people in Turkey can practice their religious practices freely	–1,38	0,03	0,25	–1,02	0,01	0,36	–0,21	0,64	0,81	–0,19	0,71	0,83	–0,82	0,09	0,44
Dummy variable for those people who give turban and headscarf ban as examples for pressures upon religious people	1,55	0,02	4,71	1,37	0,00	3,92	1,55	0,00	4,73	0,88	0,10	2,41	1,01	0,06	2,74
Region 2 Western Anatolia	0,28	0,77	1,32	–1,18	0,06	0,31	–0,66	0,33	0,52	–1,00	0,24	0,37	–0,97	0,19	0,38
Region 3 Eastern Marmara	–16,05	.	0,00	–0,39	0,46	0,67	–1,35	0,05	0,26	–0,35	0,65	0,71	–1,67	0,03	0,19
Region 4–5 Aegean and Western Marmara	–0,90	0,50	0,41	–0,02	0,97	0,98	0,47	0,46	1,60	0,76	0,31	2,15	–0,16	0,83	0,85
Region 6 Mediterranean	–1,45	0,37	0,23	–0,95	0,26	0,39	0,06	0,94	1,06	–1,89	0,17	0,15	–1,88	0,10	0,15
Region 7 Western Black Sea	1,73	0,27	5,62	0,56	0,59	1,76	–16,08	.	0,00	–1,59	0,30	0,20	–15,90	.	0,00
Region 8 Centre Anatolia	–0,92	0,51	0,40	–0,41	0,56	0,66	–0,28	0,73	0,75	–0,05	0,96	0,96	–1,39	0,12	0,25
Region 9 Eastern Black Sea	–13,65	.	0,00	–0,96	0,38	0,38	0,43	0,68	1,53	–1,72	0,25	0,18	–1,32	0,26	0,27
Region 10 Southeastern Anatolia	1,68	0,16	5,36	–0,05	0,96	0,95	–0,52	0,66	0,59	0,53	0,66	1,71	0,78	0,48	2,18
Region 11–12 Centre-east and North east Anatolia	–0,48	0,76	0,62	–1,19	0,42	0,30	0,71	0,60	2,03	–0,65	0,70	0,52	–0,27	0,87	0,76

Table 7A.3 Multi-nomial Logit Estimates of the Vote Intention Function

The Reference Category is CHP

	DEHAP			GP			Undecided			DYP		
	B	Sig.	Exp(B)	B	Sig.	Exp(B)	B	Sig.	Exp(B)	B	Sig.	Exp(B)
Intercept	3,92	0,14		3,46	0,05		2,52	0,17		–4,15	0,04	
Dummy variable for men	0,65	0,41	1,91	–0,24	0,58	0,79	–0,83	0,08	0,44	–0,29	0,55	0,75
Respondent's age	0,00	0,98	1,00	–0,03	0,08	0,97	0,02	0,25	1,02	0,02	0,15	1,03
Dummy variable for no-schooling	15,12	0,00	3,7E+06	16,13	0,00	1,0E+07	14,58	.	2,1E+06	14,25	0,00	1,5E+06
Dummy variable for primary education	0,63	0,60	1,88	1,73	0,05	5,64	–0,12	0,88	0,88	1,11	0,24	3,03
Dummy variable for high school	–1,13	0,36	0,32	–0,16	0,86	0,86	–1,85	0,03	0,16	–0,44	0,64	0,64
Dummy variable for rural areas	–0,06	0,93	0,94	–0,21	0,62	0,81	–0,23	0,62	0,79	0,50	0,28	1,65
Dummy for those who report less than or equal to 350 million TL household income per month	0,00	0,46	1,00	0,00	0,26	1,00	0,00	0,68	1,00	0,00	0,28	1,00
Dummy variable for those who can speak Kurdish	2,79	0,01	16,32	0,35	0,69	1,42	–0,67	0,52	0,51	0,31	0,75	1,36
Dummy variable for those who indicated that over the last year the economic policies followed by the incumbent government have adversely affected their family's finances	0,52	0,66	1,68	0,08	0,89	1,08	0,03	0,96	1,03	1,22	0,10	3,39
Dummy variable for those who indicated that over the last year the economic policies followed by the incumbent government have adversely affected Turkey's economy	–0,77	0,54	0,46	0,68	0,35	1,97	0,38	0,62	1,46	–0,39	0,60	0,67
Dummy variable for those who indicated that over the next year their family's economic situation will get worse	0,96	0,32	2,62	1,26	0,05	3,54	0,33	0,64	1,39	0,09	0,90	1,10
Dummy variable for those who indicated that over the next year Turkey's economic situation will get worse	–0,18	0,85	0,84	–1,18	0,07	0,31	0,61	0,35	1,84	0,58	0,41	1,79

L-R self placement	–1,00	0,00	0,37	–0,45	0,00	0,64	–0,50	0,00	0,61	–0,23	0,04	0,79
Religiosity-Faith	–0,19	0,56	0,83	–0,06	0,83	0,94	0,22	0,50	1,25	–0,22	0,43	0,81
Religiosity-Attitudes	–0,42	0,36	0,66	–0,55	0,04	0,58	–0,66	0,02	0,51	–0,14	0,65	0,87
Religiosity-Practice	–0,21	0,51	0,81	–0,48	0,02	0,62	–0,35	0,10	0,70	–0,57	0,01	0,57
Belief in destiny	–0,04	0,39	0,96	–0,05	0,13	0,95	–0,03	0,46	0,97	–0,03	0,34	0,97
Self-evaluated religiosity	–0,06	0,71	0,94	0,07	0,53	1,07	–0,09	0,43	0,91	0,10	0,37	1,11
Xenophobia	0,21	0,54	1,23	0,21	0,35	1,23	0,59	0,02	1,80	0,41	0,10	1,51
Nationalism	–0,50	0,12	0,61	–0,05	0,83	0,95	–0,19	0,47	0,83	–0,14	0,61	0,87
Political Inefficacy	0,26	0,48	1,29	0,18	0,37	1,19	0,47	0,03	1,60	0,45	0,04	1,56
Dummy variable for those who support Turkey's membership in EU	0,83	0,26	2,28	0,39	0,33	1,48	1,31	0,00	3,72	1,80	0,00	6,06
Dummy variable for those who prefer that Turkey builds closer relations with the Muslim rather than the Western countries	–1,09	0,15	0,34	–1,00	0,02	0,37	–0,10	0,84	0,91	–0,73	0,13	0,48
Dummy variable for being angry to coalition partners DSP/MHP/ANAP	1,70	0,09	5,48	–0,35	0,64	0,71	–0,31	0,72	0,73	0,32	0,69	1,38
Interest in politics	0,02	0,95	1,02	–0,62	0,02	0,54	–0,06	0,82	0,94	0,23	0,38	1,26
Interest in the election campaign	0,04	0,92	1,04	0,40	0,11	1,49	–0,19	0,48	0,83	–0,06	0,82	0,94
Tactical voters	–0,27	0,69	0,76	0,81	0,04	2,24	0,81	0,06	2,25	0,96	0,03	2,60
Dummy variable for those who indicate that people in Turkey can practice their religious practices freely	–0,56	0,40	0,57	–0,20	0,63	0,82	0,61	0,18	1,84	0,63	0,18	1,88
Dummy variable for those people who give turban and headscarf ban as examples for pressures upon religious people	0,54	0,45	1,72	0,36	0,42	1,43	0,55	0,26	1,72	–0,13	0,80	0,88
Region 2 Western Anatolia	1,25	0,26	3,50	–0,21	0,77	0,81	0,32	0,68	1,37	–0,03	0,97	0,97
Region 3 Eastern Marmara	–14,38	.	0,00	1,28	0,07	3,58	0,32	0,69	1,38	1,32	0,13	3,75
Region 4–5 Aegean and Western Marmara	–0,74	0,60	0,47	0,14	0,84	1,14	0,63	0,40	1,87	0,92	0,26	2,51
Region 6 Mediterranean	0,43	0,82	1,53	0,93	0,41	2,53	1,94	0,08	6,93	–0,01	0,99	0,99
Region 7 Western Black Sea	17,63	0,00	4,5E+07	16,47	.	1,4E+07	–0,18	.	0,84	14,31	0,00	1,6E+06
Region 8 Centre Anatolia	0,47	0,76	1,59	0,97	0,23	2,65	1,11	0,23	3,03	1,34	0,16	3,83
Region 9 Eastern Black Sea	–12,33	.	0,00	0,36	0,73	1,43	1,75	0,08	5,76	–0,39	0,78	0,68
Region 10 Southeastern Anatolia	0,90	0,49	2,45	–0,84	0,37	0,43	–1,30	0,26	0,27	–0,25	0,83	0,78
Region 11–12 Centre-east and North east Anatolia	–0,21	0,91	0,81	–0,92	0,59	0,40	0,98	0,52	2,67	–0,38	0,83	0,69

Table 7A.4 Multi-nomial Logit Estimates of the Vote Intention Function

	The Reference Category is DYP									The Reference Category is GP						The Reference Category is Undecided		
	DEHAP			GP			Undecided			DEHAP			Undecided			DEHAP		
	B	Sig.	Exp(B)	B	Sig.	Exp(B)	B	Sig.	Exp(B)	B	Sig.	Exp(B)	B	Sig.	Exp(B)	B	Sig.	Exp(B)
Intercept	8,07	0,00		7,61	0,00		6,67	0,00		0,46	0,85		–0,94	0,56		1,40	0,58	
Dummy variable for men	0,93	0,23	2,55	0,05	0,90	1,05	–0,54	0,23	0,58	0,88	0,22	2,42	–0,59	0,13	0,55	1,48	0,05	4,37
Respondent's age	–0,03	0,38	0,97	–0,05	0,00	0,95	–0,01	0,74	0,99	0,03	0,31	1,03	0,05	0,00	1,05	–0,02	0,48	0,98
Dummy variable for no-schooling	0,86	0,60	2,37	1,88	0,12	6,52	0,33	0,78	1,39	–1,01	0,49	0,36	–1,55	0,10	0,21	0,54	0,71	1,71
Dummy variable for primary education	–0,48	0,69	0,62	0,62	0,50	1,86	–1,23	0,16	0,29	–1,10	0,33	0,33	–1,85	0,02	0,16	0,75	0,49	2,13
Dummy variable for high school	–0,69	0,59	0,50	0,29	0,76	1,33	–1,41	0,12	0,24	–0,97	0,42	0,38	–1,69	0,04	0,18	0,72	0,54	2,06
Dummy variable for rural areas	–0,56	0,43	0,57	–0,71	0,09	0,49	–0,73	0,10	0,48	0,15	0,83	1,16	–0,02	0,96	0,98	0,17	0,81	1,18
Dummy for those who report less than or equal to 350 million TL household income per month	0,00	0,25	1,00	0,00	0,06	1,00	0,00	0,25	1,00	0,00	0,96	1,00	0,00	0,54	1,00	0,00	0,64	1,00
Dummy variable for those who can speak Kurdish	2,48	0,01	11,97	0,04	0,96	1,04	–0,98	0,30	0,38	2,44	0,00	11,50	–1,02	0,22	0,36	3,46	0,00	31,82
Dummy variable for those who indicated that over the last year the economic policies followed by the incumbent government have adversely affected their family's finances	–0,70	0,58	0,50	–1,14	0,11	0,32	–1,19	0,11	0,30	0,44	0,70	1,56	–0,04	0,94	0,96	0,49	0,68	1,63
Dummy variable for those who indicated that over the last year the economic policies followed by the incumbent government have adversely affected Turkey's economy	–0,38	0,76	0,68	1,07	0,13	2,93	0,77	0,30	2,17	–1,45	0,22	0,23	–0,30	0,67	0,74	–1,15	0,35	0,32
Dummy variable for those who indicated that over the next year their family's economic situation will get worse	0,87	0,35	2,39	1,17	0,06	3,23	0,23	0,72	1,26	–0,30	0,72	0,74	–0,94	0,09	0,39	0,64	0,47	1,89
Dummy variable for those who indicated that over the next year Turkey's economic situation will get worse	–0,76	0,42	0,47	–1,76	0,01	0,17	0,03	0,96	1,03	1,00	0,25	2,72	1,79	0,00	5,99	–0,79	0,38	0,45

L-R self placement	–0,76	0,00	0,47	–0,22	0,02	0,80	–0,26	0,01	0,77	–0,54	0,00	0,58	–0,04	0,62	0,96	–0,50	0,00	0,61
Religiosity-Faith	0,03	0,91	1,03	0,15	0,46	1,17	0,44	0,11	1,55	–0,13	0,61	0,88	0,29	0,29	1,33	–0,41	0,16	0,66
Religiosity-Attitudes	–0,28	0,54	0,76	–0,41	0,13	0,66	–0,53	0,07	0,59	0,13	0,76	1,14	–0,11	0,66	0,89	0,25	0,58	1,28
Religiosity-Practice	0,36	0,28	1,43	0,09	0,68	1,09	0,22	0,31	1,24	0,27	0,40	1,31	0,13	0,52	1,14	0,14	0,68	1,15
Belief in destiny	–0,01	0,86	0,99	–0,01	0,72	0,99	0,01	0,85	1,01	0,00	0,94	1,00	0,02	0,58	1,02	–0,02	0,75	0,98
Self-evaluated religiosity	–0,16	0,31	0,85	–0,04	0,73	0,96	–0,19	0,09	0,82	–0,12	0,40	0,88	–0,16	0,12	0,86	0,03	0,83	1,03
Xenophobia	–0,20	0,55	0,82	–0,20	0,39	0,82	0,18	0,47	1,20	0,00	0,99	1,00	0,38	0,09	1,46	–0,38	0,25	0,68
Nationalism	–0,35	0,26	0,70	0,09	0,69	1,10	–0,05	0,85	0,96	–0,44	0,10	0,64	–0,14	0,50	0,87	–0,31	0,29	0,74
Political Inefficacy	–0,19	0,60	0,83	–0,27	0,18	0,76	0,02	0,92	1,02	0,08	0,81	1,09	0,29	0,13	1,34	–0,21	0,55	0,81
Dummy variable for those who support Turkey's membership in EU	–0,98	0,23	0,38	–1,41	0,01	0,24	–0,49	0,39	0,61	0,43	0,54	1,54	0,92	0,03	2,52	–0,49	0,51	0,61
Dummy variable for those who prefer that Turkey builds closer relations with the Muslim rather than the Western countries	–0,36	0,63	0,70	–0,27	0,53	0,76	0,63	0,18	1,89	–0,09	0,90	0,92	0,90	0,03	2,47	–0,99	0,18	0,37
Dummy variable for being angry to coalition partners DSP/MHP/ANAP	1,38	0,15	3,96	–0,67	0,33	0,51	–0,63	0,42	0,53	2,05	0,02	7,75	0,04	0,96	1,04	2,01	0,04	7,45
Interest in politics	–0,21	0,60	0,81	–0,86	0,00	0,42	–0,30	0,26	0,74	0,65	0,09	1,91	0,56	0,02	1,75	0,09	0,82	1,09
Interest in the election campaign	0,10	0,81	1,10	0,45	0,04	1,57	–0,13	0,59	0,88	–0,36	0,34	0,70	–0,58	0,01	0,56	0,23	0,56	1,25
Tactical voters	–1,23	0,06	0,29	–0,15	0,69	0,86	–0,15	0,72	0,86	–1,08	0,08	0,34	0,00	0,99	1,00	–1,08	0,09	0,34
Dummy variable for those who indicate that people in Turkey can practice their religious practices freely	–1,19	0,08	0,30	–0,83	0,05	0,44	–0,02	0,96	0,98	–0,36	0,56	0,70	0,81	0,04	2,24	–1,17	0,08	0,31
Dummy variable for those people who give turban and headscarf ban as examples for pressures upon religious people	0,67	0,35	1,95	0,49	0,28	1,63	0,67	0,17	1,96	0,18	0,78	1,20	0,19	0,65	1,21	0,00	1,00	1,00
Region 2 Western Anatolia	1,28	0,28	3,60	–0,18	0,83	0,84	0,34	0,69	1,41	1,46	0,16	4,30	0,52	0,44	1,69	0,94	0,38	2,55
Region 3 Eastern Marmara	–15,70	.	0,00	–0,05	0,95	0,95	–1,00	0,23	0,37	–15,66	.	0,00	–0,95	0,14	0,39	–14,70	.	0,00
Region 4–5 Aegean and Western Marmara	–1,67	0,25	0,19	–0,79	0,28	0,46	–0,30	0,71	0,74	–0,88	0,52	0,41	0,49	0,42	1,63	–1,37	0,33	0,25
Region 6 Mediterranean	0,44	0,83	1,55	0,94	0,51	2,56	1,95	0,16	7,02	–0,50	0,77	0,61	1,01	0,26	2,74	–1,51	0,38	0,22
Region 7 Western Black Sea	3,32	0,09	27,69	2,16	0,13	8,65	–14,49	.	0,00	1,16	0,46	3,20	–16,65	.	0,00	17,81	0,00	5,44E+07
Region 8 Centre Anatolia	–0,88	0,57	0,42	–0,37	0,66	0,69	–0,24	0,80	0,79	–0,51	0,73	0,60	0,13	0,86	1,14	–0,64	0,67	0,53
Region 9 Eastern Black Sea	–11,94	.	0,00	0,75	0,59	2,12	2,14	0,11	8,52	–12,69	.	0,00	1,39	0,13	4,02	–14,08	.	0,00
Region 10 Southeastern Anatolia	1,14	0,41	3,14	–0,59	0,58	0,55	–1,05	0,40	0,35	1,73	0,15	5,66	–0,47	0,66	0,63	2,20	0,11	9,02
Region 11–12 Centre-east and North east Anatolia	0,17	0,93	1,18	–0,54	0,76	0,58	1,36	0,38	3,89	0,71	0,69	2,03	1,90	0,19	6,68	–1,19	0,47	0,30

8

CONCLUSION: PROSPECTS FOR TURKISH ELECTORAL POLITICS

The coming to power of the AKP as a single-party government in the aftermath of the November 2002 general election was seen by many as a turning point in many respects. Although Turkey did not have a single party government since the 1991 general elections, the ideological character of party vote shares was an outcome of a trend of nearly fifteen years. Since 1987 the centre of the Turkish ideological spectrum was already in decline. Center-right more than the centre-left seemed to be continually loosing ground in successive general elections. In response to such a decline and partially as a consequence of it, the once marginal right-of-centre pro-Islamist and nationalist parties were on the rise. By more than doubling its vote share the MHP became a partner in a three-party coalition government in the aftermath of the 1999 elections. However, as this coalition failed to deliver any successful policy during its tenure, the appeal of the right-of-center parties could easily focus on the only credible, untried and fashionably conservative right-of-center party; the AKP.

Although in hindsight such a development may not be very surprising, many questions surfaced in the public debate about the new government. How similar was the AKP to earlier pro-Islamist parties? To what extend was the economic crisis responsible for the rising electoral appeal of the new generation pro-Islamist in the AKP? To what extent is the AKP's rise an outcome of increased ideological appeal of conservative Islamism?

Our analyses provide answers to a large number of such questions concerning the reasons as to why certain developments have taken place at the electoral scene of November 2002. They are equally useful in delineating the potential paths the Turkish electorate could follow over the next couple of years.

Our focus on the November 2002 has a larger theoretical context that evolved around fundamental questions concerning political participation in the country. We first looked into the macro-level conventional participation indicator of turnout in elections. Periodic patterns arise in turnout rates over the last more than half a century of elections that impede us from evaluating participation rates in elections in a homogeneous manner. Among the three distinct periodic dimensions in Turkish turnout rates across provinces the first four elections of 1950 to 1961 comprise the first period. In this period pockets of high turnout in western provinces come together with central east and eastern Anatolian provinces. The following four elections during 1965–1977 period the high turnout province region gets smaller and the relatively low socio-economic development regions of the central and eastern Anatolia region rank relatively "high" in their turnout rates compared to most of the rest of the country. More striking finding is that the six elections of the post-1980 period clearly show that east and south-eastern Anatolia regions of the least developed provinces as a compact region score "low" in their turnout rates relative to the rest of the country. In short, periodic as well as geographic variation in turnout rates forms the basis of turnouts in modern Turkish elections.

Political participation in Turkey in conventional as well as unconventional forms has been quite dynamic and vigorous in certain aspects and comparable to the larger western democratic experience. Voting, campaigning, debating, discussing and deliberating political issues with the intent of finding solutions for them, contacting political authorities have largely been used by the masses over the last more than a century. Similarly, protest potential has shown an increasing trend in frequency as well as variety over the years. Petitions, boycotts, legal demonstrations, and wildcat strikes have all been on the increase throughout the 1990s, while such potentially violent acts as occupation of buildings are on the decline. It is remarkable that despite legal restrictions on conventional and most unconventional acts of participation, Turkish performance in both have been quite comparable with the western democracies. The most recent legal liberalization within the framework of the adjustments for the Copenhagen political criteria should only add dynamism to this phenomenon.

We believe that a considerable experience has been accumulated in the country for the application of political resources to pressure governments and influence political decisions. Turkish citizens seem to use such skills proficiently and effectively which makes the whole party system a very competitive and vigorous political competition environment. The maturation of a culture of pluralism has gained considerable momentum within especially the EU adjustment process that the country is going thru. Within an economically and politically stable environment such a development should prove to gain in effectiveness and vitality. Our analyses also point out that while religiosity is not a significant factor in the determination of conventional political participation, it has a decreasing impact upon unconventional participation or protest potential. This factor is one of the most important characteristics of the pro-Islamist movement that also underlies behind the moderation potential of the AKP government.

A major question that occupied intellectual circles in Turkey as well as abroad in the aftermath of the November 2002 election was, and still is, about the ideological character of the AKP. The usual analysis of the intellectual heritage indicates a clear affinity to the National View (*Milli Görüş*) wherein originated the MNP and MSP in the pre-1980 period and the RP-FP-SP emanated in the post-1980 era.[1] Our analyses also provide a number of clues as to the ideological character of the AKP together with several important questions about Turkish voting behavior in general. First among these concerns the nature of ideological competition in Turkey. We see that conventional left-right ideological divide is still one of the most important factors that shape party choice decisions in Turkey. Despite speculative arguments to the contrary, we find no evidence that the AKP had a centrist constituency in the November 2002 elections. Persistently in all our descriptive observations, as well as more sophisticated statistical analyses, the AKP constituency turned out to be closer to the right-end of the left-right ideological spectrum being only second to the nationalist MHP. Religiosity, nationalist and xenophobic attitudes are only secondary in shaping the decision to vote for any given party. This again is in line with the moderate ideological character of the rising right-of-center in the country.

Despite a number of previous analyses, some of which were undertaken in the past by ourselves, we observe that the new multi-nomial regression technique we adopted here reveals a peculiar aspect of the impact of religiosity in Turkish electoral politics. That concerns the limited and selective impact of religiosity upon party choice. We see that religiosity and mostly its attitudinal dimension is effective in differentiating the two "winners" of the election at the opposing ends of the ideological spectrum. Voters of the AKP and the CHP are distinguishable on the basis of religiosity from the rest of the parties in the system as well as from one another. However, other parties of the system are not easily distinguishable from one another on the basis of religiosity. This is significant because it tells us that our previous diagnoses that religiosity helps distinguish all parties in the system in comparison to all of the rest of the parties in the system has to be qualified in light of this finding. Party-to-party comparisons of the multi-nomial analysis allows us to separate party couples wherein religiosity is helpful in distinguishing one from the other and other party couples for which it is not useful. In short, the AKP seems to have attracted more religious people especially when compared to those of the CHP. However, for the rest of the system parties of the right-wing its constituency's religiosity is not a factor that helps us diagnose the AKP constituency from the rest of the parties.

As noted above, in contrast to the 1999 election, analyses suggest that the November 2002 election was not so much influenced by nationalistic and xenophobic attitudes. However, simple choices concerning Turkey's membership in the EU or Turkey's foreign policy towards the Muslim world and the West appear more effective in distinguishing party constituencies from one another. This is not only in line with earlier diagnoses asserting that the issue of the EU is here to stay as a new salient issue that reshapes the political alliances in the country and that it does not only reflect a long-term choice about Turkey's foreign policy but rather one about a new domestic agenda built on the basis of reform for fulfilling the Copenhagen political and economic criteria.[2] In this respect it is noticeable that the DYP stands out as the only party of the peripheral right-wing in Turkish political scene with a constituency having a distinctly pro-EU stance together with the centrist CHP. The AKP however, appears to have attracted constituencies that was not particularly supportive of Turkey's membership in the EU at the time of the November 2002 election. We should note here however, that the tenure of AKP appears to have been successful in changing the stance of the pro-Islamist constituencies in favor of the EU membership.

Our analyses also suggest that generational differences and the differences between men and women in Turkey are still quite effective in distinguishing party constituencies in Turkey. However, education levels appear significant in a much smaller number of party-to-party comparisons. Kurdish speakers are attracted almost solely to the DEHAP and the CHP in comparison to the other parties. This can be taken as a reflection of the isolation of the Kurdish constituencies in the party system. Our pre-election study did not explicitly attempt to diagnose Alevi identity. However, on the basis of our post-election survey we see that Alevi community is comparably isolated in their support for the CHP. Nevertheless, Çarkoğlu (2005) reports that there obviously are Alevis that support parties other than the CHP yet their numbers are not expected to be of significance among the Hanefi-Sunni pro-Islamist parties.

Despite the fact that the Turkish economy has gone through the worst economic crisis of the Republican era in nearly two years prior to the November 2002 election, we find very little in support of the economic voting hypotheses. Neither retrospective nor prospective motivations seem to shape the voters' preferences especially for the two largest vote getters in November 2002. We attribute this to the almost unanimous negative evaluations and an almost complete depletion of the credibility of the incumbent as well as the overall total collapse of the sum of the centrist opposition parties. Our explicit inclusion of the anger factor in voting decision also leads to a similar conclusion. Voters look angry in our descriptive analyses; however they are indistinguishable from one another in terms of their anger towards the incumbents. As a result, neither anger nor economic evaluations appear significant in distinguishing parties from one another on party-to-party comparisons.

Perhaps the most important finding in our analyses together with the new qualification of the impact of religiosity on voting decisions concerns the impact of the evaluations concerning freedoms of religious practice and evaluation of oppression upon religious people. We see in these evaluations that there is a large segment of the voters who believe that there are limitations upon religious practices and oppression upon religious people. A significant group also gives the turban and headscarf ban as the example of oppression upon religious people. We also see once again that these evaluations help distinguish the AKP, DYP and CHP from not only one another but also from the rest of the party constituencies in the party system. In other words, while the AKP and CHP are opposed to one another on everything that is related to religiosity and especially here on the issue of religious freedoms and the turban ban, the rest of the party constituencies (with the noticeable exception of the DYP) are mostly indistinguishable from one another. This is a clear sign of potential, if not actual, polarization. The CHP looks mostly isolated on these issues from the rest of the party system. The fact that the CHP and DYP appear similar in their constituency orientations concerning evaluations of religious freedoms is potentially very significant. This is a clear sign of break in the peripheral tradition which was carried from the days of the DP into the modern times by the AP and DYP leadership. The DYP constituency appears in agreement with the CHP in their evaluations of the state of religious freedoms and thus has a clear optimist and pro-status quo stance while the AKP constituency appears to take a critical challenging stance on these issues.

The AKP appears to have attracted electoral support from a constituency who predominantly have a pessimistic negative evaluation of the state of religious freedoms in the country and who show turban and headscarf ban as the predominant examples of oppressions upon the religious people. This issue clearly has a litmus test capacity for the credibility of the AKP leadership who will be pressured to deliver policy ameliorations appealing to the religiously sensitive Sunni constituencies. Polarization on this issue and ultimate failure of the AKP government to deliver on this policy dimension is thus likely to benefit the DYP, who can hence adopt a more palatable, status quo oriented position on the issue and build its support bases among the peripheral constituency on the basis of more easily manageable and still conservative policy stances. In other words, by not leaving the CHP alone, opposing the AKP on the issue of turban, the DYP could be signaling the continued potential of the periphery for continual electoral success in case of failure in AKP government.

In short, the November 2002 election is a step in at least two decade long progression towards electoral dominance of the right-of-center pro-Islamist forces. The collapse of the center right against the pressures of the pro-Islamist movement was in the making for more than a decade. However, the AKP which replaced the pro-Islamist old-guard is not yet ideologically consolidated with a coherent and solidified electoral backing. The party organization has not yet experienced any real inner struggles for leadership. However, it is well-known that the AKP organization is nowhere near to being a homogenous entity under strict leadership control of Tayyip Erdoğan. Accordingly, the leadership is risking a lot in their commitment to EU related reforms in the country since these controversial moves are alienating an important segment of their own, within the party ranks, as well as amongst the opposition. One reason for such a commitment might be the realization on their part that only the EU with its consolidated democratic institutional backing can provide a ground for the survival of an even moderate pro-Islamist party against the staunch secularists in the country. Second and much more *real politique* reason concerns the knife edge economic balances in the country that so tightly have linked its survival to the anchoring of the Turkish economy to the EU. If any break in this policy is diagnosed on the horizon, the economic balances will tend to worsen thus risking any political chance that the AKP has for longer term. In short, the EU may not be a love at first sight for the AKP leadership but perhaps more like a sensible marriage of necessity and reason.

The AKP looks a lot like the ANAP of the early 1980s with its mixed bag of ideological orientation and pragmatism.[3] The party looks more like a coalition of conservative as well as liberal fractions of the centre-right tradition rather than a unified and coherent elite grouping. The charismatic leadership of Erdoğan's skillful steering of the younger generation pro-Islamists away from the dogmatic and stubborn challenges of Necmettin Erbakan's older guards of the movement may not be enough to keep the party together especially facing the next presidential elections in the Spring of 2007. Going into the presidential election the AKP leadership is more likely to be pressured and possibly cornered into making concessions concerning the turban issue. Such pressures are primarily intended to break the party apart into its smaller constituent parts. In other words, given the challenges to the AKP from within the party system, and especially from a liberal right-wing opposition, the likelihood of the AKP to remain a solid and clear right-of-center party decrease. So, the AKP may never ideologically become a new ANAP, however, its historical experience in being eroded into smaller party constituencies may be repeated for the case of the AKP..

The AKP's tenure for the last three years has been primarily very successful especially on economic and foreign policy grounds. It is true that in both policy areas crises may not be too far removed from the agenda. However, compared to the coalition government that preceded the AKP, the economy has been quite healthy and after all roller coaster changes, the negotiations have started with the EU for full membership. Such a successful move has effectively pushed the main opposition party CHP to a defensive position on especially the EU related issues. The AKP was effective in transforming itself as well as its own mass following in support of the EU cause while the CHP has consistently projected a Euro-skeptic and almost an anti-EU position. Such big change is indeed quite surprising and can only show the effectiveness of the AKP leadership in convincing themselves as well as their following about the political worth of the EU cause.

Three issues that still remain to be problematic and potentially quite damaging to the AKP's long-term vitality are first the continuing conflict in Cyprus that has the potential of pushing the negotiations with the EU off the track. Second, is the uncooperative and conflict ridden Kurdish leadership within the country who may spoil the lasting peaceful developments in the southeastern provinces and thus push the AKP into a tougher and uncompromising stands with respect to ethnic cultural rights in the country again raising red flags all over the EU scene. Last is a potential conflict in the making with the secularist establishment and its intellectuals that risk revitalizing their dormant electoral bases of support who have shifted away towards inactivism and marginal movements. We leave a more in depth discussion these issues to a later point when solid data instead of speculation will become available. However, what is clear from this picture is that the political future of the AKP is an intrinsic part of the developments both at home as well as abroad that are directly linked to dynamics within the EU and Turkey's bid for full membership therein. More than ever, Turkish domestic politics is now integrated to developments in Europe both economically as well as politically. However, this does not mean that Turkish domestic politics is now an integral part of European politics. The first term, if there ever will be another, of the AKP government may just be a prelude to making the country an integral part of the European political and economic dynamics.

APPENDIX

SAMPLE DESIGN

All analyses in this book were conducted with two kinds of data. One is macro, provincial level turnout rates or election results. The other is micro, individual level survey data. While our macro-level data is collected for all fourteen general elections since 1950 our survey data comes from a panel study comprising of a pre-election survey in October 2002 followed by a post-election survey January and February 2003.

Sample Design

Our pre-election sample was designed for a total of 2000 face-to-face interviews. For post-election survey all 2000 original interviewees were contacted for a second time. After two trials, 971 of these were successfully interviewed for a second time. A control sample of comparable design was also derived for a target sample size of 1000 interviews.

At the first stage of our sample selection we factor analyzed district level election returns for 1991, 1995 and 1999 elections and 8 dimensions were derived from this analysis accounting for 69.6% of the total variation. Factor solution for this exercise is reported in Table A.1 below. It is remarkable that clear patterns of partisan geographic dimensions emerge from this analysis. At the second stage, we cluster analyzed the factor scores for all districts and obtained 20 clusters of districts as reported in Table A.2 below. Our target sample size of 2000 interviews is then distributed to these clusters according to clusters' share of voters in each cluster. We then selected 60 districts wherein our interviews were to be conducted. These 60 districts are allocated to districts again in accordance to clusters' share in total eligible voters.

In the next stage we selected the districts from within each cluster in accordance to probability proportionate to size (PPS) principle. Once the districts for each cluster are determined, the total numbers of interviews for these districts are once again determined according to PPS. For each cluster rural and urban voter shares are applied to all selected districts in a uniform manner. As such, we obtained for each cluster, and each district, the total numbers of interviews to be carried out in urban and rural settlements.

For the urban settlements we decided to carry out 2 interviews per street and 3 streets are selected per neighborhood. As such, 6 interviews were carried out in each neighborhood. The selection of streets was based on the Ministry

Table A2.1 Dimensions of District Level Election Outcomes, 1991–1999
Geographic Pattern Dimensions

	RP/FP	DSP	CHP	Extr-left	MHP vs Hadep	ANAP	DYP	Independents
	1	2	3	4	5	6	7	8
Explained variation (%)	*11,7*	*9,7*	*9,1*	*8,7*	*8,4*	*7,9*	*7,4*	*6,8*
1995 Elections RP	**–0,87**	–0,22	–0,25	–0,11	–0,08	–0,06	–0,15	0,01
1999 Elections FP	**–0,84**	–0,16	–0,25	–0,16	0,01	0,00	–0,18	0,00
1991 Elections RP	**–0,81**	–0,22	–0,22	–0,01	–0,26	–0,06	–0,16	–0,02
1999 Elections BBP	**–0,66**	–0,08	0,09	0,06	0,03	–0,09	–0,04	–0,06
1995 Elections DSP	0,35	**0,87**	0,02	0,01	0,05	–0,04	–0,03	–0,18
1991 Elections DSP	0,14	**0,85**	–0,07	0,16	0,03	0,02	–0,04	–0,16
1999 Elections DSP	0,43	**0,80**	0,16	–0,06	0,10	0,05	0,05	–0,17
1995 Elections CHP	0,15	–0,01	**0,90**	0,00	–0,04	–0,16	0,00	0,05
1999 Elections CHP	0,18	–0,09	**0,84**	–0,03	–0,03	–0,21	–0,13	0,05
1999 Elections ÖDP	0,14	0,27	**0,61**	0,04	0,02	0,09	–0,18	–0,08
1991 Elections SHP	0,34	–0,31	**0,42**	0,10	0,33	–0,29	–0,26	0,18
1991 Elections SP	0,02	0,08	–0,04	**0,82**	0,10	0,10	0,01	0,10
1999 Elections SI˙P	–0,07	0,05	–0,15	**0,77**	0,21	–0,03	0,12	–0,03
1995 Elections I˙P	0,18	0,01	0,12	**0,74**	–0,17	–0,07	–0,07	0,15
1999 Elections I˙P	0,07	–0,04	0,09	**0,73**	–0,22	–0,05	0,10	–0,07
1999 Elections EMEP	–0,11	0,06	0,35	**0,39**	0,11	–0,01	–0,04	–0,26
1999 Elections MHP	–0,09	–0,14	–0,08	0,01	**–0,87**	–0,08	0,07	–0,23
1995 Elections MHP	0,08	–0,22	–0,05	0,07	**–0,82**	–0,21	–0,02	–0,15
1995 Elections HADEP	0,25	–0,43	–0,27	0,11	**0,53**	–0,30	–0,43	0,12
1999 Elections HADEP	0,23	–0,40	–0,31	0,09	**0,51**	–0,30	–0,42	0,17
1999 Elections DTP	0,11	–0,21	–0,03	0,02	**0,32**	–0,03	0,09	–0,14
1995 Elections ANAP	0,00	0,02	–0,09	–0,07	0,02	**0,88**	–0,05	–0,10
1991 Elections ANAP	0,00	–0,03	–0,13	0,06	–0,06	**0,79**	–0,09	–0,04
1999 Elections ANAP	0,28	0,08	–0,03	–0,03	0,24	**0,75**	–0,04	–0,06
1995 Elections DYP	0,42	0,10	0,02	0,01	0,07	–0,07	**0,77**	–0,06
1999 Elections DYP	0,05	–0,18	–0,18	0,11	0,03	–0,11	**0,77**	0,02
1991 Elections DYP	0,26	0,04	–0,30	0,05	–0,14	–0,10	**0,66**	–0,17
1991 Elections Independents	0,06	0,01	0,16	0,09	–0,01	–0,08	0,04	**0,81**
1995 Elections Independents	0,02	–0,13	–0,07	–0,01	0,09	–0,07	–0,11	**0,66**
1999 Elections Independents	–0,07	–0,16	–0,02	–0,06	0,09	–0,02	–0,01	**0,62**
1995 Elections YDH	0,11	–0,13	–0,12	0,29	0,22	–0,08	–0,20	**0,44**

Extraction Method: Principal Component Analysis.
Rotation Method: Varimax with Kaiser Normalization.
Rotation converged in 61 iterations.

Table A.2 Clusters of Factor Scores from the Analysis of District Level Election Outcome Dimensions

	CLUSTERS									
	1	2	3	4	5	6	7	8	9	10
RP/FP factor score	0,32	–0,25	1,01	–0,23	0,59	0,13	0,41	1,18	–1,65	0,86
DSP factor score	0,30	–1,14	0,20	–0,45	–1,39	–0,31	–0,27	–1,43	–0,22	1,26
CHP factor score	0,07	5,35	0,58	1,75	–0,66	–0,35	0,04	–0,53	–0,40	1,43
Extreme left factor score	–0,14	0,47	6,39	–0,02	–0,44	–0,06	0,04	1,72	–0,20	1,81
MHP vs HADEP factor score	0,01	0,83	–1,58	–0,26	1,38	–1,45	–0,07	1,30	0,04	–1,06
ANAP factor score	1,35	–0,75	0,59	–0,19	–0,54	–0,39	–0,08	–1,02	–0,07	–0,73
DYP factor score	–0,36	–0,44	–0,82	–0,53	–0,70	–0,43	1,25	–1,69	0,08	–0,36
Independents factor score	–0,10	–0,56	8,65	–0,28	0,36	–0,20	–0,21	0,79	0,00	13,10
Number of Cases in each Cluster	88	7	1	65	34	132	179	10	105	2
% share in total voters	7	0	0	9	3	12	13	1	7	0
# of districts if a total of 60 is selected	4	0	0	6	2	7	8	0	4	0
Total number of interviews targeted	150	6	0	185	51	237	256	11	149	1

	CLUSTERS									
	11	12	13	14	15	16	17	18	19	20
RP/FP factor score	1,32	1,32	–0,07	–0,50	–0,02	–0,11	0,33	–4,18	1,36	0,46
DSP factor score	–1,87	0,09	–0,74	–0,53	–1,31	0,96	1,31	0,42	–3,42	–0,48
CHP factor score	–1,70	1,18	–0,23	–0,68	–0,86	–0,28	0,02	1,45	0,04	3,80
Extreme left factor score	0,51	–0,44	–0,67	–0,65	1,68	2,31	–0,54	0,11	–1,32	–0,36
MHP vs HADEP factor score	2,41	0,37	0,56	0,19	1,83	0,17	0,31	1,08	4,37	0,45
ANAP factor score	–1,82	–1,90	3,77	0,22	0,07	0,06	–0,23	–0,96	0,87	–1,17
DYP factor score	–2,29	–0,60	–0,54	0,15	–0,19	0,27	–0,24	–0,03	1,87	2,28
Independents factor score	–0,46	7,13	0,04	2,39	–0,23	–0,26	–0,14	–0,37	–2,34	6,35
Number of Cases in each Cluster	17	1	18	28	11	50	163	6	2	3
% share in total voters	2	0	1	2	0	2	40	1	0	0
# of districts if a total of 60 is selected	1	0	0	1	0	1	24	0	0	0
Total number of interviews targeted	40	0	14	46	6	34	799	13	1	0

Table A.3 Rural-Urban Divide across Clusters

CLUSTER	Rural	Urban	Total	Rural (%)	Urban (%)
1	863.973	1.949.029	2.813.002	31%	69%
2	66.796	38.589	105.385	63%	37%
3	3.933	4.570	8.503	46%	54%
4	881.052	2.600.879	3.481.931	25%	75%
5	450.276	513.957	964.233	47%	53%
6	1.803.083	2.659.308	4.462.391	40%	60%
7	2.599.919	2.197.587	4.797.506	54%	46%
8	110.210	97.139	207.349	53%	47%
9	1.265.653	1.511.991	2.777.644	46%	54%
10	3.842	16.530	20.372	19%	81%
11	254.519	490.114	744.633	34%	66%
12	4.448	2.828	7.276	61%	39%
13	125.490	138.274	263.764	48%	52%
14	372.173	482.835	855.008	44%	56%
15	78.407	37.366	115.773	68%	32%
16	448.891	192.927	641.818	70%	30%
17	3.198.654	11.690.741	14.889.395	21%	79%
18	87.264	164.833	252.097	35%	65%
19	7.924	7.252	15.176	52%	48%
20	3.499	4.775	8.274	42%	58%
Total	12.630.006	24.801.524	37.431.530	34%	66%

of Finance's list of "Current Property Values". All streets located at the selected districts were divided into three groups of "upper", "average," and "lower" values, and one principal and one auxiliary street name were selected from each group. Building numbers for the two interviews to be conducted per street were selected from the table of random numbers formed according to the initials of street names.[1] It was decide a priori that 10 interviews will be conducted per every rural settlement. For every district's total number of rural interviews, the total number of rural settlements was determined accordingly. Then rural settlements were selected at random again by according a probability proportionate to their population size.

According to the above sampling plan, a total of 2000 face-to-face interviews were envisaged, and 1984 subjects were interviewed during the application stage. In samples of this size that are selected by simple random sampling procedure, the maximum margin of error is expected to be ±2.2% at a 95% confidence level. Our sampling procedure is only an approximation to probability sampling. At the stage when we select streets the total number of households in every street was not available to us. So, equal probability of selection with the streets could not be maintained at this stage.

In selecting the control sample for our post-election survey we went to the same district neighborhoods and villages and applied the same procedure for half the sample size.

NOTES

Chapter 1

1 Turkish party names can at times be confusing for unfamiliar readers. Our convention is to use the full English name of the party in question the first time it appears in the text followed by its original Turkish name and acronym. For later references we use parties' Turkish acronyms.

2 Such a gross distortion of the link between the vote and seat shares is due to a 10 percent nationwide vote share threshold in effect for representation in the Parliament.

3 Throughout the text we use the term "pro-Islamist" to refer to the party family initiated by the founding of the MNP. We use this term not specifically to refer to a demand on the part of these parties for an Islamic state or Shari'a rule, which they could not explicitly do within the regulatory framework of the Turkish party system, but rather for their reliance on constituencies which take Islam as a primary source for their political mobilization. These parties typically rely on Islamic motives in their rhetoric and argue for valuing Islam in the private sphere as well as justifying certain public policies on Islamic grounds. This usage could have been altered for some of these parties as "political Islamist". However, for the sake of simplicity and homogeneity in our references, we use the term "pro-Islamist" instead.

4 See also Heper (1980), İnalcık (1964, 1992), Kafadar (1995), Karpat (1972), Mardin (1969).

5 See Berkes (1959, 18–22), Shaw and Shaw (1977, 302) and McCarthy (2001, 145).

6 See Mansfeld (1980, 85–117).

7 See Davison (1963), Hanioğlu (2001), Lewis (1961) and Zürcher (1993).

8 See Mardin (1962) and Lewis (2003).

9 According to Hague, Harrop and Breslin (1998, 80) "political participation is activity by individuals formally intended to influence either who governs or the decisions taken by governments." See also Verba and Nie (1972) and Verba, Nie and Kim (1978) for similar definitions. We take conventional vs. unconventional distinction from Marsh and Kaase (1979). Conventional form occurs when a citizen uses conventional channels of influence such as voting, petitioning and working in campaign. Unconventional methods appear when citizens participate in illegal strikes, protests and demonstrations, or stops traffic on a major city or intercity road, throws paint or rocks at certain politically significant figures. See Kalaycıoğlu (1994c) and our chapter five for a more indepth differentiation between conventional and unconventional forms of participation in politics.

10 For a more in-depth discussion see Zürcher (1993) and Tunaya (1952).

11 The guiding principle of the TBMM, established in 1920, was that "sovereignty belonged unconditionally and without reserve to the people (hakimiyet kayıtsız şartsız milletindir)".

12 Shortly after the dissolution of SCF in November 1930, an originally trivial demonstration in Western Anatolian town of Menemen, led by a Dervish Mehmed of the Nakshibendi

sufi order, turned into a bloody rebellion. Similar events also took place in Bursa (1933), Siirt (1935) and İskilip (1936) again by Nakshibendi leaders (Sencer, 1974, 151–152).

13 See also Ahmad (1993, 180).

14 The coup of 1980 was preceded by the so-called "coup by memorandum" of 1971. See Çarkoğlu (1993), Hale (1994), Heper and Evin (1988), Vaner (1987), Tachau and Heper (1983) on military regimes and the role of military in Turkish politics.

15 See Hale (1980), Finkel and Hale (1990), Çarkoğlu and Erdoğan (1998) for discussions of the changing election system in Turkey See Kalaycıoğlu (2002) for a discussion of the linkage between elections and governance performance in Turkey.

16 The consultative assembly of the 1980 regime passed a new law of political parties in 1983 that effectively reduced responsiveness of political parties to electoral demands. Patronage based elite oligarchy continued to dominate the inner structures of parties thus limiting accountability of party leaders to the electorate at large. See Ahmad (1993, 129–130, 186–187), Özbudun (1988, 1995), Tanör (1996) on Turkish constitutions.

17 See Taagepera and Shugart (1989) for a discussion of the effective number of parties index (E) which is calculated by using i=1, . . . N parties in the following formula: $E = {}^{1}/\Sigma_{N}(\text{Vote\%}_{i})^{2}$.

18 See Przeworski (1975) and Pedersen (1979) for a discussion of the volatility index (V) which is calculated by using i=1, . . . N parties in the following formula: $V = \{({}^{1}/_{2})(\Sigma_{N}|\text{Vote\%}_{i,t} - \text{Vote\%}_{i,t-1}|)\}$. Çarkoğlu (1998) discusses the Turkish volatility figures in a comparative context.

Chapter 2

1 See Çarkoğlu (1998), Çarkoğlu and Hinich (2006), Hale (2002) and Kalaycıoğlu (1998) for a multi-dimensional analysis of Turkish ideological space.

2 In the summer of 2002, İsmail Cem, Ecevit's Minister of Foreign Affairs, resigned from the DSP and, together with other MPs who resigned, formed a new left-leaning party, the New Turkey Party (*Yeni Türkiye Partisi*-YTP). Although YTP attracted a lot of attention at the beginning, it eventually failed to convince enough of the voters and remained well below the ten percent threshold of electoral support required to gain parliamentary seats. It eventually decided to close down and merge with CHP in 2005.

3 Turkish society is divided into two major sects of Sunnis and Alevis. The Sunnis are divided into the Hanefi and Shafi schools of law (*mezhep*), and then between those who take Sunni Islam seriously in organizing their lifestyles and those who take a secular or anti-clerical (*laik*) view of life. The Alevis historically being in a minority position have tended to support the secularist policies of the Republican era, which provided protection against Sunni infringements in their religious freedoms. Hence the term pro-Islamist here refers to Sunni reactionism to secularist Republican establishment.

4 See Çarkoğlu (2000) and Çarkoğlu and Avcı (2002) for the geographical bases of ANAP and DYP.

5 Corruption was a hotly debated issue among the elites prior to the November 2002 election. As we will note below the masses had a different take on this issue. See Adaman, Çarkoğlu and Şenatalar (2001, 2003) for a series of survey evidence on corruption from the perspectives of the laymen as well as the business community. For a more popular perspective see, among others: Arslan (2001); Şener (2001, 2002); Seymen (2001); Ünlü (2001). The above illustrate in detail how corruption of many different kinds and in many different sectors had direct intense links with the political establishment at the time and thus led to the collapse of the financial sector in the latest economic crisis.

6 See Çarkoğlu (2003a).

7 For being against the secular regime, both MNP and MSP had been banned by the military regimes of 1971 and 1980 respectively.

8 Unable to legislate, encircled by popular resistance together, with increasing resignations from the DYP, the coalition partners agreed on going to early elections under the premiership of the DYP leader Tansu Çiller. Accordingly, Erbakan resigned. However, President Süleyman Demirel asked the ANAP leader Mesut Yılmaz, who was leading the second largest parliamentary group to Erbakan's RP to form the new government. Together with the centre-left DSP and the Democratic Turkey Party (*Demokrat Türkiye Partisi*-DTP) Yılmaz' minority government obtained the vote of confidence with outside support from the centre-left CHP. The new government was also pressured by the military for implementation of the "recommended" policies in the infamous MGK meeting, and consequently delivered on the education policy front by passing the controversial 8-year mandatory education law.

9 See chapters three and six for further discussion of the economic issues in the November 2002 election.

10 See Özbudun (1975) and Çarkoğlu (1998) as well as the essays in Sayarı and Esmer (2002) for a discussion of lacking PID and the persistent volatility in Turkey.

11 See Çarkoğlu (1995, 2000, 2003), Çarkoğlu and Avcı (2002) and Çarkoğlu and Eren (2002).

12 Çarkoğlu and Eren (2002).

13 As Table 2.2 shows, fragmentation remained high despite a downturn in that trend and a relatively increased focus on one or two parties. Looking at the election results from provinces, calculations show that the overall dominant position of the local component in election results continues in the Turkish party system. The AKP and CHP vote experienced a significant rise in their national component and in the case of the AKP, the national component is now the dominant factor shaping its electoral support. As such, the AKP becomes the first party in Turkish electoral history to gather behind it a uniform swing across the nation in its favor.

14 Çarkoğlu (1996) and Çarkoğlu and Avcı (2002).

Chapter 3

1 See the contributions to the special issue in Electoral Studies (2000) on the state of the art in economic voting literature. For the case of Turkey see Çarkoğlu (1997).

2 See literature reviews in Alesina, Roubini and Cohen (1997), Drazen (2001) and Persson and Tabellini (2002). On Turkish experience with political manipulations of the economy see Çarkoğlu (1995), Ergüder (1980), Gürkan and Kasnakoğlu (1991).

3 Radikal Daily newspaper, 14 May, 2001.

4 FP's closure by the Constitutional Court in June 2001 immediately led to founding of two new parties reflecting the inner split of the pro-Islamists between the "old guards" under SP and the younger generation under AKP in 2001. The GP was founded in Summer 2002 by Cem Uzan, a business tycoon with a blemished background adopting a populist agenda. AKP and GP jointly were able to garner 41.5 percent of support in 2002 when the ruling coalition of DSP-MHP-ANAP lost 38.7 percentage points from their 1999 vote shares.

5 Perhaps it was also not possible for him to make a convincing new argument about the economy. After all, he personally was responsible for the tough austerity program that the masses found extremely unpopular.

6 Radikal, November 1, 2002, 9.

7 Radikal, 23 September, 2002, 6.

8 See Çarkoğlu (2003b, 2004b) for analyses of the popular bases of support for EU membership in Turkey.

9 See AKP's election manifesto *Herşey Türkiye İçin* (Everything is for Turkey) HtmlResAnchor http://www.akparti.org.tr/ and CHP's election manifesto *Güzel Günler Göreceğiz!* (We'll See Good Days!) HtmlResAnchor http://secim2002.chorg.tr/bildirge.asp.

10 Milliyet daily newspaper, 4.; See also Tarhan Erdem's account of the results in Radikal, October 1st, 2002, 11.

Chapter 4

1 See Özbudun (1976, 78, 83, 98, 135) for more information on those studies led by Frederick W. Frey.
2 As will be noted at more length below, a number of shorter-term analyses with aggregate geographic data exist. However, to our knowledge, the only exception with a long-term focus is Çarkoğlu and Avcı (2002).
3 Despite conceptual similarities Mardin (1973) develops his framework independently from Lipset and Rokkan's (1967) discussion of historical cleavages in Western polities.
4 For example, while 37 percent of the rural respondents agree with the statement that in democracies maintenance of public order will be difficult, among urban settlers only 26 percent seem to agree with this argument (Esmer, 1999, 80).
5 For a more comprehensive account of the heterogeneous nature of party preferences rather than participation rates see Çarkoğlu and Avcı (2002).
6 Çarkoğlu (2000), Çarkoğlu and Avcı (2002) and Secor (2001) are exceptions that have a geographical perspective.
7 See Çakmak (1985) on the three elections in 1950's and Gülmen (1979) on aggregate election results and socio-economic development. Çakmak (1990) notes emerging electoral trends in the post-military coup years of the late 1980's. Note also Albaum and Davies (1973), Srikantan (1973) and SPO (1996) about the geographical cleavages in socio-economic development of Turkish provinces. See Çarkoğlu (2000) for the link between development indicators and electoral regionalisation in 1999 general elections.
8 See Çarkoğlu (2000, 2003) for geographical analyses of 1999 and 2002 elections.
9 "T-mode factor analysis reduces a large number of elections to electoral epochs by analyzing matrices of correlations among elections over areas. Each epoch includes elections whose geographical patterns are similar to one another but distinct from those of earlier or later epochs. Thus, each epoch describes what has been termed a 'geographical normal vote" (Archer and Taylor, 1981; Archer et al., 1986).
10 See also Shelley and Archer (1984); Osei-Kwame and Taylor (1984).

Chapter 5

1 Ostensibly, it is also possible to observe political behavior that gives the impression of action which aims to influence political decisions; however it lacks any political meaning for those who carry out such behavior. Under such circumstances we need to consider such acts not as political participation, but simply as mobilized participation. Although some references will be made to mobilized behavior in this chapter, the main focus rests on acts of political participation.
2 We employ the term political resources in the same sense that Robert Dahl suggested it in his classical study of New Haven (see Dahl, 1974, 271).

Chapter 6

1 Kalaycıoğlu and Sarıbay (1991) provide evidence that a significant breakdown occurred in party identification of early childhood political socialisation in the aftermath of 1980 coup.
2 The question as to what people understand from "left" and " right" is an important one for which we have no empirically supported answer. However, what we observe from Table 6.1 is that over the last nearly 15 years the percentage of people providing no answer to our question on left and right placements has declined considerably from about 12 percent to 6.2 percent. This obviously does not tell us anything about the content of what is being understood about the "left" and the "right", but at least we see that less people do not understand anything or do not whish to express their opinion about this dimension.

3 This study is again a nationwide representative sample collected as part of the Philanthropy in Turkey project sponsored by the Ford Foundation and the Third Sector Foundation (*Türkiye Üçüncü Sektör Vakfı*-TUSEV) conducted in February and March 2004 wherein a total of 1536 interviews were carried out.

4 The placements here also fully agree with our depiction in Chapter 2.

5 It should be noted at this juncture however that this journey back to the centre could indeed be too long for the DYP. Its constituency is relatively old, and also comes from predominantly rural settlements which have both been shrinking in size. So the DYP's main constituency of appeal may be slowly disappearing. The real challenge then for the DYP is to enlarge this constituency base to include younger and more dynamic segments of Turkish society.

6 As noted in chapter four Turkish participation rates are still quite high compared to western democracies. The Primary reason for this is said to be the mobilized voting in especially the rural areas.

7 See Esmer (1995, 2001); Kalaycıoğlu (1994a,b, 1999) and Çarkoğlu and Toprak (2000) on religiosity and voting behavior.

8 Çarkoğlu and Toprak's (2000) research on political Islam finds that the FP, MHP and DYP's electorate are significantly more religious than the other parties. The other three centrist parties, namely ANAP, DSP and CHP, voters are of significantly lower level of religiosity thus favoring secularist stand on salient issues. See Çarkoğlu (2000) and Kalaycıoğlu (1999) on the claim that MHP has effectively appealed, by using the undelivered promises of religious significance, to the alienated constituencies of the now closed Pro-Islamist RP.

9 This section relies on an earlier presentation of our post-election data in Çarkoğlu (2005) and uses answers to questions in the pre-election survey.

10 Mardin's early work (1983) on religion most clearly reflects this approach to the study of religion.

11 We specifically refrained from stating the first item in this dimension as belief in *Allah* but rather used a non-Islamic wording such as God or *tanrı* in Turkish. Shankland (2003, 157) refer to the use of *tanrı* as a typical usage of the Alevis reflecting their effort to be Turkish rather than Arabic. We maintain that the connotation of the use of *Allah* makes refusal more difficult and *tanrı* gives a more neutral tone to the question.

12 It should be noted here that these items on faith reflect predominantly the Sunni orthodoxy. Çarkoğlu (2005) notes that these reflections of faith do not necessarily hold for Alevis. An important point to note here concerns the meaning attached to "belief". Given such high levels of "belief" despite many non-conformist and unorthodox views expressed by the same respondents in other questions, one is bound to question as to whether the meaning attached to "belief" is the same for all respondents. Such, subtleties concerning the link of belief and daily lives of respondents are not questioned in our survey interview setting. Deeper discussions are needed to asses how individuals differ in meanings they attach to these doctrinally important dimensions of their belief.

13 See Kuran (1995, pp.6–9) on pressures of conformity in religious belief and practice.

14 Both of these questions are problematic in some ways. The question on prayer does not refer to the daily prayer, since the options given do not reflect the frequencies required for this ritual. They only reflect the individual's private prayers. Mosque attendance is also mostly relevant for men rather than women. That is the reason why attendance rates appear to be low. In fact, on examining the same attendance question for men and women we see that there are very few women who report going to the mosque once a week or more (10.9 percent) and nearly 44 percent of the women report that they hardly ever go to the mosque. In order to correct for this gender bias in religious practice we created a dummy variable that separates those respondents (men and women) who report going to the mosque more than once a week and those women respondents who report going to the mosque during the month of Ramadan and religious festivals (*kandils*) from the rest. As

such, we imposed an equivalence between women who go to mosques during Ramadan and kandils and men going to mosques regularly more than once a week. It should also be noted that this subject of religious practice measures is problematic in reference to the examination of the Alevi tradition, which does not particularly praise mosque attendance. However, the loose usage of the term prayer (*dua*) does not necessarily entail the connotation of Sunni orthodoxy, so it could equally apply to both sectarian traditions.

15 Of course, we should caution that for all of our statements it is possible to find counter examples. A religiously very devout person who prays regularly, who fasts and abides by all different sorts of religious rules and rituals disagreeing with our statement where agreement is interpreted as being more religious than disagreement is not unthinkable.

16 Non response rates are minimal in all the statements.

17 See Çarkoğlu (2005) for a more in depth discussion on this Alevi-Sunni cleavage in Turkish politics based on the post-election data.

18 Nevertheless, Shankland (2003:97) notes that despite . . . "the higher position which religion gives to Alevi women, it is difficult . . . to assert definitively that their position is simply equal."

19 Özdalga, Elisabeth, *The Veiling Issue, Official Secularism and Popular Islam in Modern Turkey*, Curzon, (1998), p.24, notes that "Alevis have never attached much importance to the formal requirements of Islam, like namaz (ritual prayer) and fasting during Ramadan." See also Metin (1999) for a comparison of Alevism with Sunnism.

20 A very similar picture arises from the post-election data which suggests that the measurement of religiosity across our two pre and post-elections samples is quite consistent and stable.

21 Such scores make the interpretation of an individual's position among the whole set of respondents easier. If, for example, a given individual has a factor score of zero in the faith dimension, then he or she has exactly the average orientation in this dimension. Applying a standard normal curve interpretation we should keep in mind that the results denote relative positions of individuals among the sample respondents and nothing else. That is, a negative score simply means that compared to the average, the individual in question simply has a lower score, and not that he or she has negative inclinations in that particular dimension of religiosity or that he or she is not religious.

22 See Çarkoğlu (2003b, 2004b) for a detailed description of the historical developments in EU support.

23 A selection of these messages was compiled in Perinçek (2002).

24 H. Bağcı, "Karen Fogg: Victim or scapegoat?" *Turkish News*, 18 Feb. 2002 (obtained from www.foreignpolicy.org.tr) argues that the hacking of Karen Fogg's email messages is part and parcel of an effort to hinder the adoption of reforms that would open the way for Turkey's eventual accession to the EU. In the media there were also commentators who took a critical view of the hacking. See M. Yılmaz, "Alaturka bir casusluk öyküsü" *Milliyet*, 12 Feb. 2002.

25 For a coverage of these email messages from the perspective of the problem in Cyprus see Ismail and Yusuf (2002).

26 See Çarkoğlu (2003b, 2004b).

27 See Çarkoğlu, Erdem and Kabasakal (2000) on the lack of inner party democracy in Turkey.

28 See the articles in *Electoral Studies* (2002) special issue for a review of the state of art in the literature.

Chapter 7

1 See King (1997) and Achen and Shively (1995) for more recent discussions of the ecological inference problem. King's claim that ecological fallacy can be resolved is yet to be accepted as a convincing and practical assertion see the exchanges in the *Annals of the*

American Geographers by Sui (2000), Fortheringham (2000), Anselin (2000), O'Loughlin (2000) and the reply by King (2000).

2 See *Electoral Studies* (2002).

3 The empirical extension of the spatial voting theory offers a direct link to a formal mathematical model of preference formation and choice. Besides the American elections, these models have been tested in a variety of political contexts including Ukraine (Hinich, Khmelko and Ordeshook, 1999), Chile (Dow, 1998a, b), Russia (Myagov and Ordeshook, 1998), Taiwan (Lin, Chu and Hinich; 1996) and most recently Turkey (Çarkoğlu and Hinich, forthcoming 2006). These empirical applications in different country contexts offer a test of generalizability of the spatial theory.

4 See our discussion above in Chapter 6. Esmer (1995) and Kalaycıoğlu (1994a, 1999) are all based on fieldwork conducted for World Values Survey in Turkey. Esmer (2002) is based on the first post-election study completed a week after April 1999 election.

5 For our purposes this study is particularly important because it the first coherent report of an impressive array of variables in determining party choice. Party identification, left-right ideology, nationalist ideology, tolerance, are all part of the political ideology measures. Esmer (2002, 104) evaluates the PID hypothesis and reaches the conclusion that it is "rather uninteresting to elaborate on the inevitable conclusion that the more strongly a person identifies with a party the more likely they are to vote for that party and that this variable explains most of the variance in voting behavior." He thus continues without including PID in his analyses. Most likely due to lack of space the details of the sampling procedures and the fieldwork are not reported in the article of 2002. As an overall methodological observation, it is also noticeable that the simplified stepwise variable selection procedure may also be potentially problematic (see Kennedy, 1998, 52).

6 Esmer (2002) includes positions of respondents and their evaluated positions of the parties separately in the party choice equation. Çarkoğlu and Toprak (2000) takes the difference between the self-reported ideological position of the respondents and their evaluated positions of each of the parties separately for each party vote function. In this way they reflect a spatial model conceptualization of position closeness to their vote intention function.

7 See Kalaycıoğlu (1994a) and (1999) for similar results with data from inter-election period preceding the April 1999 election.

8 The list of options given include Sunnis, Alevis, Bektashis, Orthodox, Protestants, Catholics, Evangelicans, Turks, Kurds, Kırmanç, Zaza, migrants, Circassian, Georgian, Laz, Arabs, Gypsies, Greeks, Armenians and Jews.

9 The GP was in existence at the time, but had not been 'acquired' by Cem Uzan at the time

10 The results presented in Table 1 of the two articles of Başlevent et al. (2004, 2005) are the same results replicated in every detail.

11 Our objective here was not to forecast the election result and we believe that such attempts are in many ways open to simplistic assumptions. For example, the simplest method is to calculate the party vote shares amongst the decided voters or just the reported party choices. This boils down to distributing the undecided group amongst the other declared parties in accordance to their weight in the declared group. This is obviously problematic since we expect that more competitive or larger parties are more likely to have a larger share amongst the undecided group. One could also claim that we have no way of knowing how this distribution of the undecided group is going to shape up since we do not know if these individuals are actually going to cast their vote or not.

12 See Catt (1996, 46–48) for a discussion of tactical voting.

Chapter 8

1 See Atacan (2005) and Mardin (2005) on the intellectual origins of the pro-Islamist movement as it relates to the AKP.

2 See Çarkoğlu (2003) and Çarkoğlu and Hinich (2006).

3 The ANAP was gaining perhaps not an electoral ground within the masses at the time of our writing this book but an elite backing from an unlikely group; that is the unhappy CHP MPs who resign from their party to join ANAP for the next general election.

Appendix

1 After going to the households, interviewers asked the number of residents over 18 and tried to interview one of them selected at random. If the selected person could not be found at the first visit, or if the interview could not take place for some reason, the household in question was visited a second time in order to try to interview the selected person. If the interview could not take place a second time, another household on the same street was again selected at random, and the same process was repeated.

REFERENCES

Achen, C.H. and Shively, W.P. (1995). *Cross-Level Inference*. Chicago: The University of Chicago Press.

Adaman, F., Çarkoğlu, A. and Şenatalar, B. (2001). *Hanehalkı Gözünden Türkiye'de Yolsuzluğun Nedenleri ve Önlenmesine İlişkin Öneriler* (Causes and Policies against Corruption in Turkey from the Perspective of Households) in Turkish, Turkish Economic and Social Studies Foundation (**TESEV**) publications

Adaman, F., Çarkoğlu, A. and Şenatalar, B. (2003). *İş Dünyası Gözünden Türkiye'de Yolsuzluğun Nedenleri ve Önlenmesine İlişkin Öneriler* (Causes and Policies against Corruption in Turkey from the Perspective of Business Community) in Turkish, Turkish Economic and Social Studies Foundation (**TESEV**) publications.

Ahmad, F. (1993). *The Making of Modern Turkey*, London: Routledge.

Akarlı, E.D. and Ben-Dor, G. (eds.) (1975). *Political Participation in Turkey: Historical Background and Present Problems*, Istanbul: Boğaziçi University Press

Albaum, M. and Davies, C. S. (1973). 'The Spatial Structure of Socio-Economic Attributes of Turkish Provinces', *International Journal of Middle East Studies* Vol. 4, pp.288–310.

Alesina, A., Roubini, N. and Cohen, G.D. (1997). *Political Cycles and the Macroeconomy*, The MIT Press.

Alvarez, E.M., Nagler, J. and Bowler, S. (2000). 'Issues, Economics and the Dynamics of Multiparty Elections: The British 1987 General Election', *American Political Science Review*, Vol. 94, pp.131–150.

Anselin, L. (2000). 'The Alchemy of Statistics, or Creating Data where no Data Exist', *Annals of the Association of American Geographers*, Vol. 90(3), pp.586–592.

Arat, Y. (2001). 'Group-Differentiated Rights and the Liberal Democratic State: Rethinking the Headscarf Controversy in Turkey', *New Perspectives on Turkey*, Vol. 25, pp.31–46

Archer, J.C. and Taylor, P.J. (1981). *Section and Party: A Political Geography of American Presidential Elections from Andrew Jackson to Ronald Reagan*, Chicester, UK: John Wiley.

Archer, J.C., Shelley, F. M. and White, E.R. (1986). *American Electoral Mosaics*, Association of American Geographers, Washington, D.C.:Resource Publications in Geography.

Arslan, Ş. (2001). *Hortum ve Cinnet* (Syphoning and Insanity) in Turkish, Istanbul: Om Publications.

Atacan, F. (2005), "Eplaining Religious Politics at the Crossroads:AKP-SP", in the special Issue of *Turkish Politics* on Religion and Politics in Turkey, Vol. 6, No. 2, pp.187–200.

Ayata, S. (1996). 'Patronage, Party and State-The Politicization of Islam in Turkey', *Middle East Journal,* Vol. 50, pp.40–56

Barnes, S.H. and Kaase, M. (eds.). (1979). *Political Action: Mass Participation in Five Western Democracies*, Beverly Hills: California: Sage Publications.

Başlevent, C., Kirmanoğlu, H. and Şenatalar, B. (2004). 'Voter Profiles and Fragmentation in the Turkish Party System', *Party Politics*, Vol.10 (3): 307–324.

Başlevent, C., Kirmanoğlu, H. and Şenatalar, B. (2005). 'Empirical Investigation of Party

Preferences and Economic Voting in Turkey', *European Journal of Political Research* Vol. 44, pp.547–562.

Baykal, D. (1970). *Siyasal Katılma, Bir Davranış İncelemesi*, Ankara Üniversitesi, Siyasal Bilgiler Fakültesi Yayınları, No. 302, Ankara.

Berelson, B.R., Lazarfeld, P.F. and McPhee, W.N. (1954). *Voting: A Study of Opinion Formation in a Presidential Campaign*, Chicago: The University of Chicago Press.

Berkes, N. (1959). *Turkish Nationalism and Western Civilization: Selected Essays of Ziya Gökalp*, New York: Columbia University Press.Press

Berkes, N. (1964). *The Development of Secularism in Turkey*, McGill University.

Black, D. (1958). *Theory of Committees and Elections*, Cambridge: Cambridge University Press.

Cahoon, L. and Hinich, M.J. (1976). 'A Method for Locating Targets Using Range Only', *IEEE Transactions on Information Theory*, Vol.22 (2), pp.217–225.

Cahoon, L., Hinich, M.J. and Ordeshook, P.C. (1978). 'A Statistical Multidimensional Scaling Method Based on the Spatial Theory of Voting', in *Graphical Representation of Multivariate Data*, P.C.Wang (ed.), Academic Press, New York, pp.243–278.

Çakmak, C. (1985). 'An Essay on Elections of the 1950s in Turkey'. *Middle East Technical University Development Studies*, Vol.12, pp.245–283 (in Turkish).

Çakmak, C. (1990). 'A Comparison of 1987 General Elections and 1989 Local Elections'. *Middle East Technical University Development Studies* Vol.17, pp.1–24 (in Turkish).

Campbell, A., Converse, P.E., Miller, W.E. and Stokes, D.E. (1966). *Elections and the Political Order*, New York: Wiley.

Campbell, A., Converse, P.E., Miller, W.E. and Stokes, D.E. (1960). *The American Voter*, New York:Wiley.

Catt, H. (1996). *Voting Behaviour: A Radical Critique*, Leicester University Pres.

Çamuroğlu, R., (2000). *Değişen Koşullarda Alevilik* (Alevism in Changing Conditions), in Turkish, İstanbul:Doğan Kitap.

Çarkoğlu, A. (1995). 'The Interdependence of Politics and Economics in Turkey: Some Findings at the Aggregate Level of Analysis', *Boğaziçi Journal, Review of Social, Economic and Administrative Sciences*, Vol.9, No.2, pp.85–108.

Çarkoğlu, A. (1996). '24 Aralık 1995 Seçimlerinde Bölgeselleşme, Oynaklık, Parçalanma ve Temsil Adaleti' (Regionalisation, Volatility, Fractionalisation and Representational Justice in Turkey's December 24, 1995 Elections) in Turkish, *Görüş* TUSIAD (Turkish Industrialists and Businessmen Association), İstanbul, Turkey, April.

Çarkoğlu, A. (1997). 'Macroeconomic Determinants of Electoral Support for Incumbents in Turkey, 1950–1995', *New Perspectives on Turkey*, Vol.17, No.2, pp.75–96.

Çarkoğlu, A. (1998). 'Turkish Party System in Transition: The Connection Between Macro-Level Party Competition and Agenda Change in Election Manifestoes', *Political Studies*, Vol.XLVI, pp.544–571.

Çarkoğlu, A. (2000). 'Geography of April 1999 Turkish Elections', *Turkish Studies*, Vol.1, No.1, pp.149–171.

Çarkoğlu, A. (2002). 'Turkey's November 2002 Elections: A New Beginning?', *MERIA Journal (Middle East Review of International Affairs)*, Volume 6, Number 4, December 2002. http://meria.idc.ac.il/journal/2002/issue4/jv6n4a4.html.

Çarkoğlu, A. (2003a). 'The Rise of the New Generation Pro-Islamists in Turkey: The Justice and Development Party Phenomenon in the November 2002 Elections in Turkey', *South European Society & Politics*, Vol. 7, No.3, pp.123–156.

Çarkoğlu, A. (2003b). 'Who Wants Full Membership? Characteristics of Turkish Public Support for EU Membership', Special Issue on Turkey and the European Union, *Turkish Studies,* Vol. 4, No.1, pp.171–194.

Çarkoğlu, A. (2004a). 'Religiosity, Support for Şeriat and Evaluations of Secularist Public Policies in Turkey', *Middle Eastern Studies*, Vol.40, No.2, pp.111–136.

Çarkoğlu, A. (2004b). 'Societal Perceptions of Turkey's EU Membership: Causes and

Consequences of Support for EU Membership?', in *Turkey and European Integration, Accession Prospects and Issues*, Routledge, Nergis Canefe and Mehmet Uğur (eds.) pp.19–45.

Çarkoğlu, A. (2005).'Political Preferences of the Turkish Electorate: Reflections of an Alevi-Sunni Cleavage', in the special Issue of *Turkish Politics* on Religion and Politics in Turkey, Vol. 6 no. 2 June, pp.273–292.

Çarkoğlu, A. and Avcı, G. (2002). 'An Analysis of the Turkish Electorate from a Geographical Perspective', in Yılmaz Esmer and Sabri Sayarı (Eds.), *Politics, Parties and Elections in Turkey,* Boulder, CO: Lynn Rienner, p.115–136.

Çarkoğlu, A. and Erdoğan, E. (1998). 'Fairness in the Apportionment of Seats in the Turkish Legislature: Is There Room for Improvement?', *New Perspectives on Turkey*, December Vol.19, No.1, pp.97–124.

Çarkoğlu, A. and Eren, I. (2002). 'The Rise of Right-of-Centre Parties and the Nationalisation of Electoral Forces in Turkey,' *New Perspectives on Turkey*, Vol.26, No. 1 Spring, pp.95–137.

Çarkoğlu, A. and Hinich, M. J. (2006), 'A Spatial Analysis of Turkish Party Preferences', *Electoral Studies*, Vol. 25, pp. 369–392.

Çarkoğlu, A. (1993). 'Conflict and Development in Turkey: The Problem of the Coup Trap', in E.A. Ziegenhagen (ed.) *Political Conflict in Comparative Perspective*, Praeger.

Çarkoğlu, Ali and Toprak B. (2000). *Türkiye'de Din, Toplum ve Siyaset* (Religion, Society and Politics in Turkey), in Turkish, Turkish Economic and Social Studies Foundation (TESEV) Publications. İstanbul.

Dahl, R.A. (1974). *Who Governs? Democracy and Power in an American City,* New Haven and London: Yale University Pres.

Davison, R.H. (1963). *Reform in the Ottoman Empire, 1856–1876*, Princeton: Princeton University Press.

Deutsch, K. (1961). 'Social Mobilisation and Political Development' *American Political Science Review*, Vol.65, pp.493–514.

Downs, A. (1957). *An Economic Theory of Democracy*, New York, NY:Harper and Row.

Drazen, A. (2001). *Political Economy in Macroeconomics*, Princeton University Press.

Lewis-Beck, M.S. and Paldam, M. (2002). 'Economics and Elections', *Electoral Studies* (Special Issue) Vol.19. no. 2/3 June/September.

Enelow, James and Hinich, M.J. (1984). *The Spatial Theory of Voting*, New York, NY: Cambridge University Press.

Enelow, James and Hinich, M.J. (1990). 'The Theory of Predictive Mappings', in *Advances in the Spatial Theory of Voting*, J. Enelow and M. Hinich (eds.), Cambridge University Press, pp. 167–178.

Enelow, James and Hinich, M.J. (eds.) (1990). *Advances in the Spatial Theory of Voting*, Cambridge University Press.

Erder, N. (1999). *Türkiye'de Siyasi Parti Seçmenleri ve Toplum Düzeni* (Political Party Constituencies and Social Order in Turkey), in Turkish, İstanbul: TÜSES Publications.

Erder, N. (1996). *Türkiye'de Siyasi Parti Seçmenlerinin Nitelikleri, Kimlikleri ve Eğilimleri* (Identities, Characteristics and Tendencies of Political Party Constituencies in Turkey), in Turkish, İstanbul: TÜSES Publications.

Erder, N. (2002). *Türkiye'de Siyasi Partilerin Yandaş/Seçmen Profili, 1994–2002* (Profile of Political Party Constituencies in Turkey, 1994–2002), in Turkish, İstanbul: TÜSES Publications.

Ergüder, Ü. (1980). 'Politics of Agricultural Price Policy in Turkey,' in E. Özbudun and A. Ulusan, (Eds.) *The Political Economy of Income Distribution in Turkey*, NY: Holmes and Meier Publishers Ltd., pp.169–196.

Ergüder, Ü., Esmer, Y. and Kalaycıoğlu, E. (1991). *Turkish Values*. Istanbul: TUSIAD (in Turkish).

Ergüder, Ü. (1980–81). 'Changing Patterns of Electoral Behaviour in Turkey', *Boğaziçi Üniversitesi Dergisi* (Bogazici University Journal), vols.VIII–IX, pp.45–81.

Eroğlu, C. (1971). *Demokrat Parti*, Ankara: Siyasal Bilgiler Fakültesi.

Esmer, Y. (1995). Parties and the Electorate: A Comparative Analysis of Voter Profiles of

Turkish Political Parties, in *Turkey: Political, Social and Economic Challenges in the 1990s* (Ç. Balım, E. Kalaycıoğlu, C. Karataş, G. Winrow and F. Yasamee eds), Leiden, New York, Köln: E.J. Brill, pp.74–89.

Esmer, Y. (1999). *Revolution, Evolution, Status-quo: Social, Political and Economic Values in Turkey*. İstanbul: Turkish Economic and Social Studies Foundation (TESEV) Publications (in Turkish).

Esmer, Y. (2001). 'At the ballot box: determinants of voting behaviour in Turkey', in S. Sayarı and Y. Esmer (Eds) *The Democratic Challenge: Elections, Parties, and Voters in Turkey.* Lynn Rienner, pp.91–114.

Evans, J.A.J. (2004). *Voters and Voting*, London:Sage Publications.

Finkel, A. and Hale, W. M. (1990). 'Politics and Procedure in the 1987 Turkish General Election', in A. Finkel and N. Sirman (eds.) *Turkish State, Turkish Society*, London and New York: Routledge.

Fotheringham, A.S. (2000). 'A Bluffer's Guide to A Solution to the Ecological Inference Problem'. *Annals of the Association of American Geographers*, Vol.90, No.3, pp.582–586.

Frey, F.W. (1963). 'Surveying Peasant Attitudes in Turkey', *Public Opinion Quarterly*, vol.27, pp.335–355.

Glock, C.Y. and Stark, R. (1965). *Religion and Society in Tension*, Chicago: Rand McNally.

Göle, N. (1997). 'Secularism and Islamism in Turkey: The Making of Elites and CounterElites', *Middle East Journal*, Vol.51, No.1, pp.46–58.

Gülmen, Y. (1979). *Turkish Electoral Behavior, 1960–1970*. Istanbul: Istanbul University Publications, No. 2531 (in Turkish).

Gürkan, A. A. and Kasnakoğlu, H. (1991). 'The Political Economics of Agricultural Price Support in Turkey: An Empirical Assessment', *Public Choice*, Vol.70, No.3, pp. 277–298.

Hague, R., Harrop, M. and Breslin, S. (1998). *Comparative Government and Politics, An Introduction*, Third Edition, London: MacMillan Press.

Hale, W. M. (1980). 'The Role of the Electoral System in Turkish Politics', *International Journal of Middle East Studies* Vol.11, pp.401–417.

Hale, W. M. (1994). *Turkish Politics and the Military*. London: Routledge.

Hale, W. M. (2002). 'Democracy and the Party System in Turkey' in Beeley, B.W. (ed.) *Turkish Transformation, New Century, New Challenges*, The Eothen Press.

Hale, W. M. (2005).'Christian Democracy and the AKP:Parallels and Contrasts', in the special Issue of *Turkish Politics* on Religion and Politics in Turkey, Vol. 6, No.2, pp.293–310.

Hanioğlu, Ş.M. (2001). *Preparation for a Revolution: The Young Turks, 1902–1908*, Oxford:Oxford University Press.

Hassan, R., (2002). *Faithliness, Muslim Conceptions of Islam and Society*, Oxford: Oxford University Press.

Heper, M. and Evin, A. (eds.) (1988). *Democracy and the Military: Turkey in the 1980s*, Berlin and New York: Walter de Gruyter.

Heper, M. (1980). 'Center-Periphery in the Ottoman Empire with Special Reference to the Nineteenth Century', *International Political Science Review*, Vol.1. No.1, pp. 81–105.

Heper, M. (1997). 'Islam and Democracy in Turkey: Toward a Reconciliation?', *Middle East Journal*, Vol.51, No.1, pp.32–45.

Hinich, M., J (1978). 'Some Evidence on Non-Voting Models in the Spatial Theory of Electoral Competition', *Public Choice*, Vol.33, No.2, pp.83–102.

Hinich, M., J. and Khmelko, V. and Ordeshook, P. C. (1999). 'Ukraine's 1998 Parliamentary Elections: A Spatial Analysis', *Post-Soviet Affairs*, Vol.15, No.2, pp.149–185.

Hinich, M., J. and Munger, M.C. (1994). *Ideology and the Theory of Political Choice*, Ann Arbor, MI: University of Michigan Press.

Hinich, M., J. and Munger, M., C. (1997). *Analytical Politics*, Cambridge University Press.

Hinich, M., J. and Pollard, W. (1981). 'A New Approach to the Spatial Theory of Electoral Competition', *American Journal of* Political Science, Vol.25, No.2, pp.323–341.

Hotelling, H. (1929). 'Stability in Competition', *The Economic Journal*, Vol.39, No.1, pp.41–57.

İnalcık, H. (1964). 'The Nature of Traditional Society: Turkey' in R. E. Ward and D. A. Rustow (eds.) *Political Modernization in Japan and Turkey*, Princeton, NJ: Princeton University Press.

İnalcık, H. (2000). *Osmanlı'da Devlet, Hukuk, Adalet*, Istanbul: Eren Yayıncılık.

İnalcık, H.(1992). 'Comments on Sultanism: Max Weber's Classification of the Ottoman Polity' *Princeton Papers in Near Eastern Studies*, Vol.I, pp.49–72.

İncioğlu, N. (2002). 'Local Elections and Electoral Behavior', S. Sayarı and Y. Esmer (Eds.), *Politics, Parties and Elections in Turkey,* Boulder, CO: Lynn Rienner, pp.73–90.

İsmail, S. and Yusuf, H.M. (2002). *AB Karen Fogg ve Kıbrıs AB'nin KKTC Üzerinde Bitmeyen Oyunları Karen Fogg'un Hedefi: Denktaş*, İstanbul: Akdeniz Haber Ajansı Yayınları.

Kafadar, C. (1995). *Between Two Worlds, The Construction of the Ottoman State*, Berkeley, CA: University of California Press.

Kalaycıoğlu, E. (1983). *Karşılaştırmalı Siyasal Katılma*, İstanbul, İstanbul Üniversitesi S. B. F. Publications.

Kalaycıoğlu, E. (1986), "Siyasal Katılmanın Koşullarına Genel bir Bakış: Türkiye Örneği" in Ersin Kalaycıoğlu and Ali Yaşar Sarıbay (eds.), *Türk Siyasal Hayatının Gelişimi*, (İstanbul: Beta), pp.509 – 532.

Kalaycıoğlu, E. (1994a). 'Elections and Party Preferences in Turkey, Changes and Continuities in the 1990s.' *Comparative Political Studies,* Vol.27, No.4, pp.402–424.

Kalaycıoğlu, E. (1994b). 'Radical Right Parties and Voter Preferences in Turkey'(in Turkish), *Dünü ve Bugünüyle Toplum ve Ekonomi* Vol.7, pp.65–84.

Kalaycıoğlu, E. (1994c). 'Unconventional Political Participation in Turkey and Europe: Comparative Perspectives', *Il Politico*, Vol.LIX, No.3, pp.503–524.

Kalaycıoğlu, E. (1998). 'Türkiye'de Siyaset (Politics in Turkey)' in *Sivil Toplum için Kent, Yerel Siyaset ve Demokrasi Seminerleri* (Seminars in City, Local Politics and Democracy for Civil Society), in Turkish, Istanbul: World Academy for Local Government and Democracy Publications (WALD).

Kalaycıoğlu, E. (1999). 'The Shaping of Political Preferences in Turkey: Coping with the Post-Cold-War Era', *New Perspectives on Turkey*, Vol.20, No.1, pp.47–76.

Kalaycıoğlu, E. (2002). 'Elections and Governance' in Sayarı, S. and Y. Esmer (Eds.) *Politics, Parties and Elections in Turkey*, Boulder, London: Lynner Rienner Publishers, pp.55–72.

Kalaycıoğlu, E. (2005). 'The Mystery of the Türban:Participation or Revolt?', in the special Issue of *Turkish Politics* on Religion and Politics in Turkey, Vol. 6, No. 2, pp.233–252.

Kalaycıoğlu, E. and Sarıbay, A. Y. (1986). "Tanzimat: Modernleşme Arayışı ve Siyasal Değişme" in Ersin Kalaycıoğlu ve A. Yaşar Sarıbay (eds.) *Türk Siyasal Hayatının Gelişimi* (Istanbul: Beta Pubications): 9–29.

Kalaycıoğlu, E.and Sarıbay, A.Y. (1991). 'Çocukların Parti Tutmasını Belirleyen Etkiler' (On Factors Affecting Party Identitification of Children) in Turkish, *Toplum ve Ekonomi* Vol.1, pp.137–150.

Kalaycıoğlu, E. and Turan, İ. (1981). 'Measuring Political Participation: A Cross-Cultural Application' *Comparative Political Studies*, Vol. 14, No.1, pp. 123–35.

Karpat, K.H. (1972). 'The Transformation of the Ottoman State, 1789–1908', *International Journal of Middle East Studies*, Vol.3, pp.243–281.

Karpat, K. H. (1975) 'The Politics of Transition: Political Attitudes and Party Affiliation in Turkish Gecekondu,' in Akarlı, E.D., and Bendor, G. (eds) (1975) *Pc*, Istanbul.

Key, V.O. (1955). 'A Theory of Critical Elections',*Journal of Politics* Vol.17, No.1, pp.3–18.

Key, V.O. (1959). Secular Realignments and the Party System,*Journal of Politics,* Vol.21, 198–210.

Kinder, D.R. and Kiewiet, R. (1979). 'Economic Discontent and Political Behavior: The Role of Personal Grievences and Collective Economic Judgements in Congressional Voting', *American Journal of Political Science*, Vol.23, pp.495–527.

Kinder, D.R. and Kiewiet, R. (1981). 'Sociotropic Politics:the American Case', *British Journal of Political Science*, Vol.11, pp.129–161.

King, G. (1997). *A Solution to the Ecological Inference Problem: Reconstructing Individual Behavior from Aggregate Data.* Princeton: Princeton University Press.

King, G. (2000). Geography, Statistics and Ecological Inference. *Annals of the Association of American Geographers*, Vol.90, No.3, pp.601–606.

Kirişci, K. and Winrow, G. (1997). *The Kurdish Question and Turkey*, Frank Cass.

Kuran, T., (1995). *Private Truths, Public Lies, The Social Consequences of Preference Falsification*, Cambridge, MA: Harvard University Press.

Kutad, A. (1975). 'Patron – Client Relations: The State of the Art and Research in Eastern Turkey,' in Engin D. Akarlı and Gabriel Ben-Dor (eds.) *Political Participation in Turkey: Historical Background and Present Problems*, Istanbul: Boğaziçi University Press, pp. 61– 87.

Landau, J. M. (1995). *Pan-Turkism: From Irredentism to Cooperation*, London: Hurst.

Lazerfeld, P.F., Berelson, B. And Gaudet, H. (1948). *The People's Choice:How the Voter Makes up his Mind in a Presidential Campaign*, 2nd edition, New york:Columbia University Press.

Lerner, D. (1958) *The Passing of the Traditional Society*, New York, Free Press.

Lewis, B. (1961), *The Emergence of Modern Turkey*, London, Oxford University Press.

Lewis, B. (1995), *The Middle East: 2000 Years of History from the Rise of Christianity to the Present Day*, London, G. Britain: Phoenix Giant.

Lewis, B. (2003). *Demokrasinin Türkiye Serüveni* (The Adventure of Democracy in Turkey), in Turkish, İstanbul: Yapı Kredi Yayınları.

Lipset, S. M. and Rokkan, S. (1967) in 'Cleavage Structures, Party Systems, and Voter Alignments: An Introduction', in *Party Systems and Voter Alignments: Cross National Perspectives* (S.M. Lipset and S. Rokkan eds.), New York: Free Press, pp.1–64.

Long, J.S. (1997). *Regression Models for Categorical and Limited Dependent Variables*, London: Sage Publications.

Magnarella, P. J. (1967). 'Regional Voting in Turkey.' *The Muslim World,* Vol.LVII, pp.224–234, 277–287.

Mansfeld, P. (1980). *The Arabs*, Middlesex, England: Penguin Books.

Mardin, Ş. (1962). *The Genesis of Young Ottoman Thought*, Princeton: Princeton University Press.

Mardin, Ş. (1969). 'Power, Civil Society and Culture in Ottoman Empire', *Comparative Studies in Society and History*, Vol. 11, No.1, pp.258–281.

Mardin, Ş. (1973). 'Center Periphery Relations: A Key to Turkish Politics?', *Deadalus*, Vol.2, No.1, pp.169–190.

Mardin, Ş. (1983). *Din ve Ideoloji* (Religion and Politics), in Turkish, (İstanbul: İletişim Yayınları).

Mardin, Ş. (1989). *Religion and Social Change in Modern Turkey: The Case of Bediüzzaman Said Nursi*, Albany: State University of New York Press.

Mardin, Ş. (2005). "Turkish Islamic Exceptionalism Yesterday and Today: Continuity, Rupture and Reconstruction in Operational Codes", in the special Issue of *Turkish Politics* on Religion and Politics in Turkey, Vol. 6, No. 2, pp.145–166.

Marsh, A. and Kaase, M. (1979). 'Background of Political Action' in Barnes, S.H. and M. Kaase et al. (eds.) *Political Action: Mass Participation in Five Western Democracies*, Beverly Hills, London: Sage Publications, pp.97–136.

McCarthy, J. (2001). *The Ottoman People's and the End of Empire*, London: Arnold.

Metin, İ. (1999). *Aleviliğin Anayasası* (Constitution of Alevism), in Turkish, İstanbul:Akyüz Publications.

Myagov, M. and Ordeshook, P. C. (1998). 'The Spatial Character of Russia's New Democracy', *Public Choice*, Vol.97, No.3, pp.491–523.

Nuhrat, C. (1971). 'Türkiye Köylerinde Olağandışı Oy Verme', *A. Ü. Siyasal Bilgiler Fakültesi Dergisi*, Vol. XXVI, No.1, pp.219–244.

O'Loughlin, J. (2000). 'Can King's Ecological Onference Method Answer a Social Scientific Puzzle: Who Voted for the Nazi Party in Weimar Germany?' *Annals of the Association of American Geographers*, Vol.90, No.3, pp.592–601.

Osei-Kwame, P. and Taylor, P.J. (1984). 'A Politics of Failure: The Political Geography of Ghanian Elections, 1954–1979', *Annals, Association of American Geographers* Vol.74, pp.574–589.

Özbudun, E. (1975). *Türkiye'de Sosyal Değişme ve Siyasal Katılma*, Ankara, Ankara Üniversitesi Hukuk Fakültesi Yayınları.

Özbudun, E. (1976). *Social Change and Political Participation in Turkey*, Princeton, New Jersey, Princeton University Press

Özbudun, E. (1988). 'Development of Democractic Government in Turkey: Crises, Interruptions and Reequilibrations', in L.Diamond, J. Linz and S.M. Lipset (eds.) *Democracy in Developing Countries*, Lynne Rienner Publishers.

Özbudun, E. (1995). *Türk Anayasa Hukuku* (Turkish Constitutional Law), in Turkish, Yetkin Basım Yayım ve Dağıtım, Ankara.

Özbudun, E. and Tachau, F. (1975). 'Social Change and Electoral Behavior in Turkey: Toward a Critical Realignment?' *International Journal of Middle East Studies* Vol.6, pp.460–480.

Özdalga, E., *The Veiling Issue, Official Secularism and Popular Islam in Modern Turkey, Nordic Institute of Asian Studies, NIAS Report Series*, No. 33

Parla, T. and Davison, A. (2004). *Corporatist Ideology in Kemalist Turkey: Progress Or Order?*, Syracuse University Press.

Pedersen, M. N. (1979). 'The Dynamics of European Party Systems: Changing Patterns of Electoral Volatility'. *European Journal of Political Research* Vol.7, No.1, pp.1–26.

Perinçek, D. (2002). *Karen Fogg'un E-Postaları,* İstanbul: Kaynak Yayınları.

Persson, T. and Tabellini, G. (2002). *Political Economics: Explaining Economic Policy*, The MIT Press.

Pomper, G. (1967). 'Classification of Presidential Elections', *The Journal of Politics* Vol.29, pp.535–566.

Poulton, H. (1997). *Top Hat Grey Wolf and Crescent, Turkish Nationalism and the Turkish Republic*, London: Hurst and Company.

Przeworski, A. (1975). 'Institutionalization of Voting Patterns, or Is Mobilization the Source of Decay?' *American Political Science Review* Vol.69, pp.49–67.

Rabinowitz, G. and Macdonald, S.E. (1989). 'A Directional Theory of Issue Voting', *American Political Science Review*, vol. 83, no.1 pp. 93–121.

Robinson, W.S. (1950). 'Ecological Correlation and the Behavior of Individuals'. *American Sociological Review* Vol.15, pp.351–357.

Sartori, G. (1976). *Parties and Party Systems: A Framework for Analysis*, Cambridge: Cambridge University Press.

Sayarı, S. (1975). 'Some Notes on the Beginnings of Mass Political Participation' in in Engin D. Akarlı and Gabriel Ben-Dor (eds.) *Political Participation in Turkey: Historical Background and Present Problems*, Istanbul: Boğaziçi University Press, pp. 121–133.

Sayarı, S. and Esmer, Y. (2002). *Politics, Parties and Elections in Turkey*, Boulder, Co.:Lynne Rienner Publishers.

Sayarı, S.(1996). 'Turkey's Islamist Challenge', *Middle Eastern Quarterly*, Vol. 3 No:3, pp. 35–43.

Schattschneider, E. (1960). *The Semi-Sovereign People*. New York: Holt, Rinehart and Winston.

Secor, A.J. (2001). 'Ideologies in Crisis: Political Cleavages and Electoral Politics in Turkey in the 1990s'. *Political Geography* Vol.20, No.5, pp.539–560.

Selçuk, İ., Şaylan, G. and Kalkan, Ş., (1994).*Türkiye'de Alevilik ve Bektaşilik* (Alevism and Bektashism in Turkey), in Turkish, (İstanbul: Yön Publications.

Sencer, M. (1974). *Türkiye'de Siyasal Partilerin Sosyal Temelleri* (Social bases of political parties in Turkey), in Turkish, İstanbul: May Publications.

Şener, N. (2001). *Tepeden Tırnağa Yolsuzluk* (Corruption form Top Down) in Turkish, Istanbul: Metis Publications.

Şener, N. (2002). *Naylon Holding* (Nylon Holding) (Istanbul: Om Publications.

Seymen, S. (2001). *Amiral Battı: Sabah Grubunun Öyküsü* (The Admiral has Sunk: The Story of Sabah Group) in Turkish, İstanbul: Metis Publications.

Shankland, D., (2003). *The Alevis in Turkey, The Emergence of a Secular Islamic Tradition*, (London: Routledge)

Shaw, S. J. and E. K. Shaw, (1977). *History of the Ottoman Empire and Modern Turkey: Volume II: Reform, Revolution and the Republic: The Rise of Modern Turkey, 1808–1975*, Cambridge, London, New York, Melbourne: Cambridge University Press.

Shelley, F.M. and Archer, J.C. (1984). Political Habit, Political Culture and the Electoral Mosaic of a Border Region, *Geographical Perspectives* Vol.54, No.1, pp.7–20.

Shelley, F.M. and Archer, J.C., Davidson, F.M. and Brunn, S.D. (1996). *Political Geography of the United States*, New York and London: Guilford Press.

Srikantan, K.S. (1973). Regional and Rural-Urban Socio-Demographic Differences in Turkey. *Middle East Journal* Vol.27, 275–300.

State Planning Organization (SPO) (1996). *Research on Socio-Economic Development Ranking of Provinces*. Ankara: SPO (in Turkish).

Sui, D. (2000). 'New Directions in Ecological Inference: An Introduction'. *Annals of the Association of American Geographers*, Vol.90, No.3, pp.579–582.

Taagepera, R. and Shugart, M. S. (1989). *Seats and Votes: The Effects and Determinants of Electoral Systems*. New Haven: Yale University Press.

Tachau, F. (1973). with Good, M.D., 'The Anatomy of Political and Social Change, Turkish Parties, Parliaments and Elections', *Comparative Politics* Vol.5, 551–573.

Tachau, F. (2000). Turkish Political Parties and Elections, *Turkish Studies*, Vol.1, No.1, pp.128–148.

Tachau, F. and Heper, M. (1983). 'The State, Politics and the Military in Turkey'. *Comparative Politics* Vol.16, No.1, pp.17–35.

Tanpınar, A.H. (1982), *19. Asır Türk Edebiyatı Tarihi*, (5th Ed.), İstanbul: Çağlayan.

Tanör, B. (1996). *Osmanlı-Türk Anayasal Gelişmeleri, 1789–1980* (Developments in Ottoman-Turkish Constitutions, 1789–1980), in Turkish, AFA Publication, İstanbul.

Toprak, B. (1981). *Islam and Political Development in Turkey*, Leiden: Brill.

Toprak, B. (1988).'The State, Politics and Religion in Turkey', in M. Heper and A. Evin (eds.), *State, Democracy and the Military: Turkey in the 1980s*, (New York: Walter de Gruyter, pp.119–135

Toprak, B. (1996). 'Islam and the Secular State in Turkey', in Ç. Balım et al. (eds.) *Turkey: Political , Social and Economic Challenges in the 1990s*, Leiden: E.J. Brill, pp. 87–118.

Tunaya, T.Z. (1952). *Türkiye'de Siyasi partiler, 1859–1952*, İstanbul: Doğan Kardeş Yayınları.

Tuncer, E. (2003) *Osmanlı'dan Günümüze Seçimler, 1877–2002*, TESAV Yayınları, Ankara.

Turan, İ. (1991). 'Religion and Political Culture in Turkey', in R. Tapper (ed.), *Islam in Modern Turkey: Religion, Politics and Literature in a Secular State*, (London: I. B. Tauris, 1991)

Ünlü, F. (2001). *Sadettin Tantan, Bir Savaş Öyküsü* (Sadettin Tantan, A War Story) in Turkish, Istanbul: Metis Publications.

Vaner, S. (1987). The Army, in I.C. Schick E.A.Tonak (eds.) *Turkey in Transition: New Perspectives*, Oxford University Press.

Verba, S. and Nie, N. (1972). *Participation in America: Political Democracy and Social Equality*, NY: Harper and Row.

Verba, S., Nie, N. and Kim, J. (1978). *Participation and Political Equality: A Seven-Nation Comparison*, Cambridge, Mass and London:Harvard University Press.

White, J.B. (2002). *Islamist Mobilisation in Turkey, A Study in Vernacular Politics*, (Seattle: The University of Washington Press)

Yavuz, H. (1997). 'Political Islam and the Welfare (Refah) Party in Turkey', *Comparative Politics*, Vol.30, No.1, pp.63–82.

Yavuz, H. and Esposito, J.L. (eds.) (2003). *Turkish Islam and the Secular State*, Syracuse: Syracuse University Press.

Zürcher, E.J. (1993). *Turkey: A Modern History*, London-New York:I.B.Tauris.

INDEX